The VISIONS *of the* CHILDREN

The VISIONS *of the* CHILDREN

THE APPARITIONS OF THE BLESSED MOTHER AT MEDJUGORJE

JANICE T. CONNELL

With an Introduction by Father Robert Faricy, S.J.

St. Martin's Press New York

NOTE TO THE READER: At the time that this book was written, Yugoslavia was still a unified country. The Civil War has subsequently fractured that perceived unity. Since the future of the various republics has yet to be determined, it has been impossible to refer to specific regions by their new, autonomous names. Therefore, for the sake of simplicity, the various lands are still collectively referred to as Yugoslavia throughout. Nonetheless, there are various mentions of the Civil War in the text.

The decree of the Congregation for the Propagation of the Faith, A.A.S., 58, 1186 (approved by Pope Paul VI on October 14, 1966) states that the *Nihil Obstat* and *Imprimatur* are no longer required on publications that deal with private revelations, provided they contain nothing contrary to faith and morals. The author wishes to manifest her unconditional submission to the final and official judgment of the magisterium of the church regarding the events presently under investigation at Medjugorje.

Design by Judith Christensen

Library of Congress Cataloging-in-Publication Data

Connell, Janice T.
The visions of the children : the apparitions of the Blessed Mother at Medjugorje / Janice T. Connell.
p. cm.
ISBN 0-312-07879-X (hc)
ISBN 0-312-09933-9 (pbk.)
1. Mary, Blessed Virgin, Saint—Apparitions and miracles—Yugoslavia—Medugorje (Bosnia and Hercegovina) 2. Medugorje (Bosnia and Hercegovina)—Religious life and customs. 3. Children—Yugoslavia—Medugorje (Bosnia and Hercegovina)—Religious life.
I. Title.
BT660.M44C66 1992
232.91'7'0949742—dc20 92-3622
CIP

10 9 8 7 6 5 4 3 2

CONSECRATION AND DEDICATION

This book was consecrated to the Holy Trinity in the name of the Lord, Jesus Christ, during a Mass offered by Father Luke Zimmer, SS.CC., at the Carmelite convent at Coimbra, Portugal, in the presence of the sisters, one of whom is Sister Lucy, the sole living visionary of Fatima. The date was May 17, 1991.

The book is dedicated to the Eternal Father with love and gratitude.

CONTENTS

ACKNOWLEDGMENTS

The Blessed Virgin Mary, Mother of God, Queen of Peace, Mother of All People, for her help, encouragement, and guidance.

Pope John Paul II, for his faithfulness in dark times as he leads people toward the triumph of the Immaculate Heart.

The visionaries and locutionists of Medjugorje, their families, interpreters, and translators for the graciousness with which they shared their experiences.

The priests and sisters of Saint James Parish, Medjugorje, for their assistance, perseverance, and graciousness.

Jozo and Meritza Vasilj and their family, and the people of Medjugorje parish who helped me.

My good friends at the Medjugorje Centers worldwide, who have brought the messages of the Mother of Jesus to the world.

My husband, Ed, and my children, Will, Ted, Betsy, and Derek, who worked with me on this project.

My granddaughter, Mary Christian, who spent the first three weeks of her life beside me as this book was assembled.

My mother, who gave me the faith, and my father, who received the faith through this apparition.

My brothers and sisters everywhere, who have helped me in ways known by them, especially Cornelia, Louis, Glory, Cliff, Neil, Adrian, Susan, Robert, Michael, David, and Harold.

The countless children of Mary from around the world who have personally helped on this project, but in their humility are known to God alone.

The late Father Richard Byrne, O.C.S.O., Father Joseph Coyle, O.S.F.S., Father James McGuire, D.S.T., and Father Luke Zimmer, SS. CC., who graciously read this manuscript and extended their insights and expertise.

The generous staff at St. Martin's Press for its dedication and contributions, including Roy Gainsburg, Barbara Andrews, Karen Burke, Daniel Burrows, Meg Drislane, Kathy Fink, Geoffrey Kloske, Mark Kohut, Josh Marwell, Michael Pratt, Joan Vogel, and Jeanette Zwart.
My editor, Bob Weil.

AUTHOR'S NOTE

As the twentieth century draws to a close, millions of people from all parts of the planet, of all faiths or no faith, are awakening to what lies beyond the senses. The great illusion that the world of the senses is the only reality is gradually being eroded by the shared testimonies—pouring forth from every corner of the globe—of spiritual experiences so powerful that people are willing to give their reputations, their fortunes, even their lives, in defense of a transcendent reality they claim they have experienced—or are now experiencing.

Since 1987, as many as half a million people in the Ukraine claim to see or have seen the Blessed Virgin Mary.[1] In Rowanda in Africa, the Blessed Virgin appeared many times during the 1980s to "prepare the world for the return of her Son."[2] Jesus Himself is alleged also to have appeared in Rowanda, where He taught a pagan the gospel messages of love and peace and prayer to the Eternal Father.[3] A series of extraordinary events, including the presence of a speaking angel and a bleeding statue of Mary, occurred beginning in 1973 in a convent in Akita, Japan, announcing messages of conversion, of peace, of joy, of love, and of the brotherhood of mankind.[4] This series of events began with a brilliant light emanating from the tabernacle where the Eucharist was kept. Jesus, truly present in the Host, began a manifestation of Himself that left no doubt whatsoever of His divine presence in the Eucharist.[5]

The pretense that the world of the senses, which is the object of science, is the only reality is being unmasked as the twenty-first century dawns. No longer is the world viewed as independent of God, however one defines that undefinable word. The deification of man is now nearly universally viewed as the product of ignorance, spiritual blindness, or simply being out of touch with reality.

The Catholic Church, historical guardian of "truth," has traditionally taken a firm stand regarding the veracity of the content of private revelations and extraordinary experiential phenomena. No one is bound, by Church teaching authority, to accept as true the alleged prophetic messages given by visionaries, seers, or self-proclaimed prophets. Church teaching warns the faithful that private revelations may contain error, bias of the visionary, or even misinterpretation. The claims of individuals who purport to have divine messages are not to be confused with the pronouncements of the magisterium of the Catholic Church.

The happenings at Medjugorje described herein are the experiences of individuals who have shared their personal stories. The material in this book was gathered with the help of translators and interpreters. Because of the cultural and language barrier, as well as the subject matter, this material is not to be viewed as definitive. The author takes no position as to the content of the interviews except to chronicle what was perceived, seen, and heard and translated from Croatian into English during certain days in the lives of the visionaries of Medjugorje. In the final analysis, a tree is known by its fruit. Millions of lives have been touched or changed because of the extraordinary occurrences in that village.

INTRODUCTION

After more than ten years of daily apparitions, the Blessed Virgin Mary continues to come and to speak every evening to a small group of young adults of Saint James Parish of Medjugorje in Yugoslavia. Through them she speaks to all of us, and to each of us.

The consensus of theologians and the overwhelming majority of bishops, priests, and lay persons who have gone to Medjugorje is that the Blessed Virgin Mary does, in fact, appear and speak to these young people. The Pope himself has on countless occasions spoken favorably of the apparitions to pilgrims on their way to and from Medjugorje.

What importance do the events at Medjugorje have, for all of us together and for each one of us individually? What, really, does Medjugorje mean?

It means this: Jesus has sent His mother to speak to us. He has sent her in a dramatic way: daily for several years, and not to one person but to a group. When Mary came to Lourdes and to Fatima, she came only a few times. She has come thousands of times to Medjugorje. Many healings and conversions take place there. Pilgrims see special phenomena. The sun spins and changes color. Thousands of rosary chains have turned gold. Jesus wants to speak to us through Mary, and *urgently*.

And it also means this: that Mary really is our mother, a good mother who cares about her children and who wants to help them. Jesus, from the cross, gave the apostle John to His mother. John stood in for all of us, and for each of us. Jesus' mother is my mother.

Mary has a maternal love for all of us, and for each one by name. Her motherhood stands not in the order of nature or biology, but in the order of grace. Mary is the mother of grace in my life. We speak here of Mary's function as mediatrix, to use the word that the Second Vatican Council used. Mary is the Mediatrix of All Graces.

Jesus, in His Incarnation and birth, first came to us through Mary.

That is, Mary is His mother. But motherhood is a permanent relationship. After the birth of her child, a mother remains always the mother of the child, even long after the child has become an adult. Because Jesus first came to us through Mary, and because that relationship (her motherhood) is permanent, Jesus comes to us now always through Mary. She is the mother of the Christ-life in me, the mother of grace in my life, the mediatrix of the graces I receive, my mother in the order of grace.

Does that mean that I must go to Jesus through Mary? No. It means that I *can* go to Mary and let her lead me to Jesus. The principle of Cana still holds. Jesus' hour had not yet come; the time and the place and the situation were all wrong for Jesus to work the first miracle of his public life. But His mother asked Him to supply more wine to a noisy party that had already had quite a bit to drink. And He did it. Medjugorje has Mary's motherhood of each of us as part of its meaning.

The message has meaning for the personal life of each one of us. Mary, speaking for Jesus, calls the world, and me, and you, to conversion: to turn away from sin and turn toward the Lord. She calls us to faith, not just the faith that believes all the Christian truths, but the faith that holds on to Jesus, that adheres in hope to Him, that responds to His love. Mary calls us to prayer—to pray in our churches, in our families, and to have time set aside every day for personal prayer. She calls us in Jesus' name to fast, to fast intelligently and prudently, taking into consideration age and health and work, but fast somehow. Mary's program comes from Jesus. We can find it in the Gospels: conversion, faith, prayer, and fasting.

Mary tells us that this program will help greatly to bring about peace—peace in our hearts, peace in our families, peace in our nations, and peace in the world.

Little has changed since the first year of apparitions at Medjugorje. The young people who see and hear and speak with Our Lady are older now, and have grown in Christian maturity. The two young married women who first saw Our Lady in June 1981 and who see her now only infrequently remain with their husbands and children in Medjugorje. The other four are all still unmarried and travel from Medjugorje from time to time.

The Franciscan priests and sisters at Medjugorje have been replaced by other Franciscans. Rome has taken all responsibility for the apparitions away from the local bishop and given it to the bishops' conference of the combined republics and regions that historically make up the former republic of Yugoslavia. That commission, in turn, released an inconclusive report in 1990 that they could not determine as yet whether the Medjugorje events were really from God in an extraordinary manner.

As I write this, Serbian troops shell Dubrovnik and prepare to take the city and, eventually, to bring the republic of Croatia to its knees. What will happen to Medjugorje, not in Croatia but in an ethnically Croatian pocket of Bosnia-Herzegovina, remains unknown.

The local and regional governments no longer persecute those associated with Medjugorje. They fear the Serbian government in Belgrade and the Serbian army with its soldiers and tanks in Bosnia-Herzegovina. They have discovered that hundreds of thousands of foreign pilgrims can help their struggling economy, and they hope that when peace is restored the numbers of pilgrims will be even higher than before.

Our Lady still appears every evening to the few young persons, as she has from the beginning. She says basically the same things. She says them to us.

Robert Faricy, S.J.
Rome, Italy
December 1991

PROLOGUE

The fire of love is strongest when the way is dark.

Every book has a reason for being. On May 25, 1987, Mary, the Mother of God, spoke to the world through the visionaries at Medjugorje:

> *Dear children, I invite everyone [on earth] to start living in God's love. I am your eternal mother and therefore I want to lead you all to perfect holiness. I want every one of you to be happy here on earth, and every one of you to be with me in heaven. This is, dear children, the reason for my coming here [to my children on earth] and my desire. Thank you for your response to my call.*

The reason for this book is that all people on earth may know their eternal mother and have an opportunity to respond to her call.

In April 1987, my family was having a meal at a restaurant in Rancho Santa Fe, California, as we planned my youngest son, Will's, graduation from high school. We had much to celebrate. It was a large graduating class, nearly five hundred, and Will was receiving one of five academic awards. He was captain of three sports, and always was surrounded by friends of all types. We didn't get too far planning the graduation festivities, however, because the front page of *The New York Times* carried a feature article about apparitions of the Blessed Virgin Mary in the Ukraine. According to the secular reporters covering the story, at least one hundred thousand people claimed to have actually seen the Blessed Virgin Mary in the spring of 1987. "This is incredible," I said in astonishment. Suddenly all the love and longing for the Blessed Mother I had experienced as a child came flooding into my heart so quickly that I was caught quite off guard. In those days nearly everyone had heard about the eighteen apparitions of the Blessed Virgin to Saint Bernadette at Lourdes, and some fortunate ones even had little jars of blessed water from the miraculous springs in the grotto there. Everyone seemed to know the messages of Fatima and of the visions of the three little shepherd children who saw Our Lady on the thirteenth day of six consecutive months and faithfully gave her messages to an unbelieving world. People still spoke of the great "Miracle of the Sun" that happened at Fatima in 1917 before nearly seventy thousand eyewitnesses.

Now, in my own lifetime, *The New York Times* was claiming one hundred thousand people had seen the Mother of God! The possibility that Our Lady could once again be appearing *anywhere* on earth seemed like a miracle. "This is amazing," we all agreed. "Newspaper reporters probably wouldn't write like this unless there was something to it," Will commented. "Let's consider going to the Ukraine on our summer trip," I suggested, pondering the extraordinary thought. "Just to be somewhere that Our Lady might be."

One thing our family shares is great love for the Blessed Mother. My rosary-praying grandmother and mother taught us in no uncertain terms that even Jesus obeyed the Blessed Mother. "Don't all good children behave like the Child Jesus?" they would tell us when we were very young. And the nuns had taught us this prayer:

Lovely Lady dressed in blue,
Teach me how to pray.
God was just your little boy.
Tell me what to say.

The article about the apparitions in the Ukraine set the stage for three subsequent chance encounters that forever altered the path of my life, and my family's life too. A priest from Los Angeles told me that during a visit to Rome he heard of purported apparitions of the Blessed Virgin in Yugoslavia. He said he went to a tiny village hidden away in the mountains there, where six children—four girls and two boys—were seeing the mother of Jesus Christ daily. He said he was present for an apparition, and the Mother of God spoke to him. She said:

> *My son, I want to thank you for the great faith you had to come so far to show your love for my Son and I ask you now*

to spend the rest of your life spreading and teaching my messages of Medjugorje to the world.

A few days later I met another priest, this one from Ohio. He too had heard of the apparitions in Yugoslavia while in Rome. He told me he himself went there to the village of Medjugorje. He claimed the apparitions were authentic. He said he saw the Miracle of the Sun similar to the one at Fatima. He also commented that he had met the six visionaries, and they had told him the apparitions had been ongoing since 1981. "Why hasn't everybody heard about this?" I asked, incredulous that something so serious could be occurring with little recognition in the United States. "Don't forget," the priest said, "Yugoslavia is controlled by Marxist politics. It is somewhat dangerous to go there. The pastor was thrown into prison, and tortured. Other priests have been arrested and tortured. It's a dangerous place." He too said the Mother of God spoke to him. She said:

My son, I want to thank you for the great faith you had to come so far to show your love for my Son, and I ask you to spend the rest of your life spreading and teaching my messages of Medjugorje to the world.

I had just heard those very words from another priest. The coincidence was highly unusual.

Two weeks later I met yet a third priest, this time from South Africa. He also had been to the little village of Medjugorje, behind the then "Iron Curtain." He said he had seen the Blessed Mother there, and that she had spoken to him. His Adam's apple betrayed the emotion he was feeling. Shocked and somewhat embarrassed, I hesitatingly asked, "What did she say?"

"The Mother of God said to me," he responded quietly,

My son, I want to thank you for the great faith you had to come so far to show your love for my Son, and I ask you to spend the rest of your life spreading and teaching my messages of Medjugorje to the world.

I could not contain my amazement. Those same words! Something had happened to me that April day at Rancho Santa Fe, but I didn't yet know how deeply it would alter the course of my life. I have always loved the Blessed Mother more than I can say. After hearing the words "*I want to thank you for the great faith you had to come so far to show your love for me,*" three different times from three different sources, I knew that I had to go—perhaps with an unknown destiny—to Medjugorje. I felt a call so deep in my soul that I couldn't ignore it. It didn't matter any longer if the apparitions were authentic. It didn't matter that the area was dangerous.

"What are the messages?" I asked the priest.

"The Blessed Mother has come to earth for the last time," he said. "This is her final apparition. She is calling all the world back to God for the last time."

As chilling as those words were, I didn't understand the significance at the time.

"Is the apparition like Fatima?" I asked.

"It is the Fatima peace plan in action," he answered.

Just then a friend came by. "What's going on here?" he interrupted, noting my expression of incredulity and awe.

"This priest claims he has been to an apparition of the Blessed Mother behind the Iron Curtain. It's like Fatima. The Blessed Mother herself thanked him for his faith."

"Tell us about this place, Medjugorje," we asked.

"The Blessed Mother calls herself the Queen of Peace. She says peace in the world is fragile. She warns of imminent chastisements for the sins of mankind. She is urgently calling for strong faith, prayer, fasting, reconciliation, and conversion now. She says those are the peace tools."

The Blessed Mother has always requested these at her apparitions throughout the centuries. It was staggering to us to ponder the possibility that the mother of Jesus Christ might be having daily apparitions on this planet now. Such a realization would give believers little option but to respond in some way. As for unbelievers, the authenticity of such an apparition from the beyond, from heaven, would render unbelief impossible.

It was a seemingly simple situation—the Blessed Virgin was either appearing or she wasn't. It was really that basic. The messages were pure Gospel. How could anyone face Jesus at the personal judgment, knowing His mother was visiting the earth, without having gone to call on her? And, if the apparitions were false (there have indeed been some of those), a pilgrimage is still a pilgrimage. Fasting is fasting.

Prayer and penance are still prayer and penance, whether they are carried out in Auschwitz, Siberia, Pittsburgh, or Medjugorje.

It was, however, difficult to arrange a pilgrimage. Travel agents couldn't even find Medjugorje on a map in 1987. So I prayed and asked Jesus if He would let me go to Medjugorje to show my love for His mother. Then all doors opened.

There were some painful moments. Certain family members and others thought my behavior was unusual. They could not understand why I was fasting after having read various books in French and English on Medjugorje. "New diet, Mom?" the children teased after several Wednesdays and Fridays of bread and water. Fasting was easy then. It was the "honeymoon" period. Nothing else seemed important but the Blessed Mother and her urgent calls to the world—for the *last time*—that were strangely going unheeded. I knew times were dire if the Blessed Mother was asking ordinary people to fast so severely on bread and water, twice weekly. Traditionally only the strictest monasteries impose such a strenuous dietary penance. Now the call was to the whole world, to all people of all faiths and no faith to fast strictly for world peace, and to pray. Pray much. "All prayer is acceptable to God," she was calling from the mountains of Medjugorje.

I began having "coincidental" meetings with more people who had been to Medjugorje. Each had a mysterious story to relate of seeing or hearing the Blessed Mother, or an angel, or even the Lord Jesus Himself. Each spoke of a mysterious peace encountered in that remote village in Bosnia-Herzegovina. They spoke of rainbows, beautiful rainbows, that proliferated throughout the sky, even though there often was no sign of rain. Then I heard of a friend of ours, Rita Klaus, who was mysteriously and instantly healed—completely—of multiple sclerosis when she prayed to Our Lady of Medjugorje. This healing suggested to me the miracles of both Lourdes and Fatima. "The devil doesn't heal," a skeptic ventured. "He doesn't convert either." Yet both processes were occurring at Medjugorje.

My husband agreed to go to Medjugorje with me, and I prayed that each of our children (Betsy, twenty-three, a first-year law student; Ted, twenty-one, a second-year engineering student; and Will, eighteen) would also go. That happened. My brother, Louis, his wife, Susie, and their three young sons—Louis, Alex, and Chris, ages eleven, ten, and eight—also joined the family pilgrimage in July of 1987, though we did go on to Salzburg to the music festival and to

Vienna, so the motives were not purely religious for everyone.

The journey was arduous. When the ten of us arrived in the village of Medjugorje, we found unpaved roads. We saw cows plodding down the paths, escorted by old ladies in black dresses with kerchiefs wrapped around their heads. Barefoot children ran among the chickens, which pecked aimlessly at the tiny yards of the small stucco houses with red tile roofs. Sheep grazed on the sparse vegetation that sprouted through the rocky soil at the foot of Cross Mountain, where our lodgings were.

Louis, also a lawyer, was tired and hot. "We need water," he declared, for the house had no running water that evening. As we walked the dusty path in search of a pub, we carried flashlights which we didn't need. A huge neon cross glowed from afar atop Cross Mountain, lighting the path for us. We were enchanted by the beautiful light.

Despite the jet lag, we slept little the first night. There were no screens, and the flies serenaded us along with a chorus of roosters. As dawn approached, Ed and I decided to ascend the illumined mountain we had seen the night before. As we approached the tall mountain, it looked forbiddingly steep. Boulders blocked the meager path. It was 4:30 A.M., yet people were already climbing and descending the treacherous path. For years I had been plagued with a painful disc problem in my lower back. That morning, though nearly immobile after the long plane trip, the longing in my heart far outweighed the aching in my back. I had read that the Blessed Virgin herself prays before that cross on Cross Mountain every daybreak. The memory of the neon cross was still fresh as I painfully climbed the boulders, pausing at intervals to join those who were meditating upon the life-size Stations of the Cross along the way. Now barefoot people were passing us. What a penance on the sharp rocks! Young people were descending with guitars and blankets. They had spent the night on the mountain.

Finally we reached the summit. There was *no* electricity. The "neon cross" was only a tall, gray, concrete cross planted in the sharp rocks, with a chunk missing from one of its arms. We fell on our knees upon the rocks in amazement. For the first time in my life I understood—perhaps—the meaning of the word *humility*. With immense joy, I gave the Blessed Mother everything: my own life, my husband, Ed, and each of our children, those three living and those six who were not. I gave her my successes, which looked like nothing up there at the foot of the concrete cross, and I gave her my failures, which seemed insignificant too. For a brief moment, I experienced the deep joy of freely being a child of Mary. Nothing mattered anymore, for I was with my real mother and I knew she loved me just as I am. "Please, dear Blessed Mother, accept my family and every family in the whole world as your own and keep us all safe in the Heart of your Son," I prayed, knowing she was present.

Then I heard Ed say, "It's all true!"

"What's all true?" I asked.

"All the things those nuns taught. They were right," he said quietly.

"Lovely Lady dressed in blue, teach me how to pray," we said as we held hands and pondered.

My own heart, which was now Our Lady's heart, for I had given it to her (imagine the kinds of "gifts" she receives), was so full of joy that I ran down the mountain longing to share the "message of the neon cross" with our family, which was now Our Lady's family. I ran from rock to boulder, my feet barely touching the earth. Fifteen minutes later I was in the little house, exclaiming, "There's no electricity up there." My brother was looking for his glasses as he sat up in bed.

Ted came into the little room and gasped, "Mom, did you climb that mountain?"

"Yes. The neon cross up there is just concrete!" I exclaimed, not yet realizing the strangeness of what the family was witnessing.

"This is serious," Ted ventured. "Come on, Will, let's go!" Together they went out to the mountain.

My daughter, Betsy, was surrounded by her little cousins as she came in to see what the excitement was. "Mom, you're standing *straight*," she exclaimed.

"The Blessed Mother must be here," I said, almost in a whisper. We were all amazed. I have had no back pain since.

Later that morning, we walked to the English-speaking Mass. We all felt like praying the rosary, and as we did, a man approached us. "Are you from Ireland?" he asked.

"No, the U.S.," we volunteered.

"Did you hear what the Blessed Mother said last night?" he asked. Shocked at the question, we gathered around him.

"She told Ivan (the visionary) that the souls in purgatory are very lonely," he said. "The Blessed Mother asked that all the pilgrims pray for their beloved dead by name. She said the souls in purgatory can see their loved ones on earth. The Blessed Mother wants her faithful ones to pray for them by name."

"The Blessed Mother said that?" we all asked.

"She did," he said. "Please pass the word."

And then he was off. Later we learned that the time we had witnessed the "neon cross" on Cross Mountain was the exact time of the apparition to Ivan on the mountain.

After Mass we climbed the small mountain known as Apparition Hill. There I opened an envelope my eighty-one-year-old father, an invalid who had suffered several heart attacks, had sent just before our departure. It read, "If you find your Blessed Mother, and I hope you do, ask her to give me some faith for I have none. Ask her that I might believe too." We saw the "Miracle of the Sun," and Susie saw Our Lady in the sun. "What does she look like?" we asked. "She's so beautiful!" were Susie's only words. The little boys, Louis, Alex, and Chris, were kneeling on the rocks, frightened and amazed as they clung to Will. He was sobbing. So was everyone else. The Miracle of the Sun was quite extraordinary.[1] None of us would ever again be the same, for we were learning that the supernatural is really the natural in Medjugorje. We joined hands and we knelt on the ground where Mary first appeared to the visionaries on June 24, 1981, and we prayed for Dad. We prayed for all our family, and for everyone in the world. We also prayed for all our beloved dead—all the way back to Adam and Eve. When we mentioned Grandmother and Grandfather Connell, my boys Ted and Will, who were beside each other, pulled up as tall as they could stretch. Before she died, Grandmother Connell always looked to see which one of the boys was taller. There was that smile—the same one they each had long ago when she teased her youngest grandsons. "They believe," I whispered to Ed.

"I know," he responded. (One year later, my own mother and father were with us at the same spot. My father went to confession for the first time in seventy years.)

Our family witnessed many things in Medjugorje, too numerous to mention in a brief prologue. We all returned again and again to Medjugorje. Through God's graciousness we came to know the visionaries who are close in age to my children. They themselves asked us to share their messages from the Blessed Mother with all people on earth, for the messages are for everyone. We have all tried to be faithful to that request.

The visionaries of Medjugorje have spoken often to me of the Blessed Mother's heart weeping and longing for all God's children to return to the flock of the Good Shepherd. They speak of peace, prayer, penance. They speak about the gift of love from God our Father that flows from prayer and penance, the offspring of peace. They have told me the vision they see is Mary, the Mother of God, who says she is the Queen of Peace and the Mother of Life in God. There is no other life, she warns. All else is illusion. All else is the kingdom of death, despair, depravity, and destruction. She says, "Peace, my children, only peace. Be peace. Live peace. Peace is the harbor of truth. Trust my love. Trust the power of my Spouse, the Holy Spirit of love and truth."

The visionaries always speak of peace. Never fear, the Virgin tells them. Her Son Jesus is our brother, she tells the world. There is no light apart from Him. When He came into the world, His own knew Him not. So it is today. Jesus is in the world, and His own know Him not. He is the light of the world. He is the Good Shepherd.

Jesus is here for all God's children, yet they see Him not. He is calling all God's children to His Heart. Jesus drives away all darkness, all fear by the power of His love. Jesus is truth. The visionaries tell us it is in Jesus, through Jesus, and with Jesus that man lives on in God. They cite as their source the Blessed Virgin Mary whom they personally see daily.

I have learned that Medjugorje is not about visionaries, nor is it about people, places, and events. Medjugorje is the story of paradise and the Eternal Father's prodigal children. He had a plan from the beginning for His faithful ones. That plan is unfolded in the Church and the Scriptures.

We have been advised by the children of Medjugorje that the mother of Jesus brings God's plan to mankind for the last time. She pleads: "Listen well, O children of the earth. Those of you who have ears to hear, *hear* His call, for the Eternal Father loves each of you with an unfathomable love.

I am the great God of Abraham, Isaac, and Jacob.
All is Mine but your free will.
Before I made the world I called you, O beloved children of Mine.
I called to you and you came forth out of My Heart overflowing with love.

I Myself have named you.
Love of My Heart, O little ones of My earth. I, your Father, sent you Mary. I gave you Jesus.
The past and the future are Mine.
You have only now.
Choose Me, My children.
Choose My ways. Choose life.

Listen to My words.
Listen to My daughter Mary as she calls to you for the last time.
Follow my Son, Jesus, to paradise.
Follow Him to My waiting arms, O My beloved little ones of My earth.
Follow Him into My Heart.
Each one of you on My planet earth is My creature.
Everything you have is Mine.
You are just beginning to comprehend your dependence on Me for everything.

Live now, while you still have time, before My face, My children.
Then all you do and all you use and all you experience will be for Me, and with Me, and by Jesus, and Mary, all will be in Me.
There is no darkness before My face.
Keep your heart pure, My children. Cling to My ways.
Love, only love. All will be well for those who do My will.
Pray for perseverance. Pray for patience. Pray for endurance.
The fire of love is strongest when the way is dark; then the fire of love guides you.
Love untested is no love at all.
Come to Me, My children. My arms await you.

I am the Great God of Abraham.
I am the faithful one.
My words to you, My children of the covenant, are the promise of My beloved Son, Jesus, who said: "I will never leave you orphans.
I will send the Holy Spirit that you may have life."

Though your sins be as numerous as the stars in the sky,
My promise is. You are the children of My covenant with My people.
I am faithful to My covenant.
Though My people turn from Me, I am.
Though My people disregard My laws, though they forget Me in their self-esteem, I am.
The day comes when the self of man is no more.
My children live in Me.

Though all else would pass away, those who live in Me, live in My fullness.
Be a light to the world, My children.
Speak only to bless.
Be filled with love.
Stay in My Heart.
There you are safe from all the passing things of the world.
Trust My providence.
Be filled with peace, My children.
Persevere, My children.
The path to paradise is narrow.
Jesus walked that path to show you the way.
Pray always.
Fast, My children.
Be at peace.
Soon your sorrows will be joy.
Speak only to bless.
Silence is My way.
Love with My love for your love is weak and imperfect.
O creatures of Mine, trust Me.
Your true home is heaven.
Peace is My gift.
Peace must reign in the silence of your hearts. Only then will peace reign in the world.
Peace in the world is the fruit of peace in mankind's heart.

Peace is the child of forgiveness.
Forgiveness is the child of love.
Love is only possible through prayer.
Prayer is the echo of mankind's longing calling to My Heart. Peace is the fruit of prayer.

PART I

MEDJUGORJE AND THE PHENOMENON

His ways are steeped in humility.

CHAPTER 1

IN THE BEGINNING

It shall come to pass in the last days, says God, that I will pour out a portion of my spirit upon all mankind: Your sons and daughters shall prophesy, your young men shall see visions, your old men shall dream dreams. Indeed, upon my servants and my handmaids I will pour out a portion of my spirit in those days, and they shall prophesy. And I will work wonders in the heavens above, and signs on the earth below: blood, fire, and a cloud of smoke. The sun shall be turned to darkness, and the moon to blood, before the coming of that great and glorious day of the Lord. Then shall everyone be saved who calls on the name of the Lord.

Acts 2 : 17–21

In the rural hamlet of Medjugorje, nestled in the mountains of southwestern Yugoslavia, where Marxist-Leninism was once the state-imposed Communist regime, the Blessed Mother of Jesus Christ appeared quite suddenly one evening to two teenager girls. Shocked, frightened, and confused, they fled. Later that same evening, June 24, 1981, the two girls and several other teenagers again saw the Blessed Virgin Mary at the same place, Mount Podbrdo, now known as Apparition Hill. This time she was holding the Infant Jesus. Several claim she called to them and they heard her, and that they saw her and the Child quite clearly, though the distance was at least three soccer fields away. Such a humble beginning augured what may be the most profound and important series of apparitions in the history of the earth, for the Blessed Mother says this is her last apparition, and more than ten years later she continues to appear daily. She has given ten secrets that allegedly contain the final chapters in the history of the world. She states, according to the visionaries, that after the secrets are fulfilled, she will not need to come to earth again.

The place of the apparitions, which have occurred daily since 1981, is fraught with a violent, bloodstained history that goes back at least one thousand years. It continues as violently to this day. The Blessed Mother tells the visionaries:

I am the Queen of Peace
I am the Mother of God
I am the Mother of All People on Earth

They say she appears standing on a cloud wearing a gray dress, a white veil, and a crown of twelve stars. The cloud itself is significant in that never have the visionaries seen her feet or shoes. Her contact with the bloodstained earth is six young people who became the visionaries of Medjugorje: Mirjana Dragicevic Soldo, Ivanka Ivankovic Elez, Ivan Dragicevic, Marija Pavlovic, Jacov Colo, and Vicka Ivankovic (no relation to Ivanka).

Are these the last days? Does mankind stand on the abyss of self-extinction? Is that what the Blessed Mother comes to tell the world? The weapons for such a cataclysm exist. Kindergarten children have seen the means of their own global annihilation on the television screen as death and destruction have exploded for years in the Middle East. Yet the Blessed Mother calls herself the Queen of Peace. The visionaries say she is so beautiful that there are no words to describe her. They say she is "pure love." The appearance of "pure love" juxtaposed with a region so bloody produces a dramatic contrast. The area itself is harsh. The people, for the most part, give evidence in their demeanor of the lived memories of oppression and deprivation.

Medjugorje means "Between-the-Mountains," and so it is. Thousands of years ago the sea covered the valley that separates the ranges. Here in the poorest, most economically undeveloped region of Bosnia-Herzegovina, the earth itself is often stony and stingy. Though tobacco and grapes have been harvested since the Middle Ages, the crop yield is never abundant. Currency was in such short supply at the time of the first apparition that it was standard for the able-bodied men to labor as migrant workers in West Germany or Italy, while the women and children kept the fields and the animals.[1] The hard currency the men were able to earn abroad bought cars and televisions, indoor bathrooms, and even washing machines.

The grandmothers of the village still dress in the traditional black garb of widows, since most are indeed widows. World War II took its toll on the older men, and those who survived often were debilitated by excessively hard work and malnutrition. Assets that were desirable in Medjugorje, as recently as 1981, were sheep, cows, chickens, donkeys, and goats, which would wander over the dirt roads. The women and children tended the animals in this village of four hundred families, who live in small stucco houses with red roofs. Each has a little garden, but the land is rarely fertile. The grandfathers, who are the increasingly few survivors of World War II, find joy for the most part in rest. Many spend their summers sitting in the hot sun silently staring at life around them; in winter they sit by the wood stove or play cards and drink schnapps. And some do work in the fields.

For seven hundred years, the people have had a Lenten tradition of fasting only on bread and water. This tradition dates back to the days when Saint Francis of Assisi sent his first group of missionaries to the Republic of Herzegovina and on to Medjugorje. The church has been the center of village life ever since. Saint James Church is large, with twin towers. It holds about sixteen hundred people. Behind the church, across the fields, stands Cross Mountain, thirteen hundred meters high and dotted with fourteen Stations of the Cross erected along a rocky and treacherous path that culminates at the summit where a high, gray concrete cross was erected by the villagers in 1933.

The concrete cross was constructed to commemorate the nineteen hundredth anniversary of the crucifixion of Jesus Christ. There is a practical purpose to the cross. Since its erection, the devastating hailstorms that had bombarded the village, bringing destruction and death, have stopped. A popular legend in Medjugorje has it that Pope Pius XI himself had a dream in which an angel commanded him to have a high cross erected on Mount Sipovac. It is then by Pontifical Commission that Mount Sipovac became the recipient of the high cross built by the villagers themselves, who changed not only the name of the mountain to Mount Krizevac (Cross Mountain) but the very course of their lives.[2]

Opposite Mount Krizevac is another, smaller mountain known as Podbrdo. This is where the Blessed Virgin Mary first appeared to two teenage girls as they walked along a dusty road in the area of Bijakovici. They were friends of long standing. Fifteen-year-old Ivanka Ivankovic lived in Mostar but spent summers with her grandparents in Bijakovici, where her family owned a small vineyard. Mirjana Dragicevic, sixteen, who lived in the Bosnian capital of Sarajevo, also spent summers with her grandmother in Bijakovici.

On the feast day of Saint John the Baptist, June 24, 1981, a mysterious light hovered over the small mountain (Mount Podbrdo) in Medjugorje. In that brilliant light, the two teenagers saw a beautiful woman holding an infant whom she was uncovering to show to them. Incredulous, they heard her call to them. They fled in fear.

The young girls talked to their friends, and a group of them returned to the foot of the mountain. There she was! They wondered if she could really be the Blessed Virgin Mary. They all ran away in terror. "Why would she come here?" the young people's families asked. "You are not holy," someone thundered at Ivan, sixteen, who was in the group who saw. "How dare you suggest you have seen the Mother of God! It's blasphemy!" various members of the families challenged.

Sixteen-year-old Vicka, also one of the group, has a mother who was more sympathetic. "Did you really see the Virgin?" she asked. Vicka was so certain that she said she was ready to die, if it should come to that, rather than deny the apparition.

"Maybe it's the devil. Sometimes he disguises himself as an angel of light to fool people," said Vicka's wise old grandmother.

"How would I know?" asked Vicka. "She was so beautiful! I know she was from heaven."

"If you ever see her again, take holy water and throw it at the apparition. The devil can't stand holy water. Then you'll know for sure," Vicka's grandmother asserted. Soon everyone was talking.[3]

Vicka's neighbor Marinko gave Vicka and her friend Marija a ride to school the next morning. As they drove past the parish church of Saint James, Marija quietly said, "Marinko, Vicka and some others saw the Blessed Mother last night."

Marinko laughed. "Teenage girls and all their fantasies," he mumbled. "Too early for jokes."

It was 5:00 A.M. Marinko's wife looked hard at Vicka, who was silent. For Vicka that was strange. She was known for her forthright, opinionated chatter. On June 25, 1981, Vicka seemed unaware of everybody in the car. Marinko's wife asked, "Did you see the Blessed Virgin Mary, Vicka?"

Suddenly Vicka's eyes blazed. "I did. It *was* the Blessed Mother. And she held the baby Jesus, too. She was showing Him to us."

Marinko had had enough. "Who else was with you, Vicka?" he asked.

"Ivanka and Mirjana and Milka [Marija's sister] and Ivan," Vicka said.

"Ivan Dragicevic?" Marinko interrupted.

"Yes, Ivan Dragicevic," said Vicka.

"If Ivan says he saw the Virgin, I might believe you, Vicka," said Marinko. "Ivan! Amazing, he's not the kind who would have fantasies like you foolish girls."

"How I would love to be where the Blessed Mother is," Marija sighed. "Just to be near her would be enough for me." Vicka was quiet, pensive, lost in thought the rest of the road trip to Čitluk, a nearby town where Marinko dropped the two girls off for school.[4]

That evening, June 25, 1981, Vicka set off for the small mountain with a tiny jar of holy water. She encountered Mirjana, who had ten-year-old Jacov, a neighbor boy with her. He was so excited that he kept pulling at Mirjana's arm. Vicka heard him say, "I would like to see the Blessed Mother more than anything else in the whole world! Tell me again. What did she look like?" Vicka didn't know Jacov well, but everyone knew he had a difficult home life. People said it was sad, especially since his father had abandoned the family when he was young.

Marija came hurrying up the dusty road. "Milka [who had been among those in the small group who saw the Blessed Virgin the preceding night] couldn't come," she said. "My mother had chores for her to do. Just let me tag along with you," she pleaded to the group.

"I know we'll see her," Vicka said jubilantly, "and I brought the holy water. Won't Baba [Grandmother] be surprised when she finds out it really is the Blessed Mother."

"What if she doesn't come?," asked Ivan.

"She'll come, I know it," declared Vicka.

When they arrived at the place of the previous evening's sighting, they found Ivanka already there. "Do you think we'll see her again?" Ivanka questioned excitedly. "I want to ask her about my mother."[5]

By now, the whole village of Medjugorje was praying for Ivanka. Her mother had died suddenly in mid-May. A woman still young—religious and very beautiful—her death had shocked and saddened everyone. Ivanka had wept uncontrollably in the funeral procession, and at the gravesite she fell upon the coffin, not wanting the gravediggers to bury her mother. From that day on, Ivanka became a child to every family in the village. Everyone wanted to help her.

Friends of the children and other curiosity seekers arrived that evening, though no one remembers how many were there at 6:40 P.M. The six young people who were to become possibly the most famous visionaries in the history of Christianity all say they experienced an internal urge or call to come to the mountain, a summons they could not ignore. Now great flashes of light preceded the apparition.

Then they saw. Falling to their knees, the six visionaries were in ecstasy. That ecstasy has been repeated daily now for more than a decade, and the six—Mirjana, Ivanka, Ivan, Marija, Jacov, and Vicka—have, since that June night in 1981, a story to tell of God's love, God's presence in the world in people's lives, and God's plan for each person on earth. The most studied and tested visionaries in history, they were then humble, simple mountain children.[6] In the intervening years, they themselves have become symbols of humanity as they have grown into adulthood under the intense scrutiny of the ancient rites of the Roman Catholic Church and the telecommunication systems of the modern world. As far as is known, no others in the history of the Church have ever claimed to see the Blessed Mother daily for over eleven years as they deliver to the entire world messages of the final appearance on earth of the Mother of God. What truly happened that second night, June 25, 1981, when the Queen of Peace identified herself?

"We went up to the hill. In front of us we could see a big wall of light." They were all terrified to pass through it because there appeared to be no way through it. "We thought the hill was going to melt." And thinking that would happen, "We ran away."[7]

After running about thirty meters, they turned around while fleeing to see if the light was following them. To their astonishment, they saw this light moving toward the cross on top of Cross Mountain, next to Mount Podbrdo, where they were.

From behind the light began to emerge a woman of such beauty that her presence was almost blinding. The children were running even faster now. Then, after running another twenty meters in terror through thornbushes and mountain scrub, over the jagged rocks of the rugged terrain, they tried to focus on the beautiful lady who, by now, seemed to be clothed in a light so intense that they thought she was "clothed with the sun."

They heard her calling to them. They saw her beckon to them with her arms extended. Fear overwhelmed them and they continued to flee. Reaching their homes they regained their strength. The fear began to subside amid the familiar surroundings. Now the words came tumbling out of their mouths. "I saw a big light!" "So did I." Only six of them said, "After the light, I saw the Blessed Mother. She is so beautiful." The others saw only the light.[8]

No one in the village slept that night. Everyone, it seems, remembers that night and the words of the young people in the group. The villagers, for the most part, were skeptical about the claims of the visionaries. Only the little children believed them, and they said, "I want to go with you tomorrow. Will you take me? I want to see the Blessed Mother, too." Not even they could sleep because they were so excited. The rest of the townspeople couldn't sleep because of fear. The parents of the visionaries could not sleep because of an overwhelming feeling of sadness.

The persecution was about to begin, and the parents sensed it. They admonished the children not to repeat their story, begging, "Please don't say such things. It's a sin. How can you say you saw the Blessed Mother?" The parents were worried that night that the children were ill, perhaps because of the heat; perhaps they were disturbed because of Ivanka's sorrow. Perhaps there were other reasons they didn't know. What if the children, all of them, were unbalanced? They watched the children, especially the six visionaries, closely. They realized that the children seemed very normal about everything save the event on the mountain. They were wondering, "What has happened? Perhaps the children were manipulated. Perhaps somebody told them to say all these things." They rejected the visionaries, refusing to believe their extraordinary claims. "Impossible," they all agreed. "These children aren't holy. The Blessed Mother would never come here." The six visionaries found themselves repeating the same story a hundred times or more to all those who came to their houses.[9]

The night passed. And then the dawn came. Many people decided to accompany the children to the mountain the following night. They would see for themselves.

The next day, June 26, almost everyone from the village was there. Some people came on foot, others came in the back of pickup trucks, some on donkeys and in donkey-drawn carts, in a scene that suggested the nineteenth century more than the twilight of the twentieth. More than five thousand people assembled when the children began to pray. Vicka led the group in praying seven Our Fathers, seven Hail Marys, and seven Glory Be to the Fathers. Her grandmother told her it was appropriate to honor the seven sorrows of the Blessed Mother. Then Vicka led the group with the Apostles' Creed. She saw light come upon the mountain, and then great flashes of light flooded them. As the flashes finished, the beautiful lady stood there with a smile of such beauty that the children could not speak. Their eyes revealed pure love. The ecstasy had begun. Vicka stood up. She held a small jar of holy water in her left hand and a rose in her right hand. Sprinkling the holy water in the sign of the cross, she said: "If you are Satan, go away from us." The Blessed Mother, smiling with an eternal love and joy, spoke:

Do not be afraid, dear angels.
I am the Mother of God.
I am the Queen of Peace.
I am the mother of all people.

Vicka turned to the crowd and said, "Can't you see now? We are all telling the truth."

No one had seen anything but the six in their ecstasy, bathed in an immense light. "Is it the light of the Blessed Virgin?" someone shouted. They all saw the light. It was enough for them. Silence was their gift to the Blessed Mother from heaven, who was right there with them on their mountain in the strange, mystical light.

From that moment on, all the parishioners followed the children, and they believed them. They had had their sign. They saw the light. The bishop came. He and many of the priests began to believe firmly in the apparitions of the Blessed Virgin, which have continued each day at 6:40.[10]

Word, like fire racing from rooftop to rooftop, spread far and wide. The police were confused. A political plot, they reasoned. Perhaps a nationalist gathering camouflaged by religious clothes, they scoffed. They made the decision to disperse the people and prevent these gatherings. On June 27, the children were surrounded by mobs of people, many of whom were believers. Many more were skeptics determined to unmask the hoax. The pastor, Father Jozo, in contrast to the bishop, did not believe the children. Concerned that they were possibly using substances brought to Medjugorje from Sarajevo, that they were drinking alcohol, or that they might be caught up in hysteria surrounding Ivanka's mother's death, he was skeptical and rigid. He later said, "Faith is really a gift. Until I prayed and got the gift of faith, I couldn't believe even the bishop."[11]

The bishop spoke to Father Jozo five times. Twice he gave homilies to the parishioners. He said, "The children are not lying. The children are telling the truth. We have to follow them and listen to them. I am more sure of Medjugorje than of Fatima," he told the people.[12]

News of the continuing apparitions spread rapidly. Within a few days, thousands were coming to the hill. Many came to pray, some came out of curiosity, and a few came to spy. The Communist authorities felt threatened by such a huge outpouring in this region, where the Croatian population had never really accepted incorporation into the Federal Socialist Republic of Yugoslavia. The immediate interpretation of the authorities was that the alleged apparitions served as a pretext to organize a political rally, or perhaps as a call to Croatian uprising.

Not only were the six visionaries brought in for repeated questioning, but the parish priest, Father Jozo Zovko, by now a firm believer, was arrested, charged with subversion, and sentenced to a period of imprisonment. In addition, the officials prohibited access to the hill, declaring the area out of bounds.

It was then that the Franciscans, who have always served the parish, began the daily practice of rosary devotions and Mass each evening in the church. The authorities, without realizing it, created the conditions whereby the apparitions became a part of the church ceremonies, thus allowing the Franciscans the opportunity to interpret all the messages of the Blessed Mother in the light of the Gospel.[13]

Gradually the authorities came to accept the events at Medjugorje, though they continuously kept watch, even by helicopter surveillance. Over the years they grew keenly aware of the revenue potential of the millions of pilgrims coming each year to Medjugorje. In fact, rumor has it that in certain crasser circles in Yugoslavia, the Blessed Mother became known as "Our Lady of Hard Currency." How long Medjugorje will be available as a place of pilgrimage depends largely on the political stability of the region.

Traditionally, it is not the Vatican but the bishop of the diocese who must investigate and decide upon the authenticity of Marian apparitions. Bishop Pavao Zanic of Mostar has the responsibility of safeguarding the Church against the oppression of a Communist government. Initially, he publicly defended the visionaries. But then he set up an investigatory commission, and his approach to the apparitions became embroiled in a long-standing dispute between the secular clergy and the Franciscans, which has its roots deep in Croatian history.[14] Though the bishop publicly voices strenuous opposition to the apparitions at Medjugorje, he has provided pastoral care to the millions of pilgrims who have flocked to the village. A bishop of Yugoslavia has been assigned to preside at a Mass at Saint James Church at least once per month. In addition, bishops from all over the world are welcome. They come. They celebrate Mass there and they preach there.

Since Bishop Zanic's commission was making no progress, the Vatican, in May 1986, asked the Yugoslav Bishops Conference to set up a new commission. A Vatican-appointed commission, headed by Yugoslavian Cardinal Franjo Kuharic, is still investigating the apparitions. The investigation has been ongoing for several years. The Catholic Church normally does not approve apparitions until they cease. This commission has not yet issued its final decisions. It is no secret around Rome that Pope John Paul II himself is favorable to the apparitions and encourages pilgrims to go there.[15]

Meanwhile, the apparitions of the Blessed Virgin Mary continue each evening at about 6:40 P.M. in the summer, and 5:40 P.M., as a result of a time change, in the winter. An estimated fifteen to twenty million pilgrims from every part of the world have come to Medjugorje. Many physical cures have been reported, but the real miracles are the countless conversions, the return to the sacraments, prayer, and penance, and the interior peace that pilgrims of all faiths and no faith receive in Medjugorje.

At Medjugorje, the Blessed Virgin Mary told the world through the visionaries: "*I wish to continue giving you messages like never before in history since the beginning of time.*"[16]

Of extraordinary dimension, beyond the comprehension of most save perhaps the prayer warriors who have some illumination into the mystery of the Divinity, the Blessed Virgin Mary has appeared at least daily, in a human form (actually in a body that she says is "transfigured" in the resurrected Christ). These daily apparitions, without precedent in the history of mankind, occur to the Medjugorje visionaries wherever they happen to be. Conservatively, if one calculates at least daily visitations of the Blessed Virgin for ten years, the numbers would be roughly 3,650 visitations. Since there are six visionaries, that number could be conservatively multiplied again. The messages from heaven are contained in Chapter 14 of this book. There is no precedent for this apparition, though Saint Louis Grignon de Montfort wrote in about 1700 that the last days would witness an explosion of grace and heavenly blessings through Mary.[17] Could Medjugorje be what he envisioned?

Of great significance is the fact that many others, including the village children Jelena Vasilj and Marijana Vasilj (no relation), Father Jozo Zavko, O.F.M., pastor at the beginning of the apparitions, as well as untold villagers and pilgrims, and even those who have never been pilgrims, have claimed private apparitions, visions, and locutions in these days. During the spring of 1982, the visionaries asked the Blessed Mother about other alleged apparitions. They said, "People are surprised that you are appearing in so many places!" The Blessed Mother responded, "*If it is necessary, I will appear in each home.*"[18]

The visionaries asked the Blessed Mother about the many signs and phenomena people were seeing everywhere. The Blessed Mother responded, *"It is God who gives them. My children, have you not observed that the faith began to extinguish itself? There are many who do not come to [worship] except through habit . . . [the signs are] necessary to awaken the faith . . . [they are] a gift from God."*[19]

Father Jozo's story seems to typify the kind of "purification" some pilgrims undergo after their original encounter with the Mother of God at Medjugorje. Father Jozo was arrested, tried, and sentenced to a maximum security prison where it is said he was severely tortured. Eventually, the story goes, he was released because the iron door of his cell would mysteriously be open each morning at the change of the guard. Immense rays of light would emanate from inside the cell. So mysterious was the phenomenon that those who did venture a look said they saw Jozo kneeling in prayer surrounded by a light "as bright as the sun." Was the "woman clothed with the sun" (Apoc. 12:1) there with him? Father Jozo neither confirms nor denies the story.[20]

The Medjugorje pilgrims have become zealous at spreading the messages around the world. Prayer groups exist and are being formed everywhere by people of all faiths. Personal testimonies circulate around the world. Books proliferate and millions of newsletters have been disseminated. There are even audios and videos explaining the purported final apparition of the Mother of God.

Given the proliferation of information and the zealousness of the participants, it is becoming more and more obvious to all people everywhere that, in fact, Mary, the mother of Jesus Christ, is giving the world "messages like never before in history since the beginning of time."

What does this mean? Why do people honor the Virgin Mary? The Lord God has commanded that children honor their parents. He has embedded this law so deeply in nature that even the storks observe it. (Storks have such filial devotion toward their fathers and mothers that they carry their old parents on their wings to a warmer spot as winter approaches, that they may reciprocate the benefits they have received from them.) There can be no doubt that Jesus observed to the height of perfection this commandment that was engraved upon the heart of humanity. Hence His own mother Mary is necessarily endowed with the richest treasures a creature can have.[21]

"When the Lord Jesus came into this world He sought the lowest place there was and He found none lowlier in humility than the Virgin."[22]

"She gave Him a place according to His desire. Now He gives her one according to His love, exalting her above the cherubim and seraphim."[23]

Those who know Jesus love and cherish His mother, for He did. Those who do not know Him have had little reason to honor the Great Ark of the Covenant, which Mary is. Medjugorje is a paradox. People of all faiths and no faith have come there seeking God. Mary brought God in human flesh to mankind. Her presumed presence is once again drawing all humanity.

Is this love for Mary, which is inflaming the war-weary world, really the beginning of the reign of peace promised by the angels at Bethlehem to men of goodwill? She does call herself the Queen of Peace at Medjugorje.

CHAPTER 2

SIGNS, WONDERS, AND WARNINGS

Satan is strong and wants to sweep away the plan of peace and joy, and make you think that my Son is not strong in His decisions.

Signs, wonders, and warnings of possible self-destruction are part of the Marian apparitions of the twentieth century.[1] An interesting time sequence, which may be significant: from the words of the first prophet until Jesus Christ walked the earth, there was a two-thousand-year time span. Since Christ died, nearly two thousand years have elapsed.[2]

In 1917, the Blessed Virgin Mary appeared in her role as the Queen of Prophets at Fatima, Portugal, to three shepherd children, aged seven, nine, and ten.[3] Through these three visionaries, she warned the world of impending chastisements that would occur if people would not repent of their wayward lives. She spoke, of course, about the twisted legacy of World War I and of World War II, more destructive than any wars man could, at that time, fathom. She also warned that Russia, a backward country so poor and primitive in 1917 that it could not even feed its own inhabitants, let alone influence regions beyond its borders, would spread terrors worldwide.

To prevent this she said:

> *I have come to ask for consecration of Russia to my Immaculate Heart and the Communion of Reparation of the First Saturdays [of each month]. If my requests are granted, Russia will be converted and there will be peace. Otherwise, Russia will spread her errors throughout the world, provoking wars and persecutions of the Church. Many will be martyred; the Holy Father will have much to suffer; several nations will be annihilated. In the end . . . my Immaculate Heart will triumph . . . and a period of peace will be granted to the world.*

Few responded to the prophetic warnings of Mary. History records her sad prophecies as fact.

The road from Fatima, though separated by sixty-four years, leads directly to Medjugorje. Once again, Mary has come in the name of the Eternal Father, to warn the world of impending chastisements. Once again, she brings a plan to prevent the ominous doom she sees on the horizon. The visionaries at Medjugorje report the messages of the Queen of Heaven and Earth for all her imperiled children. Their words warrant an analysis by anyone who wants to live.

On August 25, 1991, Mary, the mother of Jesus Christ, gave a message to the world at Medjugorje through the visionary Marija

Pavlovic, who has been receiving messages for the world since March 1, 1984. The military coup of the Soviet Union was collapsing as the message was given, leaving great uncertainty for the world. Yugoslavia itself was tangled in the web of a violent civil war.

> *Dear children! Today also, I invite you to prayer now as never before when my plan has begun to be realized. Satan is strong and wants to sweep away the plan of peace and joy, and make you think that my Son is not strong in His decisions. Therefore, I call all of you, dear children, to pray and to fast still more firmly. I invite you to renunciation for nine days, so that with your help everything I wanted to realize through the secrets I began in Fatima may be fulfilled. I call you, dear children, to grasp the importance of my coming and the seriousness of the situation. I want to save all souls and present them to God. Therefore, let us pray that everything that I have begun be fully realized. Thank you for having responded to my call.*

This message that came forth in August of 1991 at Medjugorje was the first that actually mentioned the ominous prophecies at Fatima. The significance of this is clear, for one needs to recall that in October 1981, at Medjugorje, the Blessed Mother said of Russia: *"It is the place where God will be most glorified. The West has made civilization progress but without God, as if they were their own creators."*[4]

The divine pronouncements revealed at Fatima indicated that an era of turmoil and chastisement was likely to occur. There are strong similarities to the apparitions of the Blessed Mother at Medjugorje. The visionaries at Medjugorje speak about ten secrets—chastisements—that are the result of the sinful ways into which mankind has fallen. There may be days ahead that will bring much suffering.

Though the visionaries have been steadfast in refusing to disclose the secrets themselves, much is already known.[5] Mirjana has been chosen as the instrument through whom each of the ten secrets or calamities to befall the world will be announced three days before each event. The advance warning will serve as a proof of the authenticity of the apparitions at Medjugorje and a final call to the world for conversion. Will such conversion occur? The visionaries say there will still be unbelievers at the time of the third secret, a permanent, indestructible, and beautiful sign from heaven. When asked, "Will many people die between the time of the first secret [chastisement] and the permanent sign promised at Medjugorje?" Mirjana admitted, "After the visible sign, those still alive will have little time for conversion."[6]

There are rumors of natural disaster—earthquakes, volcanoes, typhoons and hurricanes, tidal waves. All of these can kill many quite suddenly without warning. There are also rumors of global economic collapse, droughts, famine, and rampant, uncontrolled disease. There are fears of nuclear explosions. None of this is new. Such has always been the way of life of mankind; yet, according to the Blessed Mother, mankind lives as if there is no God, no accountability, as if man is the center of the universe, and his personal whims and wishes are the center of reality. The Blessed Mother's apparitions contain these promises:

> *My children, you have forgotten. Prayer and fasting will stop war. It will change the natural law. The world must find salvation while there is time. Let it pray with fervor. May it have the spirit of faith.*[7]

The Blessed Mother continuously calls all people on earth to conversion by prayer and fasting. The children of the world, she explains, are led by their appetites because they have never learned mortification of the flesh. Instead they gratify their appetites. Today, those appetites lead them into pastures of grave danger. The world will suffer much. Suffering, however, sanctifies when it is experienced for love of God, she says. God is love. He calls to His children from the mountains at Medjugorje, and deep in the silence of their hearts, wherever they are, to stay faithful to His ways, to seek refuge among His children. The Blessed Mother calls all those who have ears to hear to join prayer groups now. There, she promises, you will find love and peace and consolation from the turmoil of the world. Those who seek God's peace and contentment on this earth know God always protects and guards them. They experience the peace and love of His children who surround them.

CHAPTER 3

MARY, MOTHER OF ALL PEOPLE

Dear children! If you want to be very happy, lead a simple, humble life; pray a great deal and do not delve into your problems, but let God solve them.

—Message to the world from the Blessed Virgin at Medjugorje, 1984.

Christians have always revered Mary as the Daughter of God the Father, Mother of God the Son, Spouse of God the Holy Spirit, and mother of all people on earth. The visionaries at Medjugorje unhesitatingly refer to her as a great and mysterious sign, and a woman possessed of inordinate beauty. This lady and queen comes in such light, they say, that she seems to be actually clothed with the sun. She has a crown of twelve stars and she stands on a cloud, as she is described in Apoc. 12:1.[1] She is surrounded by angels, little angels they say. A synonym for her is pure love. She brings such immense tenderness and love, peace and joy, that the visionaries of Medjugorje each speak of her with astonishment and wonder even though they see her with a frequency and familiarity that is unknown in the history of the Church since the dormition (death) of Mary, the exact date and place of which are unknown.

As expressed by Saint Dionysius the Areopagite, and according to Church dogma, Mary was conceived in the Divine Mind, adorned with the dignity and gifts of the humanity of the sacred Son she would bear. She received from the Trinity the gifts appropriate to her state of being, Mother of God and, as such, mother of humanity. This pure creature, conceived in the Divine Mind before all ages, formed an image of His divinity, in order that His divinity became flesh. In Mary alone are contained more treasures that honor the Lord than those contained in composite among all the multitudes of other creatures.

There is no definition for God, but Pope John Paul II has said: "God is absolute Holiness . . . absolute Grace. . . . He is Eternity and Fullness." Before God made heaven and earth and all that is seen and unseen, He was the unchanging God. He created what humanity knows as "time." Then He made the earth, and all the creatures and things of the earth; the seas and the sky with the moon and the stars, and the sun; the rivers and the land; the fishes and the animals; the trees and the plants.

Then one day it pleased Him, the Almighty Creator of all these things, to fashion an image of Himself out of the dust of the earth. Not a robot, but a man free to love his Creator, or to disregard, ignore, or even hate his Maker. He gave this man a "beloved" to share and reciprocate his love, and to care for with tenderness and joy. She was called woman. The Creator's enemy beguiled her one day and she carried the deception to her husband. He too was beguiled. In that deceptive enchantment the man and the woman fell away from the image of their Creator and Source. This mortal wound introduced sickness and death into their life of perfect love and peace and joy.

But God, their Creator, sensing their distress, intervened (Genesis 3:15). This undefinable Creator of all that is, seen and unseen, sent an angel known as Gabriel to the planet earth centuries later to an Israelite virgin named Mary, daughter of Joachim and Anne, in the small town of Nazareth in the region of Lake Galilee. That region still exists today. It is part of the Middle East.

The angel asked the Virgin if she would cooperate with the will of God. Unwed, but engaged, Mary discovered that God wanted to send His Son, the Messiah, the Promised One, to His poor, lost children. The Israelites had been awaiting the Messiah since their forebears, that first man and woman were banished from paradise and driven out into exile on earth. Life was hard for them. They always remembered paradise. They spoke of it to their children and their grandchildren. Each generation remembered that God had given them a promise in the early days of their banishment. Without that covenant, they couldn't have endured, they often said. Times were so difficult with sickness, death, pain, war, famine, drought, and family fights that often, without the promise, they would have had no reason to keep living. But God covenanted with them that if they were faithful, He would one day send the "woman." Her seed would destroy sickness and death and lead all the faithful back to paradise. Though centuries passed, they still remembered and some were faithful.

Now the angel was asking the maiden of the house of David (and hadn't the prophets said the Messiah would come of the house of David?) if she would consent to the will of God.

"I have no husband. How can I bear this mighty child who will deliver all people on earth from slavery in exile?" she asked.

The angel responded, "*Rejoice, O highly favored daughter! The Lord is with you. Blessed are you among women.*"

She was deeply troubled by these words, and wondered what his greeting meant.

The angel went on to say to her, "*Do not fear, Mary. You have found favor with God. You shall conceive and bear a Son and give him the name Jesus. Great will be His dignity and He will be called Son of the Most High, the Lord God will give him the throne of David his father. He will rule over the house of Jacob forever and his reign will be without end.*"

Knowing she had no husband, the Virgin asked the angel, "*How can this be since I do not know man?*"

The angel said: *The Holy Spirit will come upon you and the power of the Most High will overshadow you; hence the holy offspring to be born will be called the Son of God.*"

The Virgin bowed her head and responded, "*I am the servant of the Lord. Let it be done to me according to God's will.*" (Luke 1:28–38).

And the Virgin Mary became the Mother of God. Along with that Motherhood, she was raised far above other creatures.[2]

Tradition teaches that at that moment it pleased God to make Mary, the Mother of His Son, who carried in her womb an embryo minutes old—the Second Person of the Blessed Trinity made flesh—Queen of All Creation.[3] It was only fitting, after all, that she, to whom the God-Man Himself, by His own law, would owe obedience and honor, would also receive from God that same respect and honor from all created matter.[4] Only creatures with free will are at liberty to reject her queenship. They—men, women, and children—may choose to honor Mary as God does, and to obey her, as Jesus did, or to ignore her.[5]

> *It seemed due the Majesty of the Divinity that the tabernacle chosen for His indwelling should appear before [His creatures] prepared and adorned with all that was highest in dignity and perfection, in nobility and magnificence to the full extent. . . .*[6]
>
> *The Eternal Father made her entire being to shine forth the Divinity; for since the Divine Word was to issue from the bosom of the Eternal Father to descend to that of Mary, He provided for the greatest possible symmetry between the Mother and the Father.*[7]

The result of the showering of such divine gifts upon Mary produced humility such that she did not even have a suspicion of anything great or admirable in herself. On the contrary, the more God blessed her, so much the more lowly were her thoughts concerning herself.[8] She, perhaps alone among God's creatures, truly understood the chasm between the Creator and all created beings. All generations call her blessed because God became man in her womb. Who is the Virgin Mary who said yes to the archangel Gabriel? She is humble. She is the most humble of all God's creatures.

Humility is at the same time the most precious, the most delicate and perishable; for if you lose it in any respect, and if you be not humble in all things without exception, you will not be humble in anything.[9]

Humility is God's way. Humility sees all things belonging to God. Humility, like the gentle breath of a flower, is God's heart in the world. Humility is peaceful. Humility is gentle. Humility is love. Humility is God's way. Mary is humble as God is humble. Like the scent of a flower, humility is beauty. Humility is the scent of God purifying His world of the stench of pride. A humble person is one who knows God well. A humble person savors the delicacies of God's kingdom. A humble person feasts on His love. A humble person feasts on His hidden, silent ways. The noise of God clashes with the noise of the world. God's noise is sweet silence. The world's noise is disorder. A humble person purges the senses of attachments, for all is God's.

Because her most holy Son was Himself to obey this heavenly Queen of Humility who is His mother, and since He was the Creator of the elements and of all things, it follows naturally that they should obey her to whom the Creator subjected Himself and that they should be commanded by her. In her humility, she never used her sovereignty over the elements and the creatures for her own use.[10] She, the mother of the suffering Son of God, knew how valuable suffering is.

Mary knew that God made mankind out of nothing, herself included, not to be a slave to the senses but to be master of all creation out of love for the Creator. The humble soul, like Mary, is a soul that works but uses not. The humble soul, like Mary, replenishes the earth. The humble soul, like Mary, is a source of life. The humble soul, like Mary, is a soul through whom God the Father renews. The humble soul is one through whom Jesus makes all things new. Only through the humble is there life in God.

God enkindled divine love in Mary's heart when He made her the mother of the Word made flesh. She has such a sweetness in her heart that she is ready to communicate it to all people and to shelter them in her heart in order to make them participants of the divine love that was enkindled there. This heart filled with love was one of the principal dispositions required for conceiving the Eternal Word in her womb[11] for the Immaculate Heart of Mary and the Sacred Heart of Jesus are one.[12]

She is the mother of the Body of Christ. All God's children are the children and members of the Body of Christ. It is within the Heart of Jesus that God's children receive the nourishment for their life in God. All God's children are one. Jesus and the Father are one.[13] He who lives in the Heart of Jesus lives in the Heart of God. All else passes away. The Heart of Jesus is a crucible where God's children are prepared for life with the Eternal Father. The Heart of Jesus is the earthly house of God's children.

How does one get into the Heart of Jesus, which is one with the heart of Mary? Her example leads all people to surrender to Him. Surrender to His ways. Live only the life He showed all people on earth when He too walked the earth as we do now. Any other path but the path of Jesus takes God's children far away from the kingdom of the Eternal Father and His waiting arms. Life on earth is short. The prodigal children are lost in the world. Jesus came to the world through the Virgin Mary to show the way home, the way to the Eternal Father's waiting arms, the way to Him.

The purpose of Mary's creation, free from the stain of original sin, was to bring God's Word to His lost children. Like begets like, so God made Mary as close to His own pouring forth as is possible for a creature. God endowed her with perfections corresponding to the humanity of Christ. It can be said the humanity of God is the humanity of Mary, but Mary is never God. The creation of Mary implied the humanity of the Second Person of the Holy Trinity.

Mary is the ultimate fruit of God's love for His children. The Body of Christ is the fruit of the body of Mary. Mary is the fruit of God's perfection. Through Mary, who brought Jesus, God's prodigal children are brought to perfection. It is Jesus who is the means of mankind's perfection. It is Jesus who clothes mankind in His body and blood, which are Mary's body and blood, which are mankind's garments in paradise.

Mary's response to God's redemptive gift of Jesus, in the words of the Magnificat, is an echo of each soul who catches a glimpse of God's wonderful plan in his own life:

> *My being proclaims the greatness of the Lord,*
> *my spirit finds joy in God my savior,*

for He has looked upon His servant in her lowliness;
all ages to come shall call me blessed,
God who is mighty has done great things for me,
holy is His name.
His mercy is from age to age on those who fear Him.
(Luke 1:46–50)

Those who fear God know God.
Those who do not fear God live in profound ignorance and immense darkness.
To offend God's Commandments for any reason whatsoever drives all light, all protection away.
When a soul offends God's Commandments, the evil one gains immense power. He is most effective in darkness.
The soul that disobeys the Commandments brings darkness to his consciousness.
He cannot see truth. He cannot see reality.
The soul living in darkness because of sin cannot find God. Only God's mercy can intervene and bring light.
The Blessed Mother is the Light-bearer.
Many today do not want her Light.
Her Light is Jesus.

Perhaps this explains why the Blessed Mother has appeared daily for more than eleven years at Medjugorje. Based on the testimony of the visionaries at Medjugorje, and indeed visionaries in many parts of the world, a caring, participating, hands-on mother who sees mankind's heart, and loves all people with unconditional love, is being manifested on a global scale. She is seen as ministering great treasures of grace and blessings to all who ask. She weeps as her "children" blindly reject the flow of these treasures and deprive themselves of participation in the Divinity.

She begs the faithful to join her in prayer, sacrifices, humilities, and heroic acts of love of God and each other so that no one shall lose heaven. She says, "*Do not think about wars, punishments, evil, because if you do you are on the road toward them. Your task is to accept divine peace, to live it, and to spread it.*"[14]

The messages and the miracles of Medjugorje have just begun to awaken a world slumbering in fear and uncertainty. The Virgin Mary calls to an endangered world, she says, for the last time. The deepest longing of the human heart is reentry to the garden of paradise from which all children of the first man and woman were banished, for in that garden, mankind walks with God, his Creator, Source, and Goal. At Medjugorje, it seems the memories of homeland and Father are stirred as the Virgin Mary, the God-bearer, tenderly shows humanity the fulfillment of the promise, the covenant of God with His creature, man.

PART II

VISIONS

The end is really the beginning.

CHAPTER 4

THE VISIONARIES TODAY

God's will is the path He has chosen for each of His children.

The interviews that follow were conducted with the six young people from Medjugorje who assert boldly that they see the mother of Jesus Christ daily. They claim they are delivering messages from God the Father, Creator of heaven and earth, given to them by the Virgin Mary, mother of Jesus Christ. They have given their lives as surety for the authenticity of the apparitions, which have been ongoing in excess of eleven years. What do these messages contain?

The visionaries announce the fulfillment of the covenant established between God and mankind immediately following the sin of Adam and Eve when paradise was lost. God so loved His creatures—man and woman—that He promised (covenanted) to send . . . "the woman," Mary, clothed with His Son (Rev. 12) whose seed (Jesus) would crush the head of the serpent (Satan) (Gen. 3:15). Jesus, from the cross, identified His mother as that woman of the covenant, and mother of all the offspring of Adam and Eve who choose her (John 19:25:27). John took her for his own. He had the gift of wisdom even if it was clothed in mere obedience. Those who are wise also take Jesus' mother for their own in these times, say the visionaries.

All six visionaries explain that the Blessed Mother promises those who abandon themselves to the will of the Eternal Father, who pray—particularly the rosary, which she says has immense power in times of stress, sorrow, and temptation—who trust the divine mercy of her Son Jesus, who trust in her mother's heart, who trust her power, shall be taken by the hand after death to the throne of God—that is, they shall reenter paradise. How can Mary, the mother of Jesus, make such a promise? Tradition indicates it is by the power of the sacrifices of her beloved Son (the promised "seed of the woman"). Through her, Jesus brings light and eternal life to each who so chooses.

According to the visionaries, Mary at Medjugorje says a period of darkness has enveloped the planet. Today, as the teachings and beliefs of Jesus Christ are lifted high on the cross of indifference, disrespect, abuse, and death, the faithful stand at the foot of the cross as Mary and John once did. And once again Mary is at the foot of the cross (at Cross Mountain), appearing daily, loving and pleading with her children, all people on earth, to return to God while there is still time. She reminds people Jesus is the light. Jesus is life. Jesus is the way to paradise lost. Jesus is the truth (God is the Creator, man is the creature). Jesus is life (eternal life).

Mary, spotless daughter of the Father, and Jesus, perfect creature of the Trinity, and Son of Mary, always did God's will. To a lesser extent, so did the patriarchs and the prophets and the holy women. The visionaries speak of God's will as the path to paradise.

What is God's will? God's will is holiness. God's will for each child of His is reunion with Him. God's will is the path He has chosen for each of His children. When people obey God's will, they live in peace and joy. They are filled with God's love, according to the visionaries. They walk the path to paradise and to the waiting arms of God, the Father of all humanity.

How does one obey God's will? It is never God's will that people disobey His commandments. Throughout the centuries, people have been warned that it is Satan who constantly entices them to disobey God's will. The visionaries explain the presence of the evil one in the twentieth century in a way that has, according to them, never been possible before. They cite, as their source for this fact, the Blessed Virgin Mary, the "woman" of Genesis 3:15 herself.

All the visionaries are soft-spoken, though Mirjana is perhaps the most soft-spoken. All, except Vicka, are slow to speak.

Each has a smile that emits glorious joy, though Ivan smiles least.

None of the visionaries uses hand gestures.

Their body language is simple and unassuming.

They would never stand out in a crowd and, in fact, often go about the throngs in Medjugorje quite unnoticed. They seem to like being inconspicuous.

Each has said, "I am not important."

The interviews with the visionaries and locutionists were conducted, for the most part, with translators. Much of the material was filmed and recorded. Given the language and cultural barriers, every effort has been made to preserve the integrity and the intent of each of the statements of the visionaries and locutionists.

On Friday, December 2, 1988, the *Birmingham News* of Alabama carried this article about the visionaries of Medjugorje:

> *The six visionaries have willingly undergone extensive medical tests by those who seek to discredit the authenticity of the apparitions, all to no avail.*
>
> *Repeated medical tests have, in fact, tended to lend credence to the arguments in favor of the apparition. In 1983, Ludvik Stopal, a Yugoslavian psychiatrist, hypnotized Marija and found*

> *her testimony about the apparitions of the Blessed Virgin identical to her conscious testimony. His extensive tests of all six visionaries concludes they are psychologically normal.*
>
> *In 1984, the visionaries were then subjected to a series of tests by a team of French doctors. Electrocardiograms were administered. The movements of the eyes, larynx, and various reflexes were all measured. "They documented a simultaneous fixing of the gaze in an identical point, with eye movement ending at the same time. They concluded that the concurring bodily reactions were inexplicable."*

In addition, this part contains interviews with the two "locutionists" of Medjugorje, Jelena and Marijana (Chapter 11). These young women heard from the visionaries what the "Fatima peace plan in action" is (though they had never heard of Fatima at the time). Nine years old, they responded fully and enthusiastically. Their rewards have been immense.

The visionaries and locutionists have much to say—and, in fact, probably little of anything that is not already in Scripture. The Eternal Father told Adam and Eve and all their offspring of the cosmic battle between the seed of Satan and the seed of the woman, Mary, that will rage until the end of time when the "woman" Mary will crush the head of Satan (Gen. 3:15). How does one recognize Satan? Mirjana has said, among other things, anger is a mark of the children of the evil one.[1] Jelena has said that impatience is a sign of the presence of the evil one.[2] Ivan has warned that greed and avarice—when goods and services are taken for which no funds are available—are a sign of the presence of the evil one in people's lives.

What about people who have nothing? Should they steal? Since no one may ever disobey the Commandments, Vicka says, people are invited to turn to God and ask His providence. If He should provide, then people use what He provides in gratitude. If He should withhold things of the earth, people need to trust His providential care. Of course, this presumes that people work and are good stewards of all the gifts God has given them. Many who seem indigent, living without, actually do not use the gifts God has given them. Certainly some are poor because many don't share. A joyful giver wears God's joy. A sorrowful giver wears his own greed. And many today fail to help their brothers and sisters at all.

If all people on earth live the Fatima peace plan, which the visionaries at Medjugorje have outlined, all people would live in peace and abundance, the Blessed Mother reminds her children, for that is God's will.

The visionaries tell us the Blessed Virgin at Medjugorje says that God's will is for all His children to live in peace, His peace. Jacov reminds people that God's children know they may keep nothing they do not need. Anything not being used must be given away. All people must be good stewards of God's gifts. He is a God of justice, as well as a God of love, the Blessed Mother warns. She asks all people to be sensitive to the needs of those around them. At Medjugorje the Blessed Mother asks people to live in peace and simplicity. She asks people to follow the path of Jesus to paradise, for He is meek and gentle of heart (Matt. 11:29). He rescues those who get caught in the evil one's traps. The way to Jesus is surrender to His will, to His ways. His ways are gentle. His ways are steeped in humility. His ways are contained in obedience to God's commandments (John 14:15). The Blessed Mother says, "*Hurry and be converted. Do not wait. The time is now.*"

The visionaries of Medjugorje offer, perhaps more than at any time since the Scriptures were written, a glimpse of the Blessed Virgin Mary, the mother of Jesus, whom they refer to as "pure love," God's love. They bear witness to her love. They speak of her patience, which she says is His patience. Her Son is the Savior of the world.

What does the Blessed Virgin Mary, mother of Jesus Christ, want us to know? Those who have ears to hear may listen to the words of the Eternal Father once again, for He brings messages through Mary, claim the visionaries. The words issue forth, according to Mary, for the last time.

Such beliefs began with a woman whose name was Eve. They end with a woman whose name is Mary, for her Son, Jesus, promises eternal life (John 14:2–4). The end is really the beginning.

The chapters that follow present a brief glimpse into the lives of the six visionaries, followed by a deeply personal discussion about the Blessed Mother, their extraordinary visitor from heaven. The reader will note that each of the six children, who by now are young adults, has a distinct and unique appreciation and approach to his or her mission. Each is steeped in humility and simplicity, but the lived expression of these qualities varies. The visionaries today are well trained for the job they have. After more than eleven years of daily visitations with the Blessed Virgin Mary, their very lives are a testimony of the sacred trust they have been given, for they are messengers to God's prodigal children—of whom each is also one.

PRODIGAL CHILDREN

You are all the prodigal children.
I am the Prince of Peace.
My reign is a reign of love and mercy.
Hide in My mercy.
I am preparing My flock.
I Myself shall govern My people.
I shall walk among My people.
I have come to claim My people.

No one shall pillage My flock.
I am the Good Shepherd.
I know Mine and Mine know Me.
My sheep hear My voice.
Come to Me all you who fear.
Come to Me all you who labor.
Live in the safety of My Word.
Live in the protection of My Commandments.
Hold My Heart as you walk.
the path of the earth to Me.

I am the Light of the world.
Live in My light.
Live in My peace.
Live in My hope.
Live in My joy.

I am Love.
I am Peace.
I am Joy.

Live in the Holiness of My ways.
Follow Me, My very beloved, My very dear children
to My waiting arms.
My kingdom is a kingdom of Love, of Joy, of Peace.
My children dance and sing before My face.

My children eat honey and drink sweet water.
I have redeemed My children.

These are the times of My great victory.
Rest in the Immaculate Heart of My Mother.
Allow her to bring you to Me.
I am the Way, the Truth, and the Life.

CHAPTER 5

M I R J A N A

Every time I see an unbeliever, I know what awaits him.

Mirjana Dragicevic Soldo, the second visionary to see the Blessed Virgin on June 24, 1981, was the first visionary to receive all ten secrets and the first to stop seeing the Blessed Mother daily. As a young woman, she is lovely. She has a sense of fashion that reflects her life in the once cosmopolitan city of Sarajevo. Soft-spoken, Mirjana is intelligent and possesses the sophistication of one who has studied at the University of Sarajevo. She is married to fellow university student Marco Soldo, the nephew of the Franciscan psycho-theologian, Father Slavko Barbaric, who is also the spiritual director of the visionaries.[1] Both Marco and Mirjana have some facility with English and have traveled widely. Like the visionary Ivan, Marco's favorite sport is basketball. He is tall, athletic, quite spiritual himself, and takes protective care of Mirjana, who had a one-year maternity leave of absence from her job with an international tourism agency.

Born on March 18, 1965, Mirjana is the daughter of Jozo Dragicevic, a hospital radiographer; her mother formerly worked in a boutique. Mirjana has a brother fifteen years younger than herself. Her family lived in Sarajevo before the Civil War of 1991, though Mirjana's grandmother lives in Medjugorje, where Mirjana spent her childhood summers. Mirjana, Marco, and their daughter, Maria, born on December 9, 1990, have a house of their own in Medjugorje. (During the Civil War of 1992, the family lived in exile.)

Mirjana indicates she carries a heavy burden, for the Blessed Mother has communicated ten secrets to her that allegedly involve chastisements for the sins of the world. At times, when Mirjana is asked about the secrets, she gives the impression that the prophesied misfortunes are so grave for the world that, indeed, she often cannot bear the suffering that this knowledge brings. In fact, Mirjana says that if the Blessed Virgin did not help her she could not endure. While speaking about the secrets, Mirjana was asked, "Are the secrets that bad?" She responded, "Yes, every time I see an unbeliever, I know what awaits him. It is often more than I can bear."

Mirjana holds the future of the world on a mysterious piece of parchment, which only she can read. This parchment was given to her by the Blessed Mother. On it are written the days and dates of the ten secrets, chastisements for the sins of the world.

Mirjana has had some horrible encounters with Satan. She knows Satan and his wiles by personal experience. She asked me to warn people throughout the world that Satan is real and wants to deprive

God's children of their inheritance, the kingdom of heaven, won by the victory of Jesus on the cross. She said the Blessed Mother told her and, in fact, allowed her to experience the power and seduction of Satan.[2]

Mirjana says that when the first secret entrusted to her is realized, the power of Satan will be broken.[3] She says the Blessed Mother told her that is why he is so aggressive right now. Satan has had immense power throughout the twentieth century, a power he has never had before, nor will he ever have again, claims Mirjana, who says the Blessed Mother told her that. According to the visionary, a great cosmic battle is in full fury now for souls. The battle rages between the "seed" (children) of Mary and the "seed" of the serpent (Satan).[4] The Eternal Father gave Satan one last challenge at His church, the twentieth century, and even some time preceding it. According to Mirjana, there were three things Satan did not know:

1. The Eternal Father would send Mary, the "woman" of His covenant with His people,[5] throughout the century to warn, encourage, and mother the souls struggling in this time of great darkness.[6]
2. The Eternal Father would permit such vast amounts of grace in the world as has never before been known in the history of mankind.[7]
3. The Eternal Father would send chosen souls who would remain faithful no matter what the allure or attack of Satan.[8]

Compassion for the unbeliever, the wasted life, truly rests heavily on Mirjana. She states, "They are choosing things that pass away. They are wasting their lives on things they cannot keep." She knows what is to come. "Pray," she pleads. "Pray for unbelievers. They do not know what awaits them! Satan is the great liar. He promises everything. He wants to destroy all peace, all joy, all happiness. A synonym for Satan is pain." One day, Mirjana exclaimed, "I've seen heaven! Nothing, absolutely nothing of the earth is worth one unkind word." Mirjana, the spokeswoman of the final apparition of the Blessed Virgin Mary who calls herself the Queen of Peace, says, "The Blessed Virgin comes in love and mercy to the planet earth, for the last time, bringing assurances of life after death of such splendor that we can only catch glimpses now through shared love and joy. Heaven is worth any price."

Mirjana's name has two parts: *mir*—which in Croatian means *peace*; and *jana*—which means *John*. The Blessed Mother first appeared on the feast of John the Baptist, June 24, 1981. His message was: "Repent, the kingdom of heaven is at hand."

The visionaries, especially Vicka, have stated that God, Himself, named each person, each creature with free will on the planet. When asked the source of such information, Vicka volunteered, "The Blessed Mother said before God made the world He knew each one of us, He Himself named us before He made the world. He breathed us out of the love in His Heart into our mother's womb. If you want to know who you really are, ponder the Biblical meaning of your name."[9]

As one of six visionaries, Mirjana too must be faithful to the messages of the Blessed Mother. She too must pray and fast. Her life is open to the scrutiny of the world. She tolerates such intrusion into her private life for the love of God and the Blessed Mother.

A compilation of several edited interviews with Mirjana follows:

Q. Mirjana, I noticed that these days in 1991 pilgrims are coming to your doorstep here in Medjugorje. Do you give general interviews every day like the other visionaries?

A. I see pilgrims only from time to time.

Q. Do you have a message for the pilgrims?

A. My message is for all people. Pray for unbelievers. This is a special time of grace. Our prayers really matter. The Blessed Mother asks all her faithful children on the whole earth to pray for unbelievers, that they, too, may come to the kingdom of heaven.

Q. Mirjana, do you give many private interviews?

A. No. I give very few interviews.

Q. Why?

A. That's how the Blessed Mother wants it.

MIRJANA'S VISIONS

Q. Mirjana, can you describe how she looks?

A. The Blessed Mother appears to me the same way now that she did during the time that I had the daily apparitions. She is dressed the same way: the gray dress, the white veil, that beautiful face, those incredibly beautiful eyes of love. Her whole demeanor is filled with God's love.

Q. How often do you see the Blessed Mother now?

A. My *daily* apparitions with the Blessed Mother stopped in December of 1982. That was the hardest period of my life.

Q. Do you still remember the end of the apparitions with great pain, Mirjana?

A. Yes. I remember how horrible it was for me, how terribly depressed I was when the Mother of God no longer came to me every day.

Q. When you look back on those terrible days, how did you get through it?

A. The Blessed Mother promised me something very special. She promised me that she would come to me once a year on my birthday for the rest of my life. And she also promised me that she would come to me at times of very great difficulty in my life.

Q. Mirjana, you sometimes share your apparition of December 24, 1982, at your home in Sarajevo. At that time you were receiving daily apparitions. Since there were only a few people present at your house that night, do you wish to speak about that apparition?

A. It makes me sad.

Q. Why?

A. The Blessed Mother told me that it was my next-to-last apparition. She told me she would come the next day on Christmas as a gift of joy without any revelations. I already knew the tenth secret, which is particularly grave. She promised me she would come every year on my birthday, March 18, as long as I lived.

Q. Mirjana, do you remember the message you got that Christmas that upset you so much?

A. At my last meeting with the Blessed Mother, after I had [been told] all ten secrets, she told me she loved me. She prepared me for this moment for a whole month. She explained everything to me. She was very motherly. She told me that she had accomplished the task for which she had selected me. She told me that I was sufficiently informed and that I must realize that I too have a normal life, that I must return to everyday life like all girls of my age. The Blessed Mother said I must continue living without her motherly advice, and the daily conversations with her, which had been so necessary for my soul. But she promised to be always beside me and to help me in the most difficult situations of my life as long as I live with God.

Q. What does that mean?

A. As long as I stay close to God she promised she would help me. The meeting with the Blessed Mother was so hard for me I can still remember my pain. I felt it in my soul. It was such a great emptiness. It's similar to the feeling you have when you realize that the most beautiful thing in your life is gone. Our Blessed Mother was keenly aware of my torment and my pain. She prayed with me to cheer me up. She prayed that I would be happy. She asked me to sing, to praise, and to glorify God. She taught me that when I'm sad, if I sing and praise and glorify God, I won't be sad anymore.

Q. Why not?

A. Because some of God's joy falls on me too. I prayed the prayer that I always prayed when I was alone with her, the Hail Holy Queen.

Q. Mirjana, is it still your favorite prayer?

A. I love that prayer, but now I love all prayer. I always will remember the words of the Blessed Mother to me that day. She told me, "*Mirjana, I selected you and told you all that is necessary. I transferred to you many horrors that you must carry worthily. Think of me and think about how many tears I have shed because of these horrors. You must always be courageous. You quickly understood my messages and now you have to understand that I may no longer appear to you daily. Have courage.*"

Q. Did she say anything else?

A. The rest was for me, personally.

Q. You seem so happy now. What a beautiful Christmas it must have been for you with your new baby.

A. I am always happy when the Blessed Mother is near me.

Q. Mirjana, you have been having other apparitions since 1982, when your daily apparitions stopped. Are they to prepare you for the procedure that you are to follow for the revelation of the secrets?

A. Yes.

Q. Are the secrets and their unfolding imminent?

A. People should be prepared now. People should always be prepared. If people would pray more and think less, they would have more peace.

Q. Mirjana, I remember your apparition on your birthday, March

18, in 1989, the seventh of the promised apparitions on your birthday. You were twenty-four years old that year.

A. Yes. That was a long apparition and a very joyful one, but it was also grave. In these times, on the second of each month during prayer, I listen to the voice of the Blessed Mother in my heart. At that moment we normally pray together for unbelievers. On March 2 of this year [1991], the Blessed Mother told me that I would have my birthday apparition at seven-thirty in the evening. The apparition lasted approximately twenty minutes. During that time we prayed the Our Father and the Glory Be for all our brothers and sisters who do not know God, our Father, and who do not experience His presence.

The Blessed Mother was sad, very sad. Once she begged us all to pray, to help her through our prayers for unbelievers who, she says, do not have the grace to feel the experience of God in their hearts through a living faith. She says that she doesn't want to warn us once again. As a mother she wants to call to all of us and to beseech us for those who do not know anything about the secrets. She herself has suffered, she told me, because she is the mother of all people on earth. The rest of the time of this apparition was spent in conversation concerning the secrets.

Q. Going back to your apparition in 1989, the Blessed Mother identified herself as the mother of all people on earth, didn't she?

A. Yes, she did.

Q. Mirjana, you seemed so distressed after your apparition in Portland, Oregon, on February 2, 1990.

A. Yes, I'll never forget that apparition. The Blessed Mother gave a message for the world that is quite significant.

Q. As I watched you during that apparition, three times it seemed that a great wind came upon you and you swayed back as if you were being blown by this great wind. What was happening during those moments?

A. The Blessed Mother was speaking to me about very serious things. I don't recall though that my body moved. I have no recollection of my body moving at all.

Q. Mirjana, what was the message from the Blessed Mother that February 2, 1990?

A. She said, "*Dear children, I have been with you nine years to tell you that God your Father is the only way, truth, and life. To show you the way that you can reach eternal life. Give good example to your children and to* *those who do not believe. You will not have happiness on this earth; neither will you come to heaven if you do not have a pure and humble heart and if you do not fulfill the laws of God. I am asking you for your help to join me in praying for those who do not believe. You are helping me very little. You have little charity or love for your neighbors and God gave you the love and showed you how you should forgive and love others. For that reason, reconcile, and purify your souls by going to confession. Take your rosary and pray. Take all your suffering patiently. You should remember how patiently Jesus suffered for you. Do not impose your faith on the unbelievers. Show it to them with your example and pray for them, my children. Please pray for them."*

Q. You said that message is significant. So many who know about the Blessed Mother's apparitions feel that the Blessed Mother has spoken to each of us that all could do more.

A. I, myself, feel that way. I know every day that I can do more for the Blessed Mother, and I try and try. But sometimes I fail so much that I can hardly bear it.

Q. When you fail, what do you do?

A. When I fail, I pray. And when I pray, I have peace.

Q. Mirjana, do you still see the Blessed Mother on the second day of the month, every month?

A. Sometimes I see and hear her, but at other times I only hear the Blessed Mother's voice.

Q. Do you also hear the Blessed Mother at other times, that is, other than on the second of the month?

A. No.

MIRJANA'S MESSAGES

Q. Mirjana, your life seems to be very serious. Do you live in profound awe of the messages you carry?

A. I try to be faithful to the goals that the Blessed Mother has given me. I try to live in obedience to her instructions.

Q. How does the Blessed Mother appear to you now, Mirjana?

A. I see her in three dimensions, just as I see a normal person who is with me. She is as close to me and as intimate, more intimate, than even my own mother could ever be with me.

Q. In what way, Mirjana?

A. The Blessed Mother knows me and she loves me just as I am. She always wants the best for me. She trusts me. She loves me.

Q. Mirjana, she is the Mediatrix of All Graces, isn't she?[10]

A. She is filled with grace.

Q. Could you describe what it is like to be around this holy one who is filled with grace?

A. You can experience her presence here in this room with us now through faith. The whole world can experience her love and her presence through faith. All people on earth have that privilege.

Q. Mirjana, does the Blessed Mother only appear in special places?

A. No. She's always present. It is through deep prayer that we can experience her presence. She appears to me to speak to me. So she speaks to me wherever I am. If I am here at home, the apparition occurs in my bedroom.

Q. Does the apparition always occur during prayer and at a special time?

A. Yes. I know in advance when the Blessed Mother will be appearing and I prepare. My heart is so filled with longing that to just wait for her is my life.

Q. Isn't God your life?

A. To wait for the Blessed Mother is to wait for God.

Q. Why is that, Mirjana?

A. Because the Blessed Mother always brings me to her Son. The Blessed Mother always brings me to God. God is the source of all that is. The Blessed Mother herself is only a creature. I'm a creature, you're a creature. We are all just creatures before God.

Q. Why is the Blessed Mother still appearing to you on the second of the month now?

A. Well, as you know, she promised me that she would come to me at any time that I suffer anxiety because of the secrets that I have.

Q. Mirjana, are the secrets causing you great stress these days?

A. I suffer in many ways.

Q. Mirjana, you certainly seem to have great responsibilities. You are the one who has been chosen to announce the day and date of the unfolding of the ten secrets that the Blessed Mother has given for the whole world. Do you carry the responsibility for the unfolding of the final days of the planet?

A. I will announce each secret to Father Petar. He will make whatever public announcement is to come. [Father Petar Ljubicic, O.F.M., is the Franciscan friar in residence at Saint James Parish, Medjugorje, who was selected by Mirjana to reveal the secrets, one by one, to the world. He is now approximately fifty years old. There is some question whether he must reveal the secrets, or whether such announcement is within his discretion. Mirjana herself will reveal the secrets only to Father Petar.]

Q. That is an awesome responsibility. How do you manage?

A. All things are possible with God. On my own, I could do nothing. On my own, I am quite incapable of anything. That is why the Blessed Mother comes to me on the second of the month to help me.

Q. At this time, Mirjana, do you speak about the secrets during your apparition of the Blessed Mother?

A. When I meet with the Blessed Mother now she asks me to ask all people on earth for prayers to help her with the conversion of unbelievers.

THE BLESSED MOTHER AND PRAYERS

Q. Mirjana, do you know what the Blessed Mother does with all these prayers?

A. Yes. The Blessed Mother takes all the prayers and all the penance of all her children on the earth and she brings them to her divine Son, Jesus. I am an instrument. The Blessed Mother comes to all people on earth. She comes that we might know her divine Son, Jesus, better, and in knowing Jesus better we can come to know God, our Father.

Q. Mirjana, you said the Blessed Mother is asking all people on earth to pray and do penance?

A. Yes. The Blessed Mother needs the generous prayers of all her children to help with the conversion of unbelievers.

Q. Are all our prayers for unbelievers?

A. Yes. Many times the Blessed Mother speaks to me about her children. We are all children of the Blessed Mother—believers and unbelievers alike.

Q. Is the Blessed Mother's message different now than the one she gave you in Oregon? There she said her faithful children were not doing enough through prayer and penance. She said those who know about the apparitions at Medjugorje are not helping her even though many of us know of her requests.

A. Her message is the same now. We, her faithful children, are not doing enough. She asks us all to pray every day for unbelievers. Many do not do this.

THE BLESSED MOTHER ON UNBELIEVERS

Q. Mirjana, who are these unbelievers?

A. The Blessed Mother says from time to time even her most faithful children are unbelievers. We all have our moments during the day, during each day of our life, where even the most faithful among us do not believe. So the Blessed Mother prays for each of us too. Many of us who think we believe have many parts of ourselves that really do not believe. The Blessed Mother repeats this plea to her faithful ones: *"Please pray for unbelievers every day. They know not what awaits them."* She recognizes sadly that many of her children throughout the world go to church or places of worship just because it is a tradition, but they are unbelievers because they do not really know and love God. They only go to places of worship as a social custom. The Blessed Mother says they need much prayer so that they, too, can believe.

Q. Mirjana, does the Blessed Mother still speak to you these days about Satan?

A. Yes. She spoke of Satan this year on my birthday at my yearly apparition.

Q. What was the message on March 18, 1991?

A. The Blessed Mother said: *"Dear children! I am glad that you have gathered in such a large number. I desire that you often gather in prayer to my Son. Most of all, I desire that you dedicate prayers for my children who do not know my love and the love of my Son. Help them to know it. Help me as mother of all of you. My children, how many times have I already invited you here in Medjugorje to pray? I will continue because I desire you to open your hearts to my Son, to allow Him to come in and fill you with peace and love. Allow Him! Let Him enter! Help Him by your prayers in order that you might be able to spread peace and love to others, because these actions are most necessary for you now in this time of battle with Satan.*

"I have often said to you, pray, pray, pray, because only by means of prayer will you drive off Satan and all the evil that goes along with him. I promise you, my children, that I will pray for you, but I seek from you more vigorous prayers, and I wish you to spread peace and love, which I have been asking of you in Medjugorje for already almost ten years. Help me, and I will pray to my Son for you."

At the monthly apparitions and at my yearly apparition the Blessed Mother prays with me and comforts me about all the unbelievers in the world.

Q. Mirjana, you said from time to time you're an unbeliever?

A. Consciously I never do not believe.

Q. That's very interesting, Mirjana. So from time to time even the best of us are unconscious unbelievers?

A. From time to time all of us lack belief in God—in God's love—and we lack trust in God's love for us. Every day we need to pray for faith, for hope, for love so that we can be a believer—a total believer.

Q. You said you're comforted by the Blessed Mother. Why do you need to be comforted by the Blessed Mother?

A. Because of the secrets. I know what awaits unbelievers. This is a time of great grace. Those who do not believe in God, who do not know God, are wasting their lives on things they cannot keep.

Q. Mirjana, could you explain what you mean by that?

A. Yes. The Blessed Mother has taught me that nothing matters in a person's life but faithfulness to God's will. God made us for Himself. So many people today waste their earthly lives on things that pass away. So many people today do not know God. So many people today have made gods out of things, goals, and other people. For them there is only weeping and anguish because our life on earth is so short—so very short.

Q. Mirjana, in one of the Blessed Mother's monthly messages, she compared our life on earth to the life of a flower.

A. Yes. A flower's life is very beautiful while it lasts, but it is so short, like our human life on earth.

Q. Could you tell me a little bit more about your yearly apparition in Medjugorje on March 18, 1991?

A. Yes. It lasted about seven minutes. Many people were present. The Blessed Mother blessed everyone who was present just as she did last year when we were all together in Oregon and she gave a special message for all people. We then prayed one Our Father and Glory Be for the unbelievers. The second Our Father and the Glory Be was for the sick people all over the world and the third Our Father and Glory Be was for people in special need of God's help.

Q. Did the Blessed Mother define those people who are in special need of God's help?

A. She mentioned those in special need of God's help, but she didn't mention who they are.

Q. Mirjana, did the Blessed Mother mention your new baby?

A. No, the Blessed Mother never did mention my baby.

Q. Did your baby see the Blessed Mother?

A. Oh, she's too little.

Q. Was the baby in your arms during the apparition?

A. No, I was not holding her.

THE SPECIAL MEANING OF THE APPARITION

Q. You have said that the apparition of the Blessed Virgin Mary here in Medjugorje is the most important in the history of the world.

A. Yes, it is.

Q. You have said that this apparition is our Blessed Mother's last apparition on earth. Is that true?

A. Yes. Those are her own words.

Q. Do you know why this apparition is the last of the Blessed Virgin to the earth?

A. I know many things, but I do not know why this apparition is our Blessed Mother's last apparition on earth. She said after the secrets are realized she will not need to come again.

Q. Do you recall the context of her statement, which might give some indication of the deeper meaning?

A. No, I don't know what the Blessed Mother meant when she said this is her last apparition of earth. Some theologians have asked me if the Blessed Mother meant that this is her last apparition in this way. I myself do not know the underlying meaning of what our Blessed Mother has said. Her words were very simple. She said this is her last apparition on earth. She said after the secrets are realized she won't need to come again.

Q. Mirjana, in light of the secrets you know, can you tell me the significance of the Blessed Mother's statement that this is her last apparition of earth?

A. The Blessed Mother simply told me and the others that this is her last apparition on earth. She gave no explanation. I have no explanation.

Q. Mirjana, do you know anything about the Blessed Mother's other apparitions, which are occurring around the world?

A. No, I don't. If she is appearing in other places as well, no one can ever say they have not been warned.

Q. Mirjana, there is certainly great controversy surrounding this apparition.

A. Yes, I know.

Q. Does that make you sad?

A. It makes me sad, but I think it makes the Blessed Mother even sadder.

Q. Why, Mirjana?

A. Well, she hasn't exactly said, but I suspect it's because she is receiving the same response her Son Jesus had when He came to the earth. "He came to His own and His own received Him not. But to those who received Him, He gave the power to become children of God."[11] It's the same today with the Blessed Mother. To those who receive her, who welcome her, who listen to her, she brings the power to be children of God. She brings Jesus.

SUFFERING

Q. Mirjana, is all that you do for the Blessed Mother a source of great joy to you?

A. The Blessed Mother has warned us that we would suffer much, and we are.

Q. Does that bother you, Mirjana?

A. [Gentle laugh.] No one likes to suffer, especially me. The Blessed Mother helps me. She says that if I pray, I will have peace. She says we *will* have the strength to endure whatever comes.

Q. Will the suffering increase?

A. Yes. The faithful ones will have much to endure everywhere.

Q. What about the unfaithful?

A. What awaits them is terrible suffering of their own choosing.

THE EARLY DAYS FOR MIRJANA

Q. Do you remember your life before our Blessed Mother appeared to you? That was about ten years ago.

A. Yes. I remember.

Q. Mirjana, you seem so serious these days. Did you have great faith in those days before the Blessed Mother appeared to you?

A. Faith is a tradition in all the families here. We have much faith.

Q. Did you pray the rosary every day before the apparition?

A. Yes. My family life involved the daily rosary. We prayed the rosary every day as far back as I can remember.

Q. Did you pray by yourself?

A. No. We prayed as a family.

Q. Did you live in Medjugorje before the apparitions began?

A. No. I lived in Sarajevo. My family came to Medjugorje in the summers and at other times to visit my grandmother and our other relatives here.

Q. Mirjana, do you remember the first day of the apparition?

A. Yes. When Ivanka exclaimed that she was seeing the Blessed Virgin Mary, I didn't believe her.

Q. How old were you?

A. I was sixteen. I thought the Blessed Mother was in heaven. I never thought of her as being willing to come here. I didn't think I was worthy to be near the Blessed Mother. When Ivanka told me to look at the mountain, I looked at Ivanka. I thought something was wrong with her. I wondered what was happening. But, I did look and I did see her.

Q. Mirjana, some of the various books give different accounts. For example, some dispute whether you were certain the first day it really was the Blessed Mother.

A. Oh, I was certain. I knew exactly who it was.

Q. How did you know?

A. My whole being knew without doubt that this lady of unexplainable beauty was the Mother of God. That is why I had such fear.

Q. Are you still afraid when you see her?

A. Oh, no.

Q. What do you feel now?

A. Total love in her presence.

Q. It has been written that the Blessed Mother will sever the bonds that hold God's children in captivity.

A. The Blessed Mother says prayer and fasting will free God's children from the evil one.

Q. You have explained before, Mirjana, that the Blessed Mother has shown you that God's love is stronger than all the evil in the world. That His love frees, that His love redeems, His love glorifies. Is it true, that God's kingdom is coming into the world?

A. Yes. God's kingdom is a kingdom of peace and joy and love.

Q. Mirjana, do you know anything about the Second Coming of Christ?

A. The Scriptures have promised us that the reign of God is at hand. The Lord will walk among His people. His covenant is everlasting.

Q. Mirjana, the Blessed Mother has said, "*Let those who have ears to hear, listen; let those who have eyes to see, see.*" She said that God's kingdom lives now in the hearts of those who love God. She also says the fire of love in her faithful children's hearts shall consume the world as we know it. Is that why she asks us to be at total peace?

A. Yes. The Blessed Mother asks us to rest totally in God's love, to rely totally on God's power, to enjoy His providence, to never fear for anything. The Blessed Mother has taught us to live totally in Jesus. She has taught us He is our brother.

Q. Mirjana, you told me that through Jesus all things are made well. You said through Him and with Him and in Him all belongs to God forever. Is this what the Blessed Mother teaches you? That Jesus brings God's kingdom on earth?

A. That is the fulfillment of God's promise to His people.

Q. The first day when you saw the Blessed Mother on the mountain, did you experience any of this deep insight?

A. I was so frightened, I ran home to my family.

Q. Why did you run?

A. At that time I didn't know much about God, I didn't know myself at all, and I was filled with fear.

Q. What happened when you got home?

A. My grandmother asked me why we did not pray in the presence of the Mother of God. I told her I was too afraid.

Q. Did your family believe you?

A. Of course. They know I do not lie.

Q. Who else saw her the first day?

A. Ivanka, Ivan, Vicka, and all the others who came by. They also saw. The next day Marija and Jacov saw her, too.

Q. Do you know anything about that?

A. Well, I do know that when Jacov heard from me that I saw the Blessed Mother, he said he too would want to see her more than anything else in the whole world. That's why he came with me on the second day.

Q. Jacov was with you?

A. Yes.

Q. Marija told me that when her sister, Milka, told her that she saw the Blessed Mother, Marija merely wanted to be in the presence of the Blessed Mother. She didn't even care if she saw her. She said she would have been happy just to be near where the Blessed Mother is.

A. The first day Ivanka and I saw. Then Vicka, Ivan, Milka, and the others passed by. We told them and they came to look too. After all saw, we were all afraid, and we all ran home.

Q. Vicka told me that was the day she ran so fast that she ran out of her shoes and left them behind on the path. [Laughter.]

A. We all ran as fast as we could. We probably all left our sandals behind. Vicka came looking for us and then she saw and ran away. Ivan was on his way home. He too saw and he ran home. When I saw them all running, I realized that if they were running away, we should run too.

Q. Do you remember the second day, Mirjana?

A. Yes, of course.

Q. Why did you go back?

A. I felt in my heart that I must go back. Interestingly, the others felt the same way too.

Q. Oh, you had not talked about this and planned it?

A. No. We didn't plan it. We just all, about the same time, felt an immense desire to go back to that place.

Q. What was that desire like?

A. It was as if I was called to come to that place on the mountain. Many people throughout the world now know that same desire. They too have heard the call of the Mother of God to come to the mountain here in Medjugorje, and they come no matter what it costs.

Q. Approximately fifteen to twenty million people have come so far.

A. There will be more. Many more. Medjugorje is a call to the whole world. All will hear the call. Many will respond.

Q. What did you find when you returned to the mountain that night?

A. We saw the Blessed Mother alone. This time she did not have the Infant Jesus in her arms.

Q. The first time you saw the Blessed Mother she was holding the baby Jesus in her arms, and she was covering Him and uncovering Him, wasn't she?

A. Yes. She was showing Him to us.

Q. Mirjana, could you really see the Blessed Mother with your eyes?

A. Yes. Certainly.

Q. Mirjana, the distance between the spot where you first saw the Blessed Mother and the spot where you said the Blessed Mother stood is at least one thousand feet. That is the size of three soccer fields. You couldn't have seen details of the Blessed Mother's face, you couldn't have seen the baby Jesus from that distance. They would have been a mere speck up on the mountain.

A. No. I saw her very clearly as if she was right by me.

Q. Mirjana, do you think that's rather unusual? Can you see others from that far away so clearly?

A. [An embarrassed laugh.] I never thought about it. Probably not. I saw the Blessed Mother quite clearly. There is no doubt.

Q. Up on the mountain, far away?

A. Yes. I saw her most clearly.

Q. Was there a lot of light surrounding her?

A. I don't recall. It was daylight. She was quite clear.

Q. Mirjana, once again. How did you know it was the Blessed Mother?

A. I knew it. I could see her.

Q. Mirjana, the second day did she come surrounded with great light?

A. When I see the Blessed Mother she is all-encompassing. Maybe there is light around her. I don't know. I don't ever focus on the light. Her presence is so personal to me that I am not aware of any other thing except her immense love, her immense beauty, her immense presence.

Q. Mirjana, did you speak to the Blessed Mother the first day?

A. It was Ivanka who talked to her first.

Q. Do you remember when you first spoke to the Blessed Mother?

A. I had great fear. I fainted many times.

Q. Why?

A. I was quite overwhelmed to be in the holy presence of the Mother of God.

Q. Was it really that frightening?

A. It was more that I was amazed. I was filled with awe and reverence and unknowing. It was really quite more than I can speak about.

Q. Did you stay in Medjugorje and continue to see the Blessed Mother?

A. Yes. For a while. My aunt called my mother right away and explained everything to her. My mother asked my aunt if I was normal. My aunt said I seemed normal. My mother said, "Mirjana does not lie." My family knows that.

Q. Did the Blessed Mother continue to appear to you when you returned home to Sarajevo?

A. Yes. She appeared to me every day until December of 1982.

Q. Mirjana, did the Blessed Mother discuss the secrets with you immediately?

A. At first, only from time to time. Often we had conversations that were just for her and me. At other times there were messages for the whole world. The Blessed Mother herself chose the topics.

MIRJANA'S PRAYER LIFE

Q. Did the Blessed Mother lead you into a deeper prayer life right away?

A. Yes.

Q. Vicka and Marija, in fact all six of you visionaries, have explained that the Blessed Mother is present in a special way when we pray. You all have stated again and again that the Blessed Mother tells us to pray more fervently. That she asks us to experience her presence when we pray. That she asks us to experience the presence of the heavenly court, all the angels and saints, when we pray to God our Father. She tells us, "*Pray my children, and I shall pray with you.*" How long did it take you to respond to that kind of teaching, Mirjana?

A. Immediately when the Blessed Mother prayed with me I could sense a power in my prayer life that I did not have alone.

Q. How is your prayer life now, Mirjana?

A. Whenever I pray now, I hear the Blessed Mother pray with me in my heart. I sense her presence. Actually I sense her presence about me all the time.

Q. Did the Blessed Mother lead you into fasting right away?

A. Yes. She asked me and the others to fast on Fridays. Later she asked the whole world to fast on Fridays. Now she includes Wednesdays in her request, and she tells us when we really need special things that it's very beneficial for our souls if we will fast three days a week.

Q. Why is fasting so beneficial? Ivanka told me that fasting frees us from things—from their hold on us.

A. Fasting is a type of purification. It also is a type of discipline. It allows us to experience the value of our free will over ourselves and the requirements of our bodies. When we are able to fast, we really know who is in charge of our bodies.

Q. Mirjana, Father Slavko [Barbaric, the spiritual director of the visionaries] has said fasting is a gift of grace. Do you experience that?

A. Of course. I pray. I ask for the grace to be able to fast.

Q. If you don't pray what happens, Mirjana?

A. If I don't pray I am not able to fast.

Q. Even now, Mirjana?

A. Oh, I need to pray now more than ever.

Q. Did the Blessed Mother continue to appear every day no matter where you were?

A. Yes, she did.

THE REACTION OF OTHERS

Q. How did the priests treat you?

A. At first they were distant. Later they came to accept the apparitions.

Q. How did your family react to all this? It must have been shocking.

A. They suffered much. My father's hair turned gray.

Q. Were they present for these apparitions?

A. Many times.

Q. Were there messages for them?

A. You must understand, my family and I are not special to the Blessed Mother. She wouldn't have messages specifically for us. We are no more important than any other family of the Blessed Mother.

Q. What about you?

A. I am not important. I am no more special to the Blessed Mother than any of her other children are. We are all the same to the Blessed Mother. She has no preferential love. We are all her children. She loves each of us as we are because we are each her children.

Q. Mirjana, in the early days of the apparitions, did you know anything about apparitions? Had you ever heard of Lourdes or Fatima?

A. I knew nothing about the Blessed Mother appearing on earth before the apparitions. I am from Sarajevo. It was a Marxist, atheistic city. Nothing was ever mentioned in churches about apparitions to people by the Blessed Mother. I thought she was in heaven. I got a book about Fatima and Lourdes, though, after the apparitions started.

Q. Were you in an atheistic school at the time the apparitions began?

A. All schools here are government-controlled schools. There are no private or Catholic schools.

Q. So you attended an atheistic school?

A. Yes.

Q. Did the other students know what was happening to you every day—that the mother of Jesus Christ was appearing to you every day in your home?

A. They would have dismissed me from the school if they had known.

Q. Your peers really didn't know?

A. Gradually word got out. The officials told me I had to leave school. My father signed me into another school where no one knew about the apparitions.

Q. You didn't tell anyone?

A. I didn't have anyone to talk to. Most of the other students in the new school were Moslems or Orthodox. They didn't know me and they weren't interested in me and they didn't bother with me.

Q. So, Mirjana, you had to go to a new school?

A. Yes.

Q. That's quite a bit of persecution.

A. I have had much persecution. There will be more.

Q. Did you tell anybody about this apparition at school?

A. I was not permitted to speak about it.

Q. Who forbade you?

A. The school officials. They allowed no discussion of anything sacred.

Q. You must have felt very lonely at school.

A. I have known loneliness.

Q. Did you ever wear a cross?

A. Always. The Blessed Mother has asked all of us people on earth to wear a cross or a medal, a scapular, some blessed object on our body as a sign to Satan that we belong to God.

Q. When were you persecuted at school?

A. After they found out about the apparitions. As the teachers learned about the apparitions, they mocked me. They taunted me. They made fun of me in class.

Q. Were all the teachers like this?

A. There was one teacher who was different. She helped me. When it came time for final exams—and in our country everyone must pass final exams—the police called the school and told the officials that I was not permitted to pass the exams in order to finish secondary school. They ordered the school to prevent me from taking the exams. My teacher called my father and told him that if I failed the exams, it would not be my fault. She told my father she would try to conceal when I would take the exams so the officials would not interfere. In that way I was able to pass the exams. That teacher really helped me.

Q. Did the Blessed Mother ever speak about that teacher or about school?

A. The Blessed Mother has never indicated that I am in any way special. As a mother, she has encouraged me to do the very best I can with every opportunity that God places in my path each day. That includes school. There has been a problem with my schooling because of the government.

Q. When the daily apparitions stopped for you in December of 1982, how old were you?

A. Seventeen.

Q. That is quite a challenge, Mirjana, to experience so much at such a young age. How do you remember all the details of such an important apparition?

A. Without the Blessed Mother's help, I wouldn't remember anything.

THE SECRETS

Q. It has been ten years now since this monumental apparition began. Looking back, it might seem that the Blessed Mother gave you all those ten secrets concerning the future of the world very quickly.

A. I had enough time. It may seem fast to you, but I have had more one-on-one time with the Blessed Mother than the other visionaries who were here in Medjugorje. They were constantly surrounded by people. They were asking the Blessed Mother questions for priests and for all those who come here. My time with the Blessed Mother was private and quite concentrated.

Q. Can you repeat once again what you are permitted to say about the secrets?

A. The first two secrets will be warnings to the world—events that will occur before a visible sign is given to humanity. These will happen in my lifetime. Ten days before the first secret and the second secret, I will notify Father Petar Ljubicic. He will pray and fast for seven days, and then he will announce these to the world.

Q. Mirjana, many evangelists these days talk about the end of the world. Will the world survive the secrets you know?

A. God's world is unchanging. All passes away but God's will. Those who pray understand.

Q. Mirjana, do you consider yourself brighter than the other visionaries so that you could absorb these amazing facts faster?

A. No.

Q. How do you remember the secrets?

A. I have them written down.

Q. In your own handwriting?

A. No.

Q. In the Blessed Mother's handwriting?

A. I received a parchment with the secrets written on it from the Blessed Mother.

Q. Is it true only you can see the writing on the parchment?

A. Yes.

Q. Where do you keep this parchment?

A. In my family's house in Sarajevo in my bedroom there.

Q. You keep this parchment in Sarajevo? What if you need it here?

A. I keep it in Sarajevo.

Q. If I looked at that parchment, what would I see?

A. Everyone who has seen it has seen something different.

Q. But only you can read what is written on it?

A. Yes.

Q. The ten secrets are written on this parchment?

A. Yes.

Q. That means you don't have to remember the secrets. You can pull that parchment and read it?

A. I remember everything. I don't need the parchment to remember the secrets.

Q. Is it true you know the day and date of everything?

A. Yes.

Q. Mirjana, are you certain you wouldn't forget anything? Do you know the day, the minute, and the hour?

A. I know the day and the date.

Q. Does that frighten you, Mirjana, especially as the days for the fulfillment of each secret draw near? [Mirjana shrugs and looks away.] Can you share whether the secrets bring good or bad news?

A. Well, the first secret will break the power of Satan, and that is why he is so aggressive now.

Q. Mirjana, concerning the first secret, some people have quoted you as saying that a whole section of the planet would be desolate—would be totally destroyed. No life would grow in that place. Is that true?

A. I don't remember talking about that to anyone. Please ask people not to speak about secrets. Please ask those who know about the Blessed Mother's apparition here to focus on God's will. Our Blessed Mother says we should pray more, and we should love God as our Father. We should accept the messages of prayer, fasting, conversion, and reconciliation that God is sending to the world through the Blessed Mother of Jesus. If we do this, we will not be afraid of anything, no matter what the future may hold.

Q. Mirjana, people are talking about three days of darkness, about tidal waves, earthquakes, catastrophes. Do you know anything about these sorts of occurrences in the future?

A. I am not speaking about any of those things, nor have I ever spoken about those things. God is peace. God is love. The messages of the Blessed Mother here are messages of peace so that all her children of the earth may experience God's love.

MIRJANA'S LASTING MISSION

Q. Mirjana, there are six visionaries here in Medjugorje. What is your particular mission?

A. For now I am to pray for the conversion of unbelievers.

Q. Mirjana, once you told me that we are to view everyone as a baby in God's arms. That we are to surrender ourselves so that we are as comfortable in God's arms as His own baby.[12] That requires a great act of surrender of our own willfulness. Have you been able to do this?

A. I try to do this every day with the help of the Blessed Mother.

Q. Mirjana, will you have a different mission later?

A. Yes.

Q. What is that?

A. I am not at liberty to say right now.

Q. Mirjana, how do you now pray for the conversion of sinners?

A. With a great love for all those who don't know anything about the Catholic Church.

Q. Do our prayers help?

A. They do—very much. The Blessed Mother has told me that we will not fully comprehend the value of our prayers in this life.

Q. Why not?

A. Our prayers are part of the things of faith.

Q. Mirjana, one Our Father doesn't seem like much.

A. It is very much if you pray it with love.

Q. Do you and Marco enjoy being here in Medjugorje full-time?

A. Yes. Very much.

Q. Does Marco miss working in Sarajevo?

A. We moved here because neither of us was able to find a job in Sarajevo.

Q. Many thought your move here might be motivated by the imminence of the secrets you know, since both you and Father Petar are here in residence in Medjugorje. Some have thought the secrets might begin to unfold soon. Will you comment?

A. The secrets will unfold during my lifetime. I can say no more. Please ask people not to focus on the future. Our life is one day at a time. Tomorrow is no threat for those who trust God.

GLOBAL ECONOMIC COLLAPSE

Q. Other alleged visionaries in different parts of the world have suggested that part of the chastisements predicted involve not only natural disaster but also global economic collapse.[13]

A. I don't know anything about that.

Q. Some international economists are beginning to discuss that possibility even now, Mirjana. You are an economist by education, aren't you? Wasn't your course of studies at the university in economics?

A. Yes.

Q. Do you have an opinion about the global economy?

A. No.

Q. Is global economic collapse one of the secrets?

A. I don't wish to comment about the secrets now.

Q. Does it bother your husband, Marco, to be here without work?

A. No. Marco prays frequently. He tries to be obedient to God's will. He has much work to do daily to care for our property and the duties of finishing our house and caring for those who come here as our guests.

Q. Is it God's will that he is here now?

A. Circumstances have placed us here. We have much peace.

Q. Mirjana, there are military tanks eighteen miles from here. We were told this morning [early May 1991] that all the roads into and out of Medjugorje are blocked by convoys of farm equipment, all types of vehicles, huge rocks. Does this worry you?

A. No.

Q. Why not?

A. We will be safe here in Medjugorje.

Q. How do you know that, Mirjana?

A. I know.

Q. Has the Blessed Mother spoken to you about this incident?

A. The Blessed Mother always says to pray. Those who pray have peace.

WAR IN MEDJUGORJE?

Q. Mirjana, many people here in Medjugorje seem worried today, especially some of the pilgrims. The village is silent. There is an ominous, almost eerie silence around the church. The stores, the shops, the cafés are closed. Cabdrivers are nonexistent except for a few strangers who are parked near the church, and even they have no business. It's hard to find a male in this town. We were told that every man is armed and guarding all the roadways into Medjugorje. I notice that Marco is not armed and out guarding a road. He's right here with you.

A. Those who do God's will need never worry about anything. The people here pray much. Those who pray experience God as their loving, providential Father. They can go to His house—the church, synagogue, mosque, or other place of worship—and tell Him their needs, their hurts, their desires, knowing He hears everything and knows everything and loves each of His children with an unfathomable love. The Blessed Mother says His love for each of us is so great that we will never be able to comprehend its vastness or its uniqueness or its personal dimension in this life.

Q. What do you make of all this civil unrest—the vigilantism, the guns, the people fighting, people being killed, their bodies being desecrated. We were told yesterday that twelve Catholics were brutally massacred and skinned, that even their eyes . . . you are living with this at your doorstep.

A. People are concerned here. They are aware. People are familiar with the idea of war. They have some fear about this situation and they will fight. People don't think about work anymore, they are concerned with how to protect life and home and property against the present threat.

Q. We have heard that the men in the village had some meetings to decide whether they need to use guns to protect life and property.

A. The main problem here is that there is to be a change in the government on the fifteenth of this month [May 1991]. Some who disagree are trying to stop it. They are using the army to create an international incident. They want to prevent the newly elected officials from assuming their government posts.

Q. They believe this civil unrest is a way to manipulate the government transition?

A. As bad as things look, people here of faith are patient. They are trying to prevent a quiet occupation [by military force with army tanks].

Q. Do you know what the outcome will be?

A. I know the Blessed Mother. She is the Queen of Peace. She says prayer, especially the Mass, the rosary, and fasting, especially on bread and water only, can stop war, can change the natural law, particularly if they are done with great faith and great trust and great love.

Q. Mirjana, what does the Blessed Mother want particularly in these circumstances here in Medjugorje? Do the people here know God's will for them?

A. Those who pray with their hearts know.

MIRJANA'S DAILY LIFE

Q. Mirjana, are you happy here in Medjugorje with your husband, your little daughter, Maria, your mother next door, your cute little dog, this beautiful house, the Church, Cross Mountain visible from your front door and Apparition Hill at your back door?

A. Yes. Very happy.

Q. But do you miss Sarajevo?

A. My father works there at the hospital.

Q. What does he do?

A. He's a radiologist. My brother goes to school in Sarajevo. We go often to our family house there so I really do not have any reason to miss Sarajevo.

Q. Mirjana, have you graduated from the university?

A. Not yet. I still have two examinations to finish.

Q. What about Marco?

A. The same. He also has two examinations to finish.

Q. It is really difficult to get a job as an economist?

A. Yes.

Q. Does your religion have anything to do with your ability to get a job?

A. Not now. Religion has nothing to do with these jobs. Many people throughout Yugoslavia are losing their jobs these days.

Q. The tensions here in Bosnia-Herzegovina are certainly a test for the Blessed Mother's peace formula. Do you have any advice or messages to send?

A. Yes. Ask all people on earth to pray and fast more. Prayer and fasting will bring peace.

Q. Do you recommend any particular prayer?

A. Yes. The rosary will protect all who pray it with their hearts. For those who are able, the Mass and the Eucharist are armor.

MIRJANA'S ADVICE

Q. Many don't believe there is a God. They don't believe in a hereafter. They are certainly not into prayer and, fasting as a way to stop war. Do you have any advice or messages for the unbelievers?

A. I will send a message to those who *say* they believe. Tell them they are not to force others to believe, or to tell others how to live.

They must be examples to these people. Their lives should be examples of God's existence and God's love. Their lives should be examples for all those people who do not believe.

Q. What should believers do, Mirjana?

A. First of all, the Blessed Mother says those who know are particularly requested by her to pray fervently, intensely, and frequently for those who do not believe. She is pleading with her faithful children who know about God, who know about her presence here in Medjugorje, to pray. And she will pray with us for all the unbelievers on the planet, especially our own loved ones.

Q. How do we experience the prayers of the Blessed Mother?

A. Our Blessed Mother is most humble. She will never interfere in our lives. She is God's most faithful creature. She will never forsake any child of God who calls to her. She will bless and protect and defend any person who calls to her. She, herself, will pray with and for any child of God who invites her.

Q. Who is this "child of God" who can obtain the personal blessing and protection of the mother of Jesus on demand?

A. All people on earth.

Q. How do you know that?

A. The Blessed Mother told me that Jesus, her Son, redeemed all people on earth by His passion and death on the cross. Jesus gave all people on earth to His mother before he died on Calvary.

Q. What about people who don't know Jesus or who may know of Him, but who have no belief or respect for Him?

A. Because Jesus gave these people to the Blessed Mother, she accepts all people on earth with love and respect. She asks us to do the same out of love for God. Jesus gave Mary to all people on earth as the mother of their eternal life, if they choose her.[14] She, like Jesus, is too humble to force herself upon anyone. She invites. We choose.

CHOOSE JESUS AND MARY

Q. How do we choose Jesus or His mother, Mary, Mirjana? Do you know?

A. Well, the Blessed Mother says that to choose Jesus, we must be like Him.

Q. Otherwise we won't be able to find Him to choose Him, will we?

A. Many people call themselves believers. They speak the right words, they do the right things, but they lead pagan lives. A real Christian is Christified.

Q. What does that mean?

A. A true Christian is like Jesus.

Q. Do you know what Jesus is like?

A. Jesus is the way, and the truth, and the light for our life.

Q. Has the Blessed Mother taught you that?

A. Yes. She says the way is spelled out in the Scriptures. The truth is in Scripture and in the Church. The light comes from God to those who are faithful. She is always asking her faithful ones to read Scripture so we might learn about God.

Q. Mirjana, what about those who have never heard of Jesus or Mary? Does the Blessed Mother speak of these people?

A. Yes. Each comes into the world with the covenant of God's love in his heart. Each person hears God in the silence of his heart. Some hear better than others because they listen better.

Q. Mirjana, Marija told me that the Blessed Mother has said that if Catholics lived their faith, the whole world would be Catholic.

A. She has said that. Today many people have forgotten. Many people choose things that pass away. Many are unaware of truth, drunk on the pleasures of the world, blinded by the intellect, and crippled by selfishness.

Q. What about these people?

A. The Blessed Mother says, "God makes all things well for those who trust Him." That is why the Blessed Mother asks those who say they believe to live the life of Jesus on earth. Jesus shows us the path to paradise. His life is the pattern for believers to follow. If believers live that pattern, they will be faithful followers of the Gospel. Their lives will be examples that there is a God who loves us and nurtures us and sustains us in all things. The Blessed Mother says it is prayer and our changed lives that free us. She mentions many times that prayer, fasting, choosing a life like Jesus lived, is so powerful that it can not only stop wars, but it can alter the natural laws.

Q. With the environment in such disrepair that is really important to know.

A. The messages of Medjugorje are the path to eternal peace and fullness.

Q. Mirjana, what does the Blessed Mother want?

A. She is here to call the entire world back to God.

Q. What does our Blessed Mother ask?

A. She says, *"First of all I ask all of you for your help. Pray for yourselves and for others. Fast for yourselves and others. I ask nothing else. Just pray and fast."*

Q. She asks nothing else?

A. For believers, prayer is our way of life. Those who pray should be living examples of God's love, God's mercy, God's goodness for all those people who do not believe. It is the believer's joy and peace and fullness that is the proof of God's existence. Believers must be examples. The Blessed Mother has mentioned many times that all things are possible through prayer, even the avoidance of war.

Q. Many people pray a lot but still bad things happen. Do you know why that is?

A. God's will is the only criterion that has value. Not my opinion. Whenever we pray, we should always say, "Let Your will be done, not mine, dear God." The Blessed Mother has shown us her Son, Jesus, during His passion. He suffered much. Bad things happened to Him. He obeyed our Father's will.

Q. Do you know what our Father's will for Jesus was, Mirjana?

A. The same will that He has for us—to love Him [God] with our whole heart, soul, and mind, and to love our neighbor as ourself.

Q. How was the crucifixion God's will? Do you know, Mirjana?

A. Those who crucified Jesus were children of our Father. They did not know what they were doing. Jesus explained that to us from the cross. They were blind to God's presence in their life. Jesus honored our Father, God the Creator and sustainer of all people and places and things, by loving His Father's children even as they crucified Him. He suffered and died in silence and obedience and love for all our Father's children.

Q. Why did He accept such abuse?

A. He took all sin upon Himself.

Q. Is it God's will to accept abuse from our brothers and sisters?

A. It is not God's will that any of His children abuse one another. That is sin. Whenever abuse occurs, Satan is involved.

Q. God's love is stronger than all the pain and even death, isn't it, Mirjana?

A. God's love is eternal. He invites us to that same love.

Q. So, Mirjana, God is calling all of us to be great lovers?

A. God is the great lover. We are the object of God's love. The Blessed Mother says, *"God is love."* And we can block His love. We can refuse it.

Q. You have also said that prayer and fasting will break the power of Satan. That it will change the world as we know it. You have said that prayer and fasting will convert unbelievers, including those who claim they believe and those who claim they don't. Will this happen in our lifetime?

A. Yes, because we will pray to God that we have a long life.

Q. Lucy of Fatima has certainly had a long life. Do you know that many people today believe there is no devil, there is no Blessed Mother, there is no God?

A. Yes. I know many people like this personally because of where I grew up. Sarajevo is a city where atheism is taught from grammar school through the university.

Q. Do you know whether people with belief like that will convert?

A. Many people with belief like that are converting. Many more will convert.

Q. Mirjana, for those who don't convert, will they end up in hell, or can they come to heaven too?

A. You can ask that of the Blessed Mother. I'm not sure.

Q. Mirjana, do you know what happens to people who don't believe in God?

A. I don't know. The Blessed Mother says we may never judge one another. She herself judges no one. She loves, she teaches, she guides. God alone judges.

HELL, HEAVEN, AND PURGATORY

Q. Mirjana, did you see hell?

A. No. I did not want to see it.

Q. Did the Blessed Mother offer to show you hell?

A. Yes, she did. The Blessed Mother gave me the choice. I opted not to have the experience of hell.

Q. Do you know for sure that you will not go to hell?

A. No one can be sure. I pray every day to be filled with God's strength. On my own, I can do nothing. I depend on God's love and His mercy for everything.

Q. Do you know when you are going to die?

A. No.

Q. You have seen heaven?

A. Yes.

Q. Did you experience heaven with your heart, or did you really see it with your eyes?

A. I saw heaven with my eyes.

Q. What did you see?

A. Heaven was like a video unfolding before my eyes. I saw happy, healthy people, both men and women. The grass was of a beauty I can't describe. The flowers were so beautiful I can't describe them.

Q. Why did the Blessed Mother want you to see heaven?

A. She told me many people on earth today do not believe heaven exists. She said God has chosen us six visionaries to be instruments of His love and mercy. I have personally seen heaven. It exists! I've seen it! Those who stay faithful to God to the end will see heaven as a reward for their faithfulness.

Q. Why do some people who seem to be doing God's will suffer so much? The Blessed Mother herself suffered terribly as she stood at the foot of the cross.

A. She was filled with God's love, God's peace, and God's strength. There is love and peace in doing God's will even in the midst of the worst perceived suffering.

Q. How do you know that?

A. The Blessed Mother has shared that with me. Every day I pray for the light to see God's will and the strength to obey God's will.

Q. But do you always know and obey God's will?

A. No. I am a sinner. When I fall, I know I have not prayed enough and I know I have not obeyed.

Q. What happens when you sin?

A. I go to confession and I get some strength from the sacrament to help me avoid sin. The Blessed Mother says to pray always for God's grace. She herself guards us with her angels.

Q. Ivanka speaks often about the Blessed Mother as the Queen of Angels.

A. She always comes with angels, but we must choose her help in order to experience her help.

Q. Why is that?

A. The Blessed Mother is too humble to impose herself upon us. She only comes where she is invited.

Q. Have you ever truly seen purgatory?

A. Yes.

Q. Is it a place?

A. Yes.

Q. Is it geographically part of the planet earth, or is it somewhere else?

A. I saw one place. Many people were there. They were suffering immensely.

Q. What kind of suffering?

A. It was physical suffering.

Q. Where is this place?

A. I don't know.

Q. What kind of people were there? Old, young, fat, thin?

A. They were normal people, all kinds. There was much physical suffering.

Q. Can you describe the suffering you saw? Was it like leprosy or something similar to that?

A. I could see the people shivering, thrashing, and writhing in pain.

Q. Were the people cold? Was the place cold?

A. I saw this place for a short time. I didn't personally experience the temperature. The Blessed Mother was with me. She explained to me that she wanted me to see purgatory. She said so many people on earth today do not even know about purgatory.

Q. Have many people today forgotten about the justice of God?

A. Since nothing can live in the sight of God but pure love, God's justice cleanses. That's why we have purgatory.

Q. Mirjana, are you saying purgatory is an instrument of God's justice? We have been taught that God's justice is not like man's justice, for God has no cruelty. Cruelty is an attribute of pride.

A. The Blessed Mother has said God is pure love.

Q. Were the people in purgatory screaming?

A. I could not hear them. I only saw them.

Q. Why did the Blessed Mother want to show you purgatory?

A. She said so many people who die are quite abandoned by their loved ones. They cannot help themselves in purgatory. They are totally dependent on the prayers and sacrifices of the generous people on earth who remember them. Our Blessed Mother hopes her own children will help the souls in purgatory by prayer and fasting and various penances for the poor souls to make restitution for them.

Q. Mirjana, why do people of the earth have to make restitution for people who have died?

A. Because those who have died no longer have free will as they had on earth.[15] They no longer have a body. It's no longer possible for them to make up for the things that they did when they had their body that hurt and harmed themselves and others.[16] On July 24, 1982, the Blessed Mother said: *"We go to heaven in full conscience: that which we have now. At the moment of death, we are conscious of the separation of the body and soul. It is false to teach people that we are reborn many times and that we pass to different bodies. One is born only once. The body, drawn from the earth, decomposes after death. It never comes back to life again. Man receives a transfigured body. Whoever has done very much evil during his life can go straight to heaven if he confesses, is [truly] sorry for what he has done, and receives Communion at the end of his life."*[17]

Q. The good thief who died next to Jesus was the first canonized saint, wasn't he, Mirjana?

A. Jesus Himself promised him paradise that very day!

Q. Mirjana, how do the prayers of those who are still on earth and the penances help those who have died?

A. The Blessed Mother explained that the prayers and the penance of those on the earth soften hearts of stone, melt hearts of stone. When the hearts of stone of God's children are melted, great love is possible, even on this earth.

Q. Mirjana, is it true or do you know whether the poor souls in purgatory can see us on the earth?

A. They can see their loved ones during those moments when we pray for them by name.

Q. Ivan told me the Blessed Mother said they are very lonely and she herself goes there often to comfort them.

A. We too can comfort them with our prayers and sacrifices.

Q. Mirjana, do you pray for the souls in purgatory?

A. Yes. I have given my life to the Blessed Mother for the sake of the unbelievers.

Q. Why, Mirjana?

A. Because I know what awaits them. The Blessed Mother asks all her faithful children to consecrate their lives to her, to pray and fast and do penance that all might gain the kingdom of heaven.

Q. Is this apparition just for the faithful ones?

A. No. This apparition is for all people on earth. Each person on earth will have a role to play as the secrets unfold. Many already know their role in this apparition, as I do. There will be suffering. Those who follow the Blessed Mother's messages will know persecution, but in the end all will be well. The rewards are great. They are worth every bit of persecution and suffering.

Q. Will the bishop come to believe in these messages?

A. The Blessed Mother wants us to pray for the bishop and to love him and obey him. God's will is always realized. Sometimes great suffering must occur because the free will of mankind is a sacred trust from God.

Q. The free will of man is a sacred trust?

A. Yes. Many abuse that sacred trust.

Q. Why? I suspect that it must be through ignorance. No one would voluntarily abuse a sacred trust from God.

A. Jesus said it on the cross: "Father, forgive them, they do not know what they do." It takes much prayer to keep all these mysteries in perspective.

Q. Mirjana, do you know if suffering is part of God's plan?[18]

A. Disobedience to God's plan causes suffering.

Q. God intends paradise for all His children, doesn't He?

A. That is His will. For those who love God all things work together for good, even suffering.

Q. Mirjana, that takes great faith. The deeper the suffering, the more faith it takes.

A. That's why the Blessed Mother tells us to pray for strong faith. Our faith must be stronger than death. For those who know God's love, who trust God's love, there is only peace.

Q. What does it take to experience that peace? Do you know, Mirjana?

A. Faith in God's love, trust in God's goodness, and love for His will that is strong enough to obey His will no matter what happens in a lifetime.

Q. Mirjana, how do we know God's will?

A. The Blessed Mother says we can know God's will through faith, the Scriptures, prayer, obedience to the Commandments, the Church, and lawful authority.

CHAPTER 6

I V A N K A

Allow God to be our Father.

Ivanka Ivankovic Elez is, besides Mirjana, the other visionary who says she knows ten secrets, which involve the final chapters in the history of the planet earth. As with Mirjana, the secrets were given to her by the Blessed Mother. It is Ivanka who has told us that God will not destroy the world.[1] She says it is man's sinful heart that is capable of such destruction. She reminds people daily by her faithfulness to the ordinary life of a wife and mother that God is our Father, that the Blessed Mother has come as the Queen of Peace, and that all things are possible for those who love God.

Ivanka was asked about the three days of darkness that were prophesied by Padro Pio. She was asked if she knew anything about fire raining from heaven, the alleged third secret of Fatima. Ivanka was also consulted about the message of Akita, an ecclesiastically approved apparition of the Blessed Mother in Japan in 1973 in which the Blessed Mother said:

> *The Heavenly Father is ready to [allow] a great chastisement on the whole of mankind. If mankind does not repent and amend its lives, the Heavenly Father will [permit] a supreme chastisement . . . worse than the deluge. Fire will plunge from the sky . . . a great part of humanity will be annihilated. The good will die with the bad. Those who survive will suffer so much that they will envy the dead.*[2]

Ivanka is serene and she is silent. Her life is a powerful message that God is love.

A gentle woman of great simplicity, Ivanka's prayer life is based on her deep love for God. She has learned silence. She is learning to prefer God's will. She is His choice for a great project involving the final chapters in the history of the planet earth. She is known for her faithfulness to God's ways. She is gracious. She understands God's graciousness—that His graciousness accommodates the weakness of all His children. His graciousness is silence when He is not asked. His graciousness is absence when He is not invited. His graciousness forbears when His children seek to exploit His graciousness. He withholds rewards to those who abuse his graciousness.

Ivanka, tall and strong, is married to Raico Elez, one of six sons who owns a local restaurant. She has a quiet demeanor and a radiant smile. Her first child, Kristina, is nineteen months older than Josef, who was born in June 1990. One afternoon, as Ivanka held newborn Josef, she had a faraway look in her eyes. This young woman has seen heaven, hell, and purgatory. She has also had four visits from her dead mother. Her favorite encounter, she says, was most unique.

"The third time was so happy. I had completed a difficult assignment for the Blessed Mother. As a reward, she brought my mother to me. I had seen her two other times, but the third time she came over to me, and embraced me and said, "Dearest Ivanka, I'm so proud of you!" When Ivanka tells the story she has tears of joy and longing in her eyes.

"The Blessed Mother always comes surrounded with angels—little angels. They look like babies," Ivanka recalls. She said the Blessed Mother has even invited her to play with the angels, and she does. She calls the angels her playmates and confidants. Angels seem to have the mission of intervening in the world as instruments of divine power. They are believed to preside over the different domains of the universe—the stars, the meteors, the planets, and even the animals. All things of the earth are said to be governed by the angels, and each child of God, each creature of free will, is assigned a particular and personal guardian angel.

Ivanka and her children pray to the angels every day. Her family prays the daily rosary together, and Ivanka has a yearly apparition with the Blessed Mother on the anniversary of her first apparition, June 25. Ivanka will enjoy this privilege for the rest of her life.

Ivanka says that those who experience the light of Medjugorje are usually aware that God sees all places and ideas, remote and proximate; that God alone is the fullness of life; and that God alone fills. She says the Blessed Mother has told her that God alone brings the joy and peace and delight all men seek.

Ivanka seems to live these words, for her life in Medjugorje is a life of simplicity, peace, and joy, notwithstanding the fact that she carries with her all ten secrets concerning the final days of the planet earth.

What are those secrets? If we pray and listen, will we too know?

A compilation of several edited interviews with Ivanka follows:

Q. Ivanka, do you know why the Blessed Mother has come to Medjugorje?

A. Yes. She has come here to Medjugorje to call all people on earth to her Son, Jesus, to His ways, for the last time.

Q. Why?

A. Jesus is the way home to God, who longs for all His children of the earth.

OF LOVE AND ANGELS

Q. Ivanka, you said that the Blessed Mother always appears to you surrounded by angels.

A. Yes. They are small, like babies.

Q. How often do you have your apparitions now?

A. Yearly, on June 25.

Q. Do the angels ever speak to you?

A. The Blessed Mother has helped me to know the angels.

Q. In what way?

A. The Blessed Mother brings great interior illumination of the things of heaven and of earth.

Q. You said that you pray to the angels every day.

A. Yes. I love the angels very much. They are filled with God's love.

Q. How do you experience that?

A. The Blessed Mother has shown me many things about the angels. She is the Queen of the Angels.

Q. What do you say to the angels?

A. I always ask them to help me, and my family, and all those who come here to love God as He deserves to be loved.

Q. Can the angels do that?

A. Yes.

Q. Do we need to allow them to help us?

A. We can turn away from the help of the angels. We can refuse them. These angels are especially caring to babies and the elderly, the sick and the weak, and those in trouble. They are most solicitous to help those who pray to them.

Q. Do you know how angels help people?

A. Many ways. Each person on earth has a special angel assigned to him or her by God.

Q. Did the Blessed Mother tell you that?

A. Yes. The Blessed Mother said that before God made the world He knew each of us. He Himself named us and He assigned a guardian angel to us.

Q. He assigned a guardian angel to us before He made the world?

So our personal angel waited all those centuries for each of us to be born?

A. Where God is, all is the eternal now. There is no time. The angels are with God.

Q. Do the angels have names?

A. Yes. God named each one of them. If you pray, you too can know your angel's name.

Q. Will our guardian angels communicate their names to all who ask?

A. Of course, and much more too.

Q. What sorts of things will our guardian angels communicate to us?

A. They always see God. They also may see the plan God has for each one of us.

Q. What is that plan, do you know?

A. It is the path each must walk to get home to heaven.

Q. Will our guardian angel show us the path God has for us that leads us to heaven?

A. Yes—if we respond to the help our angel gives.

Q. How do we turn away from our guardian angel?

A. By sin.

Q. Then what happens?

A. The angels keep prodding us to get back on the path to heaven.

Q. What do they want?

A. Repentance for sins.

REPENTANCE AND GRACE

Q. Ivanka, what is repentance for sin?

A. Repentance is a great grace. But we need to accept the grace. When our heart is hard we don't want God's grace. We block it.

Q. How do we stop blocking the grace?

A. By prayer. We ask every day when we pray the Lord's Prayer.

Q. Why the Lord's Prayer?

A. The Lord's Prayer, which Jesus taught us, really can open our hearts, if we say it with love.[3]

Q. How beautiful that hope is, Ivanka. You have seen your mother on four visits to you from heaven. You mentioned that she had come to you during your visits with the Blessed Mother.

A. Yes. The Blessed Mother has given me many gifts. She gives many gifts to all her children on earth. Most people don't even know their heavenly mother, but she is always watching over her children. She always gives us good things. It pleases God very much when we come to know and love the Blessed Mother He has given us.

Q. In what way, Ivanka?

A. God has a plan for all of us that He tells us about in the Bible. That plan is realized through Mary, the mother of Jesus, who is also our mother. There wouldn't be any Jesus if first there was not Mary. That is God's plan.

THE RETURN OF IVANKA'S MOTHER

Q. What was it like to see your mother, Ivanka, especially knowing she lives in heaven?

A. It was a great joy. She was here last year with our Blessed Mother. She saw Kristina, and newborn Josef. The Blessed Mother thanked Raico and me for choosing life, for having Josef and Kristina.

Q. Did your mother say anything to you, or did she hug you?

A. No, not this time. She just smiled and looked at us with great love.

Q. Why did the Blessed Mother bring your mother?

A. She always knows what is in my heart. She knows what is in all hearts. God created her the mother of all people on earth when He created her to be the mother of Jesus. This is true whether they know about her or not. She has been given immense powers in heaven and on earth for the care of her children.

Q. Where did she get these powers?

A. From God. That is His plan. All those who turn to the Blessed Mother experience her love, her power, her tenderness. No one is ever refused. I am certain of that.

Q. What about those who don't turn to her?

A. She is our mother. She cares for each of her children whether they know of her or not. She loves with God's love.

Q. Ivanka, what is this "power" of the Blessed Mother you speak of?

A. Jesus' love for her.

Q. Ivanka, do you know why each of us has a guardian angel?

A. His job is to guard our soul. He protects us unless we block his efforts.

Q. How do we do that?

A. By sin, or neglect, or ignorance. Lots of ways.

Q. How do we permit our guardian angel to help us?

A. While we are on the earth we each have freedom of choice. We can ignore God, ignore our guardian angel. We can pretend these angels don't exist, even though God gives us everything we have—and our guardian angel makes himself known to us all the time. This angel's real job is to keep us on the path to heaven. Our angel always sees God. He wants us to see, too. That is why the Blessed Mother wants us to make Mass the center of our lives.

Q. But Ivanka, many people on this earth are not Catholic.

A. The Blessed Mother says the Mass is offered for them too even if they don't know about it. The Mass is for all people on earth. The Mass is the power of Jesus' sacrifice on the cross that gives us the strength to walk our path of the earth to God's waiting arms. That is God's will for us. That is why our guardian angel always helps us to stay on that path to heaven, if we allow it.

Q. Ivanka, is it true that the angels are meant to be our playmates and confidants?

A. The angels are our true friends. They are wonderful playmates and the best confidants.

Q. Do we offend them when we forget to turn to them?

A. We offend God. The angels await us day and night. They never stop serving us when we are in our bodies of the earth. We make the angels very happy when we kneel in the presence of the Blessed Mother or her divine Son.

Q. Why?

A. They love to see us honor the Lord Jesus and their queen, His mother. When we no longer have our body, we will experience great joy that we knelt in their presence when we could choose to do so.

Q. Is the Blessed Mother always present when we pray the rosary?

A. Yes. She is always present.

THE LIFE GOD WANTS US TO LIVE

Q. Vicka said the Blessed Mother is always looking at us; that she never leaves the presence of any of her children. Every act of our lives is committed by an act of our will in her presence and the presence of God.[4] Soon all her children of the earth will become aware of that truth, won't they?

A. Sooner than many believe.

Q. How soon? [Ivanka looks at the sky and shrugs.] Ivanka, these pilgrimages to Medjugorje have been quite a blessing for quite a few people in the world. The visits seem to free us from so many attachments.

A. God has granted much light to His children who come to Medjugorje.

Q. Ivanka, some eminent theologians are saying that Medjugorje is a means of disclosing the true role of the Blessed Mother in salvation history. God's children of the earth belong to the Blessed Mother in a relationship that is just now being disclosed. Do you know anything about that?

A. I know some things. Some people already know much about the Blessed Mother.

Q. All things of the earth are subject to her for the use of her children's salvation, aren't they?

A. Yes. But she is most respectful of our freedom of choice.

Q. Will the day come when all people on earth will understand that the Blessed Mother has all the goods of the earth to give them?

A. That day is here for many.

Q. What kind of life does God want us to live, do you know?

A. He wills the discomfort of none of His children.

Q. What about luxuries?

A. When a person is too comfortable, the spiritual life can decline. That is why the Blessed Mother asks us to fast. She says a person who does not fast does not know God.

Q. Voluntary fasting is a sign of kinship with God, isn't it, Ivanka?

A. Yes. Voluntary fasting greatly pleases God.

Q. What about involuntary fasting?

A. God loves His people. For those who won't or cannot fast, He gives them involuntary fasting.

Q. Why?

A. Fasting cures us of the sickness of sin.

Q. The Blessed Mother has asked us to fast from sinful places, sinful situations, and sinful sensual experiences, hasn't she?

A. She says her children must fast with their eyes, their tongue, their hands, their feet, their ears.

Q. Through fasting, does the will of a person bend to the breath of God?

A. Exactly! Without fasting, we cannot experience God.

Q. How do we fast from people?

A. Often we choose companions. It is here that we can show our love for God by our choices.

Q. Sometimes, Ivanka, people have difficult family relationships or work relationships that are impossible to change. What does one do in these circumstances?

A. Pray. Consecrate the person and the situation to the Immaculate Heart of Mary, and trust Jesus.

Q. For those who love God, all things and circumstances work together for good, don't they?

A. Yes, but our Blessed Mother warns us never to judge others. She always tells us to love others and serve others. Sometimes the problem that looks so big in others is really our problem that we need to solve. If we pray and fast we can get the help from God to solve very difficult relationships and circumstances.

Q. How do we fast from places?

A. The Blessed Mother wants us to avoid places that have been sources of temptation to us, or that take our mind or heart off God and His ways.

Q. What about things? Things don't take us to heaven, but they can keep us from getting there, can't they?

A. Yes. By taking first place in our lives.

Q. Are you saying the Blessed Mother wants us to fast from people, places, and things that take us off the path to the kingdom of heaven?

A. If we love God, we will do that.

Q. Is that why we have to go through sickness, suffering, old age, and death?

A. These experiences free us from attachments that are transitory. The Blessed Mother asks us to fast with love because the reward is very great.

MOTHER OF THE BRIDE

Q. Ivanka, tell us a little about your wedding. It must have been difficult for you since your mother was in heaven, but the Blessed Mother is really the mother of all brides.

A. She helped me a great deal.

Q. In what way?

A. She asked me to prepare for the wedding with much prayer so that we could experience great joy and peace at the wedding. She asked me to turn to her with every detail.

Q. Did you do that?

A. Yes. She helped me much with everything.

Q. Ivanka, you seem to be a person of deep humility.

A. The Blessed Mother is truly humble. I don't know if I'm humble. We can never judge ourselves.

Q. She said once, Ivanka: *"I am humble because I know God. The more you know God the more humility is a fiber of your soul. Humility is not an external characteristic. Humility is a sign of our relationship with God. Humility cannot be ascertained with the senses. Humility is a condition of the soul."*

A. That is why she always tells us a person must never judge another person.

IVANKA ON DAILY LIFE AND ANGELS

Q. Ivanka, you have a lovely home, two beautiful children, a hard-working husband of faith—you apparently lead a life of much peace and simplicity.

A. These are the fruits of prayer and fasting. They are God's gifts.

Q. Do you ever think about fashion?

A. Before the Blessed Mother began to appear to me, I thought of it often. As my prayer life grew, following fashion became boring.

Q. Fashion is transitory, like everything of the earth, isn't it?

A. Yes. Now I try to buy nothing I do not need.

Q. Ivanka, young mothers often have jobs that take them away from their babies and young children for many hours. Sometimes these mothers feel guilty.

A. They should never feel guilty. If mothers pray, they will experience in their hearts what the answer for them is. If they work and feel peace in their hearts, then they know they are within God's will. If they experience no peace, then they must pray to find God's will for themselves and their children.

Q. Ivanka, do you still see angels?

A. Sometimes.

Q. What do they look like?

A. They are most beautiful.

Q. Do you always see angels?

A. I always see them when the Blessed Mother comes.

Q. Do you see them other times?

A. I am aware of them when I pray. All people who pray frequently understand this. The angels are great helps to us when we turn to them.

Q. They find immense joy in serving God's children of the earth, don't they?

A. Yes, when we can give them projects, assign them tasks, we see and experience their presence in our lives.

Q. Do you know what humility is, Ivanka?

A. It is part of the things of heaven.

Q. You have seen heaven, haven't you?

A. Yes.

Q. Can you explain heaven?

A. Words can never describe heaven. Those who love God know about heaven. Those who do not love God yet must pray. In that way all can understand and long for heaven.

Q. What else do the angels do?

A. They communicate to us when we offend God. It troubles them, and they let us know.

Q. In what way?

A. The angels give us no peace until the action that offends God stops. Those who have a prayer life understand.

Q. What else do you know about the angels, Ivanka?

A. They are spirits of peace and gentleness. They are quite powerful. They are most respectful of us as children of God.

Q. Whenever there is an absence of peace and gentleness, do we know we have turned our backs on the angelic court?

A. We need to pray immediately when that happens.

Q. When we turn our back on the angelic court, do we then come into contact with Satan?

A. You recognize the presence of Satan where there is hatred, rage, violence, disorder. When actions are harsh and agitated, his presence is obvious. The Blessed Mother told us to pray and he will have no power over us.

Q. How do we develop a harmonious relationship with the holy angels?

A. They never leave our side. We only need to speak to them. They hear even the feeblest cry. They like to comfort us in our times of suffering and disappointment and pain. They also like to share in our times of joy.

Q. Ivanka, the Blessed Mother has introduced you to a whole unseen world all around us, hasn't she?

A. That world can be seen by everyone through the eyes of faith. It has always been part of the Church.

Q. Do you know the angels of your two children?

A. Yes. Most mothers know their children's angels. We've lived together as a family before my children were born. So it is with all mothers and their unborn babies and the angels of the unborn babies.

Q. You seem happy and peaceful, Ivanka, and your children are happy and peaceful.

A. Our angels are gentle and peaceful. They awaken in us much joy and expectation.

Q. In what way?

A. Every day we await the wonders of God that unfold before our eyes. This happens in all families who pray and fast and trust God.

Q. Do you and your husband pray together?

A. Yes. We pray the rosary every day. And we pray with our children. When we pray, we know the Blessed Mother and all the angels and saints pray with us. When we pray, we are all one family before God.

Q. Ivanka, the Blessed Mother has often said here at Medjugorje that when we pray she prays with us. Now we learn that her angels and all the saints join her in praying with us. Do you know anything about the fallen angels who follow Satan?

A. They are real. Their job is to destroy God's children.

Q. Do you ever worry about the fallen angels—the devils?

A. Never. When we are people of prayer, we fear nothing but offending God.

PRAYER

Q. How often do you pray?

A. I try to pray always.

Q. How do you do that?

A. The Blessed Mother has taught me to put the things of heaven first.

Q. What does that mean?

A. I pray as soon as I awaken. Then I try to accept peacefully everything that happens each day, the good things, and the things that don't seem good at the time.

Q. How do you handle stressful situations, Ivanka? There is a roadblock on the way to your house. The local men are armed to prevent attack on your life and property. The country is on the verge of a civil war. Many have already died [as of 1991]. There is economic uncertainty. The local bishop has not accepted the authenticity of this apparition, yet you seem tranquil.

A. The Blessed Mother has taught me to pray and to trust God.

Q. Does the Blessed Mother bring many gifts?

A. Oh yes! She is our mother. She always knows what we need before we ask.

Q. Ivanka, is it true that Satan assigns followers of his to tempt and torment us?

A. So it is. That is why the Blessed Mother taught us to pray and fast. Those who pray and fast have no worries.

Q. Ivanka, given the severity of our age, and knowing all ten secrets as you do, as well as the dates each secret will occur, what do you recommend?

A. Allow God to be our Father. Love God our Father. Accept the loving plan He has for each of us.

Q. Ivanka, is it true that the smallest prayer awakens in man a longing for God?

A. So it is. His promises live in the hearts of all His children.

CHAPTER 7

J A C O V

The human heart, on its own, is most untrustworthy.

Words are feeble purveyors of truth. So it is with the visionary Jacov Colo. When the first apparition of the Blessed Virgin occurred at Medjugorje on June 24, 1981, it was three weeks to the day after he turned ten. The photos of those early ecstasies reveal a radiant little face turned to the heavens, a boy filled with love and joy and longing. More than a decade later, Jacov is quiet, unassuming, hidden. He is also highly intelligent and insightful. He shuns publicity, yet endeavors to be faithful to his calling as a messenger of God's words, delivered to the world by the Blessed Virgin Mary, and given through him and five other, older children.

Jacov is an orphan. He was the only child of a father who abandoned the family when he was eight years old. His mother, who had suffered from alcoholism, died when he was twelve. He has been told by the Blessed Mother that his mother is with her in heaven.

Is Jacov sensitive? Imagine for a moment the relationship with the unseen world we have only heard or read about, that Jacov Colo experiences daily. He has been inside the place known as heaven. The memory is powerful for him. He said if he thought of heaven too much, he would die of loneliness. As for hell, he has been there, too. His words are haunting—"Hell is the ultimate waste because no one needs to go there."[1] And as for purgatory, he has been there as well—Jacov always asks those who speak to him to pray often for the poor souls stranded there, especially their own family members. "If you knew how much your prayers help them, you would pray always for them," he pleads.

Mirjana lives a few short steps from Jacov's uncle's house, where he now resides. She told me that in the first few days of the apparitions, the Blessed Mother was most gracious about the fear of the six visionaries, and gentle about the personal suffering each was enduring. She told the children: *"Do you know my real birthday is August fifth?"* The children said no, they did not know that. The Blessed Mother continued: *"Would you children like to give me some presents?"*

Jacov sorrowfully blurted, "Dear Blessed Mother, I don't have any money!"

The Blessed Mother smiled joyfully and said: *"Oh Jacov, my dearest little one, you don't need money for my birthday presents! Tonight when you go home, no matter what your feelings tell you, no matter how you are stimulated, rather than speak the pain in your heart, run outside and look at the heavens and cry out 'It's all for the love of You, dear Jesus.' "*

Mirjana said the next evening at the apparition, the Blessed Mother thanked Jacov for his "gifts" from the previous evening. By the time the Blessed Mother's birthday arrived, Mirjana said that Jacov was "just bursting." He had "billions of presents for the Blessed Mother!" High-strung and nervous by nature, young Jacov could hardly contain himself during the long rosary prayers that preceded the apparition. Finally the moment came. The great flashes of light announced the arrival of the Queen of Heaven and Earth, the gentle mother of all people, especially little ones with broken hearts. As Jacov saw her he literally reached up and grabbed at the Mother of God as he cried out. "Happy birthday, dear Blessed Mother!" Realizing what he had done, Jacov fell on the floor in shame and fear. Mirjana said she saw the Blessed Mother tenderly lean down and pick him up as she took his little nail-bitten hand in hers and kissed it.

When I asked Jacov what it was like to be kissed by the Mother of God, he blushed a deep crimson. Embarrassed, he struggled: "There are no words to describe what it is like to be kissed by the Mother of God. It is part of the things of heaven."[2]

That Jacov is faithful to his daily duties seems evident to pilgrims. He works in the Franciscan bookstore every day. He is fast with the calculator and can convert the different currencies at an amazing rate. In the afternoons, he does computer work in the rectory. Trained as a locksmith, Jacov says nothing about his future. He is the only one of the visionaries who refused to disclose whether he will be alive when the permanent sign comes.[3] The other five have said they will be alive. Jacov says it is a secret.[4] (In early 1992, Jacov was not in Yugoslavia; he was known to be living in exile in Italy.)

Jacov is private, gracious, and deep. No stranger to suffering, he brings joy wherever he is. Is that, after all, the paradox of the Medjugorje apparitions?

A compilation of edited interviews with Jacov follows:

Q. Jacov, you have been seeing the Blessed Mother every day since you were ten years old?

A. Yes. She comes every evening at six-forty.

Q. Where do you see her?

A. Either at church during the rosary that precedes Mass, or at home where I have a special place I have prepared.

Q. Why do you have this special place?

A. The Blessed Mother has asked all people on earth to have a special "prayer corner" in their home, to set aside a special time each day to give to God. I have done that.

Q. What do you have in your "prayer corner"?

A. A statue, a crucifix, some special pictures, and my rosaries.

Q. Jacov, have you ever felt a resistance to the apparitions of the Blessed Mother? Have you ever been too busy to be there for the apparition?

A. Absolutely not. It is the highlight of the day for me.

Q. Why?

A. The Blessed Mother fills my heart with the things of heaven. I often count the minutes until the time of her arrival comes.

Q. Jacov, many children's favorite place to go is Disneyland. If they were permitted to go to Disneyland every day for ten years, they would have resisted strenuously after several years.

A. There is nothing of earth that can satisfy the human heart. I, too, have been to Disneyland in California [in the winter of 1991]. Though it was a pleasant excursion, it is very much a place of this world. The Blessed Mother comes from heaven. She brings things of heaven with her.

THE THINGS OF HEAVEN

Q. Tell us about the things of heaven, Jacov.

A. There really are no words.

Q. Jacov, the philosophers and theologians have written many things about heaven. Do you know about the philosophers and theologians?

A. I am a simple man. I have seen some of the books that speak about the things of heaven.

Q. What do you think of the books?

A. They have a lot of words in them.

Q. Are the words correct?

A. It is tedious to work through all the words. If that were my avenue to heaven, I might have no understanding at all [laughter].

Q. Tell us your understanding of heaven.

A. I have been there. It is difficult for me to talk about it.

Q. Is it difficult to live on earth once you have been in heaven?

A. That is an understatement.

Q. Jacov, you said that if you thought about heaven too much, you would die of loneliness.[5] How do you handle the memories of heaven, hell, and purgatory?

A. The Blessed Mother asks us to be careful of the problem of the tyranny of memories.

Q. What does that mean?

A. She asks us to trust God's love to make all things well. She asks us to surrender the past to her maternal care and to remember only in the light of God's love.

Q. Does that mean you do not dwell on the past?

A. I try not to even think of the past or the future. The Blessed Mother has taught me that I have enough to do just today.

Q. Why did she show you heaven, hell, and purgatory?

A. That I might be a more effective witness of life itself, that I might see the reality of those places.

Q. Do you know whether you will go to heaven when you die?

A. For me the path is most difficult.

Q. In what way?

A. I have been chosen to be a messenger of this apparition. I do not want to disobey God. My path is difficult.

Q. Jacov, are you saying that those who receive great spiritual blessings also receive heavy crosses?

A. I have had some suffering. There will be more. I do not choose to talk about it.

Q. Jacov, you have said that the Blessed Mother wants you to make the Mass the center of your life. Has that happened?

A. She wants us to know Jesus very intimately as our brother, our Savior, our Lord. The means to this knowledge is deep interior prayer. The greatest prayer is the Mass.

Q. Jacov, do you have a relationship with the Eternal Father?

A. Yes. All creation has a relationship with the Eternal Father. The more intimate our relationship with Jesus is, the more intimate our relationship with the Eternal Father is.

Q. Do you know why, Jacov?

A. Yes, Jesus said, "*The Father and I are one. He who sees Me, sees the Father.*"

Q. Jacov, you said the Blessed Mother wants you to make your heart a tabernacle where the Holy Trinity likes to dwell. Can you tell us a little bit about that?

A. I'm not sure, but it's a process. The human heart is filled with longing that, at first, just involves people and things. The purpose of people and things is to show us the providential care of each of us by God. Many of us don't see that. We allow our hearts to get attached to the people and things for themselves, not as gifts of God. When that happens, we lose our hearts to the people and things.

Q. Are you saying that we, in effect, lose our freedom?

A. In a way, yes, because our heart is no longer ours, and things or others control us. Often, we don't even realize this has happened.

Q. What kind of freedom are we talking about?

A. The freedom to choose God. To give God first place in our lives.

Q. You are speaking of interior freedom, aren't you?

A. When my heart is all mine, I can choose to love with a love that is untainted by false attachments.

Q. Why are the attachments false?

A. Because they are only illusions. God is the source of love. All love comes from God. All that is made comes from God. When I open my heart so that God's love can enter, then it drives out all the illusions, and the false attachments. My heart becomes a conduit through which the love of God flows. As it flows through me to give to you or others, I myself am filled.

Q. Is that what the Blessed Mother teaches you?

A. She herself is a perfect conduit through which the love of God flows. None of God's love is diverted to her for herself alone. She is a transparency of sorts through which the love of God flows to the world. Do you see why I can never get too busy to receive her?

Q. Jacov, are these thoughts of yours hints of the depths of the mystery of heaven?

A. I, of myself, am nothing. My thoughts are nothing. God in His mightiness has chosen to give me life. And He has chosen to touch that life with His presence.

Q. Is that what makes your heart a "tabernacle where the Holy Trinity likes to dwell"?

A. I don't know.

Q. Do you experience this divine presence all the time?

A. I have good days and bad days.

Q. What is a good day, Jacov?

A. A day where I am constantly aware, all day long, of the presence of God.

Q. What is a bad day?

A. The opposite.

Q. How do you survive a bad day?

A. It is very painful.

Q. What do you do?

A. I have tried lots of things.

Q. Do you know the solution?

A. There is no solution. We are totally dependent on God's mercy.

GOD'S MERCY

Q. Do we have to ask for God's mercy?

A. We can refuse it.

Q. Who would refuse God's mercy?

A. Often the human heart, on its own, is most untrustworthy. That is why the Blessed Mother says it is urgent that all people on earth pray and fast. No one is exempted. Without prayer and fasting, the human heart is helpless to hear God or see God—to choose God.

Q. Jacov, we have been told that all God's children hear His voice in the quiet of their hearts. The responses of His children to His calls are known to Him alone. He is God. He alone judges.

A. People have the law of God, which is the path to heaven, written in their hearts. But the Blessed Mother is often sad. She often cries because so many reject God. They choose momentary pleasure and toss God and God's ways aside. I do this myself.

Q. You do? What does the Blessed Mother say?

A. She never criticizes me. She never judges me. Sin hurts her very much.

Q. Why?

A. Because it hurts us so much.

Q. What do you do?

A. I always try to do better.

Q. Do you succeed?

A. Sometimes yes, sometimes no.

Q. Jacov, if you, who sees the Blessed Mother every day, have such a hard time, what about the rest of us?

A. The Blessed Mother says we must pray. Sometimes, I am not as faithful to prayer as I should be. The Blessed Mother says we must fast. Sometimes, when I fast, I don't have love in my heart. Then my fasting isn't much. The Blessed Mother says we must forgive, especially our enemies. Sometimes I fail here. The Blessed Mother says we must be converted. Sometimes I turn my heart right back to the world and its pull. So you see, the human heart is very weak. It is prayer, fasting, forgiveness, and reconciliation that free the human heart. Every day I try to do better.

Q. Why do you have to fast with love, Jacov?

A. Because if we fast without love for God, the fasting hardens out hearts. The Blessed Mother says the motive behind all that we do needs to be love for God.

Q. What about those who do not understand love for God as a motive? Some fast out of fear. Some out of obedience. Some out of vanity. Some out of expediency.

A. When fasting is for love of self instead of love for God, it is like a boomerang. It has no lasting value and in many cases is hurtful either to the person himself or to others. The Blessed Mother says our motives are most important. We need to pray about our motives, that they can become pure.

Q. Why do we need to forgive our enemies?

A. The Blessed Mother says not to forgive them hurts us more than it hurts them.

Q. Why?

A. Because the unforgiveness sickens our heart. It fills it with poison.

Q. Do you have peace in your heart, Jacov?

A. When I pray and fast and truly forgive, I have much peace. So it is for everyone. This is what the Blessed Mother wants for the whole world.

JACOV'S ADVICE

Q. Do you have any advice for us from the Blessed Mother?

A. If your family owns very much, limit the use of these luxuries. Give away what you don't use, and share what you keep. If your family has little, enjoy what you have and share. For those who trust God's providence, who pray and fast and forgive, who share the talents and goods He has given, their hearts are a center of peace. For those who do not trust God, who do not pray and fast and forgive, and who refuse to love and share, their hearts are a pit of anguish. The Blessed Mother says that those who know God love God. Those who love God are a sign of His love, His peace, His generosity.

Q. Jacov, is that the future? Will only those who know God, love God, and live His ways survive the days that are prophesied at all the Marian apparitions throughout the world?

A. Only those who do God's will live on. All else is illusion. All else is death. The Blessed Mother has said: "*My children, you have forgotten. Prayer and fasting will stop war. It will change the natural law.*"

Q. Jacov, will there be war?

A. There is much war now, in hearts, in families, in towns and cities and countries.

Q. Jacov, do you know anything more about this tyranny of feelings you mentioned?

A. I don't understand.

Q. Mirjana said we need to be most careful of our feelings.[6] Do feelings lie?

A. I think so.

Q. Does the Blessed Mother speak about our feelings?

A. She wants us to ask God to purify our feelings, our emotions, so that we can have real love in our hearts.

Q. Jacov, you say the Blessed Mother has reminded us here in Medjugorje that God has written His law of love in the hearts of all His children. If that is true—and I have no reason to doubt it—could it be that there really are no unbelievers?

A. Many people may say they don't believe, but how do they live? Only God knows our hearts. There is not one creature who is unloved by God.

Q. Do you know when the permanent sign is coming, Jacov?

A. Yes. When the permanent sign comes people will come here from all over the world in even larger numbers. Many more will believe.

Q. Will all people believe because of the permanent sign, Jacov?

A. The Blessed Mother said that there will still be some who will not believe even after the permanent sign comes.

Q. Do you know what the permanent sign is, Jacov?

A. Yes.

Q. Can you tell us anything about it?

A. It will be something that has never been on the earth before.

Q. Jacov, why will some still not believe?

A. They will not put themselves in a position to be converted.

Q. Is conversion something we can't do for ourselves?

A. I don't know. It is an operation of grace, and grace comes from God. A person can say yes to the possibility of conversion. That is why the Blessed Mother asks us to pray and to fast. It is the prayer and fasting that allow our hearts to open to God. Conversion really means to become aware of God all around us. God has always been all around us, only most of us don't realize it.

Q. What do you recommend?

A. All people on earth who hear the Blessed Mother's messages and respond to them with a generous heart filled with love will experience conversion.

Q. Jacov, you six visionaries have received such a singular grace. Even the Blessed Mother says that never in the history of the Church have any persons had the grace you six children of Medjugorje have been given.

A. We have been chosen in a special way only to serve God, but not because we are better or because we are special, or because we will get more. Our role is to be messengers of God's great plan for the world, which is being manifested here at Medjugorje. Nothing more.

Q. What is that plan, Jacov?

A. The Blessed Mother is here to convert and reconcile the whole world.

Q. What do you know about suffering?

A. Some are more capable of suffering than others. God knows us. God gives us only what we can bear. The Blessed Mother knows about suffering. She suffered much herself. She always helps those who suffer.

Q. Jacov, the tiny violet is as beautiful to God as the giant sunflower. Is that the same with suffering?

A. Those who have little suffering are dear to God, as are those who suffer much. It is our attitude toward suffering that matters, not the degree. We must never compare. Any comparison is our own judgment. Only God can see the human heart.

CHAPTER 8

V I C K A

The Lord often shows great favors to the unworthy in order to manifest His goodness.

Vicka Ivankovic was born July 3, 1964. Of medium height, she has curly black hair, large flashing brown eyes, and a radiant smile. She exudes joy. Forthright and earnest, Vicka always says what she thinks. She is fearless. Those who knew Vicka in the early days of the apparitions were sometimes taken aback by her quick temper and her shortness, which bordered on curtness. Today, the gentleness, compassion, and patience of a more mature Vicka are evident, not only to those who know her well but also to all who come to see her speak about the Blessed Mother, who "loves us so much we could die for joy."

Summers are typically very hot in Medjugorje. A normal day might find Vicka wearing a lilac-and-white striped shirt with white jeans, brought to her by a generous pilgrim. Invariably, she will be leaning on the iron railing of her porch, with that penetrating smile, welcoming those who flock to her doorstep. She is thin now. No longer is she the husky Croatian farm girl, though she still works in the fields. Her spirit is truly ebullient. Her smile is joyful and quite contagious. Her bare feet are caked with mud, and a piece of skin hangs from her left heel as if she has cut it climbing the rocky and jagged mountains of Medjugorje. Vicka doesn't seem to notice. Her hair is long. Her body is beginning to have a fragile look. Penance does that.

The Blessed Mother has been giving the details of her life on earth to Vicka who has filled three notebooks with these facts. "When can we read it, too?" people ask. Vicka smiles graciously as she muses, "I don't know. I do only what the Blessed Mother tells me."

"Will it be soon?" someone volunteers.

"She didn't say," responds Vicka.

Another suggests, "Why would the Blessed Mother dictate her life history to Vicka if the world were going to end? Vicka, do you know if the last apparition of the Blessed Mother on earth means the end of the world?" Vicka laughs now. "She didn't say anything about the end of the world, did she?" Vicka does not respond.

She knows much about the unseen world. She has been to heaven. She describes heaven as a place that is not beyond the horizon. She says it is not tomorrow. Vicka says heaven is all around us, and indeed within us, even on earth, for those who live right in the center of God's will—those who experience an awareness of God's presence, in effect, experience the presence of God in all that is. Though Vicka says the experience is not constant on earth as it is in heaven, she claims that, for those who really know God, heaven is possible to experience while still on earth. All this is the fruit of God's love, His grace, His mercy, she says.

Vicka describes heaven as a vast place; conceptually, she says, it is "unlimited" and, given the language and education barrier, she may have been attempting to explain that heaven is in some way infinite, because God is infinite, and heaven is a union with God in all that is. She describes people, very happy people. They were dressed, she says daily to those who ask, in pink, gray, and yellow robes. "They are so happy. You can see it on their faces."

"What kind of happiness?" someone asks.

"They are full," she responds.

"What does that mean?"

"Well," Vicka volunteers, "the Blessed Mother said, '*See how happy they are. And they know they deserve it.*' "

Vicka speaks of a great light that is in heaven. "Is it a physical light, like the light from the sun? Or is it light that floods the intellect to illumine all those mysteries that have been hidden throughout the ages?"

It is even more than that, she says. "There are no mere words to describe heaven. You just have to experience it." Heaven is a reward for those who stay faithful to God until the end, she says. Vicka announces now that when our body dies, nothing changes for us except that we no longer have a body. We are exactly the same person, she says, except the physical body is gone. Also, we no longer have free will (see note 15 to Chapter 5). We must now face, in God's light, all the results of our free choices, which we made while we had a body. We now can see, she says, the results of our choices until the end of time. We can't remedy anything now. We are totally dependent upon God's mercy and the love and kindness of those still on earth to repair and restore any harm we have done to any person, place, or thing on earth.

Vicka also has been to purgatory. After the journey to purgatory, she was so horrified by the plight of the abandoned souls there that she pleaded with the Blessed Mother, who brought her there, to allow her to help them, for the Blessed Mother told her they cannot help themselves. They are totally dependent upon the prayers and penance of the people of earth to be freed from their place of purgation—and go to heaven. The Blessed Mother warned Vicka of the seriousness of her request. She advised Vicka to discuss this offer on behalf of the poor souls in purgatory with her confessor, Father Janko Bubalo. Vicka did. Father Bubalo asked Vicka to pray and fast for three days that she might have the strength to persevere in her desire to help the poor souls. On the third day she received permission from her spiritual director to undertake this sacrifice to help the souls in purgatory. Thus began Vicka's spiritual odyssey on their behalf, that they might be freed from that place of purgation and go to heaven.

When I asked, "Do you know the poor souls well?" she replied, "Yes. I can feel them. They suffer so much! They are so needy. They are so abandoned by their loved ones on earth! It is a joy, a privilege to help them."

Vicka became ill as quickly and mysteriously as her sacrifice was accepted by the Blessed Mother. Some believed her illness was a mystical illness. She had, in fact, a medically diagnosed brain tumor, swelling of the joints which eventually resulted in high fevers and comas. Throughout her illness, Vicka's joy was obvious to all who saw her. "I know the value of suffering," she said. "All suffering is for someone. It is a privilege to suffer with Jesus."[1]

As quickly as Vicka's sacrifice was completed, she was instantly cured on the exact date the Blessed Mother had promised many months earlier. The medical community attending Vicka, as well as the Franciscans of Saint James Parish who were aware of the mysterious circumstances surrounding Vicka's illness, had medically verifiable evidence of Vicka's commitment to the poor souls in purgatory.

Vicka has visited hell as well as purgatory and heaven. The Blessed Mother showed her hell that she might understand the consequences to those who turn away from God.[2] Satan is real, she warns. "He watches day and night. He hates God and really hates us. He wants to snatch us away from God and keep us in his power for all eternity. He [Satan] can't touch us unless we let him. The suffering in hell is horrible. The people there are not free, they are constrained. They must do Satan's bidding for all eternity."

Nothing is too much for Vicka to do, she says, if it can keep *one* person from condemning himself to hell for all eternity. So many fall into Satan's snares by ignorance, she laments. He is the father of lies. He always promises people everything so they will break God's Commandments "just a little bit." Then Satan is in charge.

God's Commandments are God's walls of safety for souls on earth. When we voluntarily kick in the walls of safety God has provided for us, we allow Satan to rush in and take over our lives.

How do we rebuild God's walls of safety around us? Repentance, sacramental confession, Vicka says. The Eucharist is armor against Satan. Also, she tells us, the Blessed Mother has told her how valuable wearing blessed objects like medals and crosses is to give protection from Satan. Every day Vicka says to pilgrims, "Always wear medals, or a cross, and the scapular. These blessed items are protection from Satan. Oh—and holy water too!" she remembers. "Keep holy water in your house." Then she holds up the rosary. "The Blessed Mother said, *'My dear children, always have the rosary in your hand as a sign to Satan that you belong to me!'* "

Vicka has developed a special ministry to alcoholics and drug addicts. "Their wounds are deep," she suggests. Many come to Medjugorje, and Vicka prays over them, and for them and with them. Miraculous cures have been claimed by former addicts from all over the world who have come to Medjugorje and been freed of the cravings of substance abuse.

Vicka is one of the visionaries who has remained in Medjugorje during the terrible bloodshed of the civil war. She has had invitations to the United States, to Europe, and to South America, especially as the civil war becomes more intense in her homeland. Vicka, however, chooses to be with her family. She is filled with joy as usual, and has her daily apparitions with the Blessed Virgin even as the fighting escalates.

Vicka says that miraculous healings will occur all over the world when the permanent sign comes. In the meantime, those who respond to the messages of the Mother of God at Medjugorje are already reporting miraculous healings of addiction, divorce, broken relationships, and also physical healings. The reports continue that the blind see, the lame walk, cancer and heart disease are healed, congential illnesses disappear.

Vicka works tirelessly all day, every day to spread the message of the Blessed Mother. These days she travels worldwide to deliver her messages. When she is home, she stands in the sun, or the rain, or the cold and delivers the messages of the Mother of God to all who will listen. And every day she has a private apparition with the Mother of

God. Of the original six visionaries, she is one of four who still receives daily apparitions.

Who is this woman "clothed with the sun" who brings such gifts? Let us draw near as Vicka, who knows nine secrets concerning the future of the world, tells us some of her experiences with the mother of Jesus Christ whose heart is "filled with such love, such compassion, such tenderness, such joy!"

A compilation of several edited interviews with Vicka follows:

Q. You have been in heaven, Vicka. What is it like? You have described flowers, trees, people in yellow, pink, and gray robes.[3]

A. The Blessed Mother took Jacov and me to heaven. It is a kingdom of love, of joy, of peace. God made every child of His to live in that kingdom. It is sin that keeps us out.

Q. You have told us that some people are able to experience heaven while on earth through obedience to God's will. You said that those who do God's will have love and peace and joy even in the midst of great suffering.[4]

A. Yes. It is sin that interrupts love. It is sin that destroys peace. It is sin that kills joy.

Q. Do you know whether Mary and Jesus lived in love and joy and peace when they were on earth?

A. When they were together, yes. Jesus would have died of loneliness without the holiness and perfection of Mary.

Q. Vicka, God the Father promised to send "the woman" whose seed would destroy the seed of Satan.[5] Do you know anything about that?

A. She is the mother of Jesus. She was in God's mind before He made the world. She is God's plan, His way for Jesus to lead us to heaven.

Q. Vicka, you mentioned that the Blessed Mother is dictating her life to you. Has she completed that project with you yet?

A. She always shows me things.

Q. Why is the Blessed Mother His plan?

A. God loves us. He wanted to become one of us. He did this through Mary.

Q. I suspect we can't comprehend Mary's dignity. God alone knows her. But that is true of all of us, isn't it?

A. The Blessed Mother says it is impossible for us while we are in a body to understand our dignity and nobility and value as children of God. That is why Jesus and Mary redeemed us.

Q. Mary and Jesus redeemed us? What does that mean?

A. Jesus is God. Mary, His mother, is God's most highly favored daughter. Mary is the way the Son of God chose to become the man, Jesus. Jesus, with the help of His mother Mary, was born, lived, and died on the cross to pay the price of our readmission to the garden of paradise. Jesus and Mary opened the door to heaven for all people whether they know it or not. The Blessed Mother is the only one of all God's children who always obeyed God's will perfectly.

Q. What does that mean?

A. It is sin that blinds us to God's will. The Blessed Mother is sinless.

GOD'S WILL

Q. Do you know what God's will is, Vicka?

A. I try to do God's will.

Q. How?

A. We have the Commandments. We have the Bible. We have prayer. I'm never sure I am doing God's will, but I always try.

Q. Does the Blessed Mother help you?

A. She is teaching me to love God more and more. It is only through love that we can follow God's will.

Q. Why?

A. God's love is stronger than all the evil in the world, all the temptation in the world. Our love is feeble. When God's love leads us we can live in peace and joy even in the midst of great suffering and temptation.

Q. Vicka, I've heard that obedience is the marrow of love. Does that mean that people must obey God's laws and the words of Jesus instead of their own perceptions of right and wrong?

A. Our own perceptions of right and wrong often come from ourselves, not God. That is why He sent Jesus, who is truth. That is why the Blessed Mother always tells us to read the Bible. She knows God, she sees God, she is able to obey God perfectly. That is why she is a perfect mother, sister, servant of God. That is why she is able to teach us about God. That is why she is a perfect example to us.

Q. But all Mary's gifts come from God.

A. Everything comes from God. He has sent her to us with messages for the whole world. Those who respond to these messages will be in heaven.

Q. Do you have any messages to share from Our Lady?

A. Yes. The Blessed Mother wants us, all people on earth, to have firm faith. She really wants us to pray, not just with our lips, but with our hearts.

Q. Does all life come from God?

A. Yes, but especially people. We are His children. He has given us free will. That is how we are different from the trees or the flowers or the fishes or birds. We can choose every minute whether to obey God our Father or not. No other creatures of God have that possibility.

Q. Do you know why God our Father has given us free will?

A. He loves us. He wants us to love Him in return. He serves us day and night.

Q. God is the servant of His creature, man?

A. Oh, yes! God is so humble. He serves us the sun that warms our face and the rain that quenches our thirst and the little seed that is planted in the earth and grows into grain for us to bake bread.

He is almighty. He is the creator and sustainer of heaven and earth, yet He serves each of us, His good children and His bad children, day and night. He gives us everything. *The sun that warms our face and the rain that quenches our thirst, and the grain that feeds us.* He gives us the stars, and the fishes and the birds. He gives us love and joy and laughter and we can use it all, and choose never to see Him or hear Him, choose never to thank Him. Yet He continues to bless us while we are on the earth. We can pollute His earth and burn His forests and poison His waters and kill His children, and still He calls to us day and night. He loves us and cares for us and longs for us with a heart filled with patience. He calls to us in the wind and in the sweetness of a flower and in the words of Jesus and now, for the last time, in the tender voice of the Blessed Mother of Jesus.

Q. Most of us never think of God our Father as our servant, Vicka.

A. And the Blessed Mother is so good. Hardly anyone realizes anymore that God is serving His children all the time. Many of us never even say thank you. And the Blessed Mother is sad because often God's children won't even serve each other as He serves us.

Q. How does this realization find expression in prayer with the heart?

A. To pray is to talk to God so that you can come to know Him and to listen as He talks to you. Many people today don't see God in the world. They don't even hear God.

Q. How do you see God in the world?

A. When you see a bird, it is God our Father who gives us that bird. When you eat some fruit, God our Father has given us the tree. He sustains the tree and it bears fruit. That fruit is served to us by God. All we have to do is eat it. Do we say, "Thank you, God, your grapes are delicious"? When we hear the bird sing, we know the bird belongs to God. It is here for our enjoyment. When it sings it praises God. The bird has no choice. It was made by God to obey Him. So were we. But we have a choice! We can love God and thank Him and enjoy His whole earth, which He gives us. That is prayer with the heart.

Q. So to see God's gifts to us, and to acknowledge them, is to pray with the heart?

A. To experience God's gifts is to experience God. God sustains us. He looks at each one of us day and night. He knows us; He made us for Himself. He longs to communicate with us.

Q. What can we do to expedite this communication?

A. Listen to Him. Look at Him. Obey Him. Return His love.

THE BLESSED MOTHER AND HER SECRETS

Q. Is this what the Blessed Mother asks of all of us?

A. She invites all people on earth to total conversion. She says, *"All my children think Jesus and I are far away from them, but dear children, we are always right beside you. We never leave you, not even for a moment. If you open your hearts you will be able to recognize us with your hearts and you will know how much we love you."*

Q. Have you experienced this, Vicka?

A. Yes. Through prayer. Just by obeying the Blessed Mother, I have learned that all of us on this earth live our whole life right before the face of God our Father, surrounded by all the angels and saints. I have discovered, through prayer, that everything that comes upon my path each day comes from God. He allows it. Often He wills it. My only choice is to accept what comes upon my path with love and trust in God as my Father, or to rebel.

Q. The Blessed Mother has told you that?

A. Yes. She has helped me in many ways, and she wants me to share what I know with others.

Q. Can you tell us more?

A. The Blessed Mother always tells me, *"I'm giving you my peace and my love so you will be able to share that peace and love with all who come here. I desire that they take my peace and love from here back home to their family and friends. I bless all who come here with my own mother's blessing."*

Q. What is this blessing the Mother of God imparts?

A. Her own personal intercession for us before God.

Q. Does she do this only for the pilgrims who come here?

A. She especially does it for those who come here to honor God. People are seeing that. The pilgrims from Medjugorje are different. They wear the blessing of the Mother of God and they know it.

Q. What about those who cannot come to Medjugorje?

A. Medjugorje is a condition of the heart.

Q. In what way?

A. All people on earth are called to have the messages of Medjugorje. That is why the Blessed Mother has come.

Q. What is this blessing of the Mother of God you mentioned?

A. The gift of holiness.

Q. What about those who have not responded to her messages?

A. We are all free. Medjugorje is a wellspring of holiness. Not everyone chooses to drink.

Q. Is there any special prayer the Blessed Mother asks us to pray?

A. Yes. In fact, the Blessed Mother pleads with us to renew the family rosary. When the parents are praying for the children, and the children are praying for the parents, when they are gathered in love with the rosary in their hands, the Blessed Mother says we can see why the rosary is the chain that binds generations to eternal life. When families pray the rosary, Satan is helpless.

Q. What about families where some don't want to pray?

A. They desperately need the prayers of those who will pray.

Q. What about children who are away from home, or too busy or too indifferent to pray the rosary with their parents?

A. In a special way the Blessed Mother recommends that we should *all* be praying for the youth of the world. They face severe problems, not only here, but all over the world. The world as we know it is passing away. We can *all* help the youth with our love and our prayers.

Q. Vicka, you know many secrets concerning future events. Do the youth of the world have problems connected with those unfolding secrets?

A. The youth are and will be facing many problems. That is why the Blessed Mother asks us to pray very hard for them. Satan is actively trying to destroy this planet, the environment, and even nature. These actions of Satan bring great suffering and hardship. Only through prayer and fasting can he be stopped.

Q. Why, Vicka?

A. Because prayer and fasting open our eyes to truth. Suffering opens our eyes to truth too, but often by the time the suffering arrives, it is too late to eliminate the cause.

Q. We have certainly seen some of that with the burning of the oil fields in the Middle East, the polluting of waters and streams, the manufacture and detonation of nuclear weapons.

A. People who are serious in their prayer life change. Peace and love are possible. The only way to peace and love is prayer and fasting.

Q. Why?

A. Prayer is the way to God. Only with God can a person truly love another person, for God is love. Without God we only love ourselves. When we only love ourselves, we take what we think we want, and we do what we think we want to do, and pretty soon the whole world is running around stepping on each other. No one is happy. No one has enough.

Q. What does the Blessed Mother specifically say to youth in terms of the secrets you know?

A. She says: "*Dear youth, nowadays what the world is offering you is just transitory. Through the things the world offers you, you can realize that Satan uses these opportunities every moment to win you for himself. Satan particularly wishes to destroy families and family life. He wishes to destroy peace and love within families, and he works through you, dear youth, by attracting you to the world's allures. Dear children: This is a time of great grace. I want you to renew my messages. Please live my messages with your hearts. Be carriers of my peace and love. Pray for peace in the world. First, dear children, pray for peace in your hearts, then peace in your families. Satan wants to destroy marriages. Children, pray for the safety of your parents'* *marriage. Parents, pray for the safety of your marriage with each other. With your children, then pray for peace in the world."*

Q. Vicka, these past few years have been dedicated to prayer for youth and families at the request of the Blessed Mother. Does she speak about this now?

A. Yes. The Blessed Mother asks that we increase our prayer for youth and family life. It is only through prayer and fasting that families can withstand the attacks of Satan in these days. She says the strongest weapon against Satan is the rosary in our hands and in our hearts.

Q. Is there any special way the Blessed Mother asks us to pray?

A. Yes. She recommends that Holy Mass become the center of our lives.

Q. What about non-Catholics?

A. They are welcome too. She wants Mass to be a special part of our everyday life. She says we have no idea of the power of the Mass to solve human problems.

Q. Vicka, you say the real prayer weapons in this battle with Satan and his forces are the Mass and the rosary. Many people on earth have no access to the Mass or the rosary. What about them?

A. We can help them by our own prayers and sacrifices for them. They are our brothers and sisters. They need the Mass and the rosary just as we do, so we offer our Mass for them. We pray our rosary for them. In that way they, too, are helped.

Q. Are other prayers effective?

A. All prayer is effective. Prayer is the key to the heart of God.

Q. Do you know why the Mass is so important that the Blessed Mother wants us to attend every day?

A. The Blessed Mother says that during each Mass, Jesus comes in person, in tangible form. We can take Jesus, in physical form, into our body. In this way, we can truly understand what it means to have Jesus in our hearts. This is our way to accept Jesus into our heart. Jesus comes alive to us through the Eucharist.[6] It is up to us. Do we accept Him or do we reject Him?

Q. Vicka, a lady in Korea named Julia Kim was given the Holy Eucharist on her tongue by a priest who told me that he saw it change to flesh and bleed.

A. That priest had a great gift.

Q. Have you ever experienced that?

A. No, but I believe Jesus is alive. The Blessed Mother asks us to prepare ourselves for that holy moment so that we can welcome Jesus properly as He comes to us alive at Holy Mass.

Q. How do we prepare, Vicka?

A. The Blessed Mother wants us to have a pure heart to receive her Son Jesus.

LOVE WITH A PURE HEART

Q. What is a pure heart, Vicka?

A. A heart that is not attached to things or people or places, but that loves God for Himself and everything else for Him too.

Q. You speak as if the Blessed Mother wants us to have detachment and distance from created things.

A. Exactly. When that happens, our hearts are capable of much greater love.

Q. Why?

A. Because then it may be possible to love with God's love, which is infinite, instead of with our own love, which is small and self-centered.

Q. How do we come to this kind of love?

A. The Blessed Mother recommends sacramental confession to prepare ourselves for Jesus.

Q. How often?

A. As often as we need to go. Some people's life choices expose them to more sin than other people's lives. For them the way is harder. They need to go to confession more often.

Q. Is their temptation stronger?

A. Yes. Often by their own choice.

Q. Should people quit their jobs if they are a source of temptation?

A. Our faith teaches us that we have a duty to avoid temptation.

Q. Why don't people know that?

A. The pull of the world is very strong. Satan is very strong these days. That is why the Blessed Mother is warning us and calling us back on the path of her Son Jesus. She wants all God's children to go to heaven.

Q. Did the Blessed Mother say more about confession?

A. Yes. She says confession does not mean just going to a priest to recite our sins and then returning to the same life we had. We need to change, to become a new person after each confession.

Q. How do we do that?

A. The Blessed Mother says the grace of the sacrament is so strong that it gives us the power to begin again, to leave the path of sin.

Q. How often do you go to confession?

A. Every time I feel I have disobeyed God.

Q. Does confession help you to do better?

A. The Blessed Mother says it does. She tells me to ask the advice of my confessor so I can take further steps along the path of holiness.

Q. Vicka, you said holiness is simply being faithful to God in good times and bad times.[7] Is it getting easier for you to discern God's will in all things?

A. I don't know [sad laugh]. I can never do enough.

Q. Does the Blessed Mother say anything about that?

A. She always encourages me. She always appreciates every little thing I do for her. I would like to do so much more!

Q. Does the Blessed Mother say anything else?

A. Yes. She keeps emphasizing how strong Satan is and how much he likes to disturb us in everything. That is why she is asking us to pray more. She needs our prayers. She asks us to pray for the success of God's plan, which is being manifested here at Medjugorje.

Q. She wants us to pray. Is there anything else?

A. Yes. She always asks us to give up something very dear to us to show our love. She says over and over that when you give up something you like for the love of God, you show God you love Him more than the thing you gave up.

Q. Does she recommend anything else?

A. Yes. The Blessed Mother wants us to take the Bible every day and read a few sentences. For that day we should try to live those passages.

VICKA'S EXPERIENCE OF APPARITIONS

Q. Vicka, you know the Blessed Mother in a personal way, which most people on earth never experience. Can you describe her to us so that we might share a bit of your experience?

A. She comes preceded by an immense, almost blinding light. She usually wears a long gray dress, a white veil, a beautiful crown made of twelve stars. She has blue eyes, black hair, and rosy cheeks. She floats on a cloud, which never touches the ground. On her feast days, anniversaries, and birthdays, she comes dressed all in gold. For

Christmas every year she brings the baby Jesus in her arms. Some Good Fridays, the Blessed Mother came with Jesus; He was all covered with wounds. All His clothes were torn. He wore a crown of thorns.

Q. Vicka, what a shocking sight.

A. It hurt me very much to see Him that way.

Q. Did He speak to you?

A. No, He only looked at me with those hurt eyes so full of love. The Blessed Mother said, "*I came here with Jesus to show you how much Jesus has suffered for all of you.*"

Q. What did you think when you heard that?

A. I thought of heaven, of how wonderful it is there, and I was sad that it cost Jesus so much for us to have the chance to go there. Then I thought of purgatory.

Q. In what way?

A. I was remembering that purgatory is an endless space of ashy color. It was quite dark. I could feel people strangling and suffering there. The Blessed Mother told us we should be praying for the souls stranded in purgatory. She said only our prayers and sacrifices can release them from that place. I looked at Jesus, all bruised and beaten, and I really experienced how much He does love us—how much He has done for us.

PURGATORY AND HELL

Q. How does purgatory relate to that experience?

A. The people there are helpless. They are really suffering. We can be like Jesus a little bit if we just do some voluntary penance for the souls in purgatory, especially for the ones who are abandoned by their families on earth.

Q. Vicka, you said you can "feel" the presence of the souls in purgatory, but you did not see them. What does that mean?

A. It means I experience their presence. I am aware of their suffering. I know some of their torment. I know how desperately they need our prayers. They are so lonely that it is almost sickening to remember those moments I was there. It is really a great joy to do penance for the poor souls because I know how much it helps them.

Q. Do you know for certain whether our loved ones who have passed away hear our prayers?

A. Of course. And many of our family members who have died desperately need our prayers. The Blessed Mother says we must pray courageously for them so that they might go to heaven. They are powerless to help themselves.

Q. You saw hell, didn't you?

A. Yes. It is a vast sea of fire in hell. I saw people filled with rage enter the fire. When they came out of the fire they looked as if they had never been human.

Q. You described a beautiful young woman who was filled with anger whom you saw enter the fire. You said when she emerged she looked like a type of nonhuman, that she was so ugly you could hardly bear to look. Does that mean that people lose the image and likeness of God that they are born with, as they enter the fire?

A. Maybe.

Q. What causes this?

A. People turn away from God by the choices they make. In this way they choose to enter the fire of hell where they burn away all connection to God. That's why they can never get back to God. It takes God's mercy to get back to Him. In hell, they no longer have access to God's mercy.

Q. They burn away their personal image and likeness of God by their choices?

A. Yes. They choose to destroy their beauty and goodness. They choose to be ugly and horrible. People do this all the time. Each choice that is against God, God's commandments, God's will, singes God's image in us.

Q. Is that why Marija said many people choose hell right here on earth?

A. Yes, they become one with hell even while they have their body. At death they go on as they were when they had a body.

Q. Are you saying that we are either God's children or Satan's children?

A. Yes. We are either for God and with God and in God, or we are victims of Satan. We choose to be one with him.

Q. Isn't there any middle ground?

A. No.

Q. What about people who sin?

A. We all sin. That's why the Blessed Mother calls us to reconciliation with God and our brothers and sisters now. The more we rebel against God's ways, the farther we are from God's kingdom.

Q. How do we get back?

A. As long as we live on earth, we can always get back to God by sorrow for our sins.

Q. How do we get to the point where we feel sorrow for our sins?

A. God's grace.

Q. How do we experience God's grace?

A. Through His mercy.

Q. And how do we get God's mercy?

A. We ask for it.

THE PRIMARY MESSAGES OF THE BLESSED MOTHER

Q. What are Our Lady's primary messages?

A. The Blessed Mother's primary messages are prayer, conversion, fasting, penance, and peace. She urges us every day to pray all three mysteries of the rosary—the joyful, the sorrowful, and the glorious. To fast on bread and water every Friday and, if possible, on Wednesdays, too. The Blessed Mother wants us to deprive ourselves of that thing which we love the most.

She personally would be very happy if each of us would stop committing sin.

Q. She has been saying these things for over ten years, hasn't she?

A. Yes. The Blessed Mother recommends that Holy Mass take the first place in all our lives. It is absolutely the most sacred, the holiest of moments.

Q. Can you explain why, Vicka?

A. At that moment, Jesus comes to us in a physical way. He is alive. That is why we have to prepare ourselves so that we can receive Jesus with love in an honorable way. Also, the Blessed Mother recommends sacramental confession once a month for all people. Again, it depends upon us. *She tells us we should not use confession as a place to get rid of sin, then go back to the sinful lifestyle. We should change ourselves.* We should become new persons in Jesus. Also, the Blessed Mother recommends that all people on earth pray with a special intensity for all the youth in the world. They are in a very serious and very difficult situation. We can help the youth of the world only with our love and with prayer that comes from our hearts.

Q. Do the apparitions still occur every day?

A. Yes. At twenty minutes until six.

Q. Will you speak of any of the secrets?

A. The Blessed Mother has promised to leave a permanent sign on Apparition Hill. This is the third secret.

Q. Do you know when it will occur?

A. Yes. The Blessed Mother has told me. I may not discuss it.

Q. Can you speak of any of the other secrets?

A. The seventh secret has been abated by our prayers. That is why the Blessed Mother begs for our prayers, fasting, and penance, that other chastisements will be lessened.

Q. Can you tell us about the chastisements?

A. With prayer and penance they can be substantially lessened.

Q. Regarding people who are sick with incurable illnesses, is there a message for them from the Blessed Mother?

A. Yes. When God gives us a big suffering, we should accept it with love. The Blessed Mother says God knows the reason He has given this suffering to a person. He knows when He will take the suffering away. The only thing He asks from us is patience. That is why we should never ask, "Why me?" We should accept the suffering as a gift, and out of love ask God if there is something more we can do to endure for Him.

Q. How long will the Blessed Mother be appearing in Medjugorje?

A. I don't know. She has said these are her last apparitions on earth. She has not said when the apparitions will end.

Q. Is there a message for priests?

A. The Blessed Mother has said priests must preserve and protect the faith of the people. They should pray the rosary with the people. Recently the Blessed Mother asked us to pray for vocations to the priesthood because of the shortage of good priests.

Q. Has the Blessed Mother spoken at all about the situation in Eastern Europe?

A. The Blessed Mother has said that peace can only come through prayer and penance. With prayer and fasting, she says that even war can be stopped. That is how strong prayer and penance are. She says we must do penance out of love, not our of fear or compulsion. The Blessed Mother warns that if we are excessive in our penance, we will not be able to persevere and we will soon stop. She says it is better to begin our penance slowly and to be faithful to our practice of penance.

The Blessed Mother pleads with all people on earth to live her messages faithfully.

A STRANGE EXPERIENCE

Q. Vicka, today a strange thing happened at the Mass.

A. Which Mass?

Q. The nine A.M. German Mass. When we walked into the church [Saint James], the whole sanctuary was filled with a mist. We could only see the top of the heads of the priests who were concelebrating the Mass. It was quite unusual. In fact, there was a mystical reality about the Mass. It was like seeing a cloud resting on the floor of the sanctuary and all those who were standing in the sanctuary were standing in the cloud. Do you know anything about that?

A. You saw that with your eyes?

Q. Yes.

A. You had the "veil" lifted from your eyes during that Mass. The "cloud" you saw was really the splendor of all the angels who always surround the altar when the Mass is celebrated.

Q. Vicka, how do you know that?

A. Everyone knows that! The angels are very much a part of our everyday world. They understand better than we do the holiness of the Eucharist. The angels *know* who is present. We only know by faith.

THE GIFT OF FAITH

Q. Faith is a great gift, isn't it, Vicka?

A. Yes. But like all gifts, it can be thrown away.

Q. Vicka, who would throw this gift of faith away?

A. Many people do and have. Faith is a precious gift. It takes work to protect the gift of faith.

Q. What kind of work?

A. It takes prayer to get God's help. And it takes practice. Those with the gift of faith need to live the truths they know, no matter what it costs them.

Q. How so?

A. For me, I know many things because the Blessed Mother has shown and taught me. My whole life is a witness of the faith I have in her divine Son and His way. The Blessed Mother is calling all people on earth to lives of faith in the word of God, Jesus. She says we can all live that life of faith by obedience to God's word, Jesus.

Q. Many people on earth don't know Jesus. Do you know anything about that?

A. That is why the Blessed Mother is here. Many "Christians" are not living a Christian life. So many have forgotten God. So many don't believe anymore. She is calling us to strong faith.

Q. How do you get strong faith, Vicka?

A. From God.

Q. How do you get to God?

A. Through prayer and fasting.

Q. What about those who have no faith at all? Those who don't know how to pray and fast?

A. The prayers, fasting, penances, and offered suffering of the faithful can be like a mantle that covers those with no faith. That is what the Blessed Mother wants from us: a total surrender to God's will. The Blessed Mother pleads with us to pray and fast and do penance for ourselves and for those who can't or won't.

Q. Do our prayers and fasting really help?

A. The Blessed Mother says they do.

Q. Many have family members who do not believe, even in the presence of God, or the fact of God.

A. I know all about that. The Blessed Mother says if one member of a family is faithful, all will be blessed.

Q. Sometimes it is lonely to be in a family where few or none believe.

A. For those who know God, the only loneliness is to be separated from Him.

Q. Are you saying faith is its own reward?

A. The Blessed Mother says faith practiced leads to hope; hope lived leads to love. God is love. Those who live in love live in God and God lives in them.

Q. Those are the words of Jesus?

A. Exactly. Do you see now how all comes from God and all leads to God?

Q. I'm not sure.

A. Jesus is the path to heaven. Those who follow Jesus have heaven even on earth.

Q. Why?

A. Because Jesus' path that He showed us is God's perfect will for us. Those who live right in the center of God's will have heaven.

MARY, THE BEARER OF LIGHT

Q. Once as I sat with Jacov, for a moment, there may have been an experience, or a glimpse of what you are speaking about. Looking into his eyes, I became aware that his human eyes view the Mother of God (she died almost two thousand years ago) every day. You too have that privilege.

A. Yes. She is the bearer of light. The light is Jesus.

Q. What is the Blessed Mother really like, Vicka?

A. She is so humble.

Q. Why?

A. Because she knows God. She says those who know God well are humble because God is humble.

Q. Do you know why this is the last time the Blessed Mother will come to earth in an apparition?

A. She says she won't need to come again after the secrets are realized.

Q. Marjana has said that the power of Satan will be broken after the first secret is realized.

A. That is right.

Q. What does that mean?

A. The Blessed Mother calls everyone on earth to immediate conversion now.

Q. Vicka, do you know what conversion is?

A. Conversion is awareness that we live before the face of God day and night and we are accountable for everything we are and have.

Q. You speak with such great urgency.

A. The Blessed Mother is weeping for all her children who do not know God, who turn away from Him, who disobey His Commandments.

Q. Why are the Commandments so important?

A. When we voluntarily disobey the Commandments through ignorance or weakness, we give Satan power over our lives. It takes God's grace to rescue us. But we have to cooperate.

Q. Is that why Marija tells us the Blessed Mother "implores us" to go to confession at least monthly?

A. Yes. Sacramental confession is a great gift of God's compassion for our weak human frailty.

Q. What about those faith traditions that don't have sacramental confession?

A. The Catholic Church is open to all.

Q. Is the Blessed Mother calling all people on earth to be Catholic?

A. No. The Blessed Mother says all religions are dear to her and her Son. She says it is we on earth who have made division. She says we are all children of God our Father. Jesus redeemed all. Not everyone accepts redemption. We have to choose God, to choose heaven.

Q. Vicka, doesn't everyone choose heaven?

A. The Blessed Mother says today many people choose hell.

Q. Who would choose hell?

A. Those who have made themselves, their earthly appetites, god.

Q. That is hard to believe.

A. It's not so hard to believe. Look at all the suffering on the earth. Father turns against son, daughter against mother. Brothers and sisters have grudges against each other. The divorce rate is high everywhere, unborn babies are killed, old people are afforded no respect, children don't obey parents. These conditions show that many people all over the world are already living in hell even on earth. The kingdom of heaven is a kingdom of love. Those who are without love, who live without God, are already in hell.

SUFFERING

Q. How does suffering fit into the world and God's plan for His people?

A. Suffering is always *for something*. People either suffer for the kingdom of love [heaven] or for the kingdom of hate [hell]. There has always been much suffering on earth. But when we offer our suffering for love, it is not really suffering. It is joy because the fruit of the suffering is heaven. I have seen hell. There the suffering has no value. It does not lead to love, to peace, to joy. It is self-perpetuating. Those who know God are filled with immense joy to do the least little thing to bring someone near to God.

Q. Why?

A. Once people begin to know the goodness of God, they want nothing else.

Q. Isn't God so big that He can reach down from heaven and lift the least little one up into heaven with Him?

A. He has done that in and through and with Jesus.

Q. Do you know why the Blessed Mother is here?

A. Yes, I know why she is here. She wants everyone in the world to be in heaven. People don't really understand how much the Blessed Virgin Mary loves each one of us, and how much she wants each one of us to know her as a mother. She asks us to pray for each other along with her. She always intercedes before God for each one of us. She wants us to pray for each other as children. There is great power in group prayer. If only people understood how pleasing it is to God to see all His children kneeling before Him with the heavenly mother He gave them through His Son Jesus.

Q. What do you recommend that we do to make the future better?

A. There is a prayer that basically goes: Bloom where you are planted. If everybody is blooming—where God plants them—the world will be a beautiful, holy place to live. But not everyone is doing this. Sometimes people stop blooming. They reject God's plan for them. Those who accept God's will live in great peace and joy and love because they know God's love. That is what the Blessed Mother wants for all her children.

CHAPTER 9

M A R I J A

Help one another and I will help you.

Marija Pavlovic was born April 1, 1965. She is tall and quite thin. Her soft, brown eyes hold a hint of suffering. Her family is poor. It is said that Marija suffered malnutrition as a child. Today she is filled with an effusive love and quite naturally extends a warm embrace to old friends. She is genuinely pretty. She has dimples and a wonderful smile. She has been described in the various international tabloids as "a beautiful, giving woman."

Visiting her in her parents' home at the foot of Apparition Hill, one notices that Marija has a prayer life that few can comprehend. She received a remarkable gift from the Blessed Mother. "From time to time when the Blessed Mother has an interest in a pilgrim's soul, she will send that pilgrim to me. Though I speak my native Croatian, the pilgrim will hear me in his or her native tongue," Marija says quietly of this gift that she shares with the first Christians. Another remarkable gift Marija has is a type of "infused" knowledge of the Italian language, which the Blessed Mother gave her one day in preparation for a visit in Medjugorje by a group of Italian clergy. It is Marija who explains that the Blessed Mother only goes where she is invited. Many who have heard have begun to pray and fast. Then they invite the Blessed Mother to come to their town or house.

One of these places is Birmingham, Alabama. In November of 1988, Marija came there to donate a kidney to her older brother, whose life was in danger from kidney failure. The people in the area had been praying and fasting and inviting the Blessed Mother to come to them for eight months. During the time Marija was hospitalized, and during her recuperation time, many apparitions occurred in Birmingham, during which the Blessed Mother spoke several times in Hebrew, and Marija was able to understand completely.

The apparitions occurred daily in a bedroom of a home where Marija stayed. Marija knelt at the foot of a four-poster bed and began to pray the rosary about 10:00 A.M. Several people knelt beside her and around her. At 10:40 the Blessed Virgin appeared.[1] Silence marked the eight minutes or so the apparitions lasted. Those present saw nothing but Marija's trancelike ecstasy, though they agreed that they all felt profound peace. Father Richard Foley, S.J., of London, was one of the theologians who found himself in Alabama during those momentous days. Also there were members of the international news media who tend to follow Marija wherever she goes. Father Foley said he experienced a "heavenly peace" during the apparitions.

The Blessed Mother gives "special blessings" through Marija to those who are present during the apparitions. The recipients are asked to extend this blessing of the Mother of God to all whom they encounter for the rest of their lives. What kind of blessing is it? There are several. One is the blessing of peace; another is the blessing of conversion; another is the blessing of love.

Marija said that on August 15, 1988, the Blessed Mother, dressed in golden robes and a veil of luminous gold, with a crown of twelve stars, appeared on Apparition Hill at 11:00 P.M. to her and Ivan. A crowd of at least one hundred thousand pilgrims from around the world had assembled on the mountain. There was absolute stillness among the crowd, which included cripples on litters and in wheelchairs, the elderly, babies, young people, priests, rabbis, ministers, nuns, and men and women of all races and creeds.

The Blessed Mother, accompanied by three angels, was radiantly happy as she gazed over the crowd. She said: *"My dear children, blessed be Jesus Christ."* She extended her hands and blessed everyone on the hill with a *special blessing*. She then said: *"My dear children, for you, from this evening, starts a new time—the time of the youth. In this time, pray for the youth; talk with the young, because the situation is very difficult in the world for them. The youth today hold a special place in the Church. Help one another, and I will help you. Pray much, my dear children. Go in the peace of God."* She left in a luminous cross of glory.

Eyewitnesses in the village, who were not on the hill, reported that around the hour of the apparition they saw a huge white light move from Cross Mountain slowly toward Apparition Hill, where it lingered for about ten minutes. Those in the fields at the foot of the mountains said there appeared to be a rosary of light stretched vertically from the cloud of light hovering over Apparition Hill. There was an aura of peace everywhere in the village, notwithstanding the crowds and the heat.

Marija revealed that during the 11:00 P.M. apparition on August 15, those present were given a special blessing, with which they in turn could bless others, after having received this signal gift from the Blessed Mother. Marija said that this blessing could be silently given to nonbelievers to help them convert, for it was a blessing of conversion. No one there would ever be the same, for a little bit of heaven had descended unto their souls that night, she said. "Please share this blessing of conversion!" Marija begged. "The whole world longs for that blessing. It is only in God that there is peace and joy and love. Through conversion we will discover that."

Those present on the mountain that night have reported many extraordinary experiences. Some claim to have seen the luminous cross. Some say they saw immense light. Some experienced the scent of incense; some the scent of roses and other beautiful aromas "like many fresh flowers."

People experienced physical, psychological, and emotional healings, they would claim. Later, around 2:00 A.M. (for the dining facilities were open all night to accommodate those who participated at the all-night vigil at the church), a young engineer from California was heard to say over beer and pizza, "I found the faith of my childhood tonight on that mountain. There were luminary signs in that sky that had to come from God. I've studied celestial navigation for over ten years. I *know* what's supposed to be in that sky! Tonight was unbelievable, but I saw it." A quiet man, tall, athletic, with flashing blue eyes, he was so excited he said he wanted to tell the whole world that "God is real." But everyone around him already knew. They had been there too. They had the blessing.

The Blessed Mother has been giving special blessings to those present in Medjugorje for special feasts for many years now, so that the pilgrims may bring the blessings back to their families, their communities, and ultimately, the whole world. Marija said for believers it is a great grace of the Holy Spirit to pass the blessings to all whom one ever encounters. Those who receive the special blessings of the Mother of God can transmit to others in her name. All blessings come from God, Marija quickly adds, and it is up to His children to extend His blessings.

This was apparently the first time since the Assumption of Mary that people of the earth were once again receiving the blessings of the Mother of God. The power of the blessings, of course, depends ultimately upon the faith of the recipients. The blessings last forever because they have been received directly from the Mother of God. When asked how to extend the blessings, Marija smiled and actually giggled as she said: "We are not priests. Certainly we never use any gestures." Then she became pensive. "The Blessed Mother is very humble. Any blessings of hers are always given with great humility, so those who know her and love her will be humble. They will always give her blessings with great humility, knowing all comes from God."

Marija gently continues: "There are no geographical barriers to her blessing. We can bless people anywhere from anywhere." In that way, Marija says, each of us who has these special blessings can give them to anyone and everyone. In 1988, Marija and several others formed a prayer community in Italy to live the messages of the Blessed Mother. Many, including those with terminal illnesses such as AIDS, came to this community. There exists medically documented evidence that those who lived the messages saw their lives physically improve.

In the summer of 1991, Marija remained a quiet symbol of God's compassion. She was arranging to live with her younger sister Milka in a house near the Peace House where young people from all over the world have congregated to live the messages of the Blessed Mother. From her modest house, Marija planned to continue to receive the pilgrims, to have her daily apparition with the Mother of God, and to spend her remaining life on earth as a witness to the reality of the presence of the Mother of God, the awesome simplicity of her messages, and the power of God to redeem and sanctify all His children on earth. Like Vicka, Marija has remained in Medjugorje during much of the war that has desecrated her homeland. Its spread has troubled her profoundly, and she speaks often of the dire human and spiritual waste. Characteristically, Marija seems most troubled by the terrible pain inflicted on the little ones and the helpless. She laments as she talks of God's "beautiful children" who are insensitive to the suffering of their brothers and sisters.

Several years before the war clouds darkened the skies over Medjugorje, Marija became the benefactress of a very special gift. On March 1, 1984, the Blessed Mother gave a momentous, and heretofore unheard-of, gift to Marija for the parish of Medjugorje and ultimately for the entire world: a weekly message. Later the message became a monthly event. Those messages are meant to guide and instruct and warn, enrich, and sanctify the whole world. They are included in Chapter 14 of this book.

A compilation of several edited interviews with Marija follows:

Q. Marija, why did the Blessed Mother choose to come to Medjugorje?

A. The Blessed Mother told me the Eternal Father permitted the Blessed Mother to choose any place on earth to bring these messages to the world. She chose Medjugorje because the faith is so strong here.

Q. Is it because the people here are better or holier?

A. Oh, no! She said it is because the people here have strong faith.

Q. Marija, do you go to Mount Krizevac often these days?

A. As often as I can. I love to climb that mountain because of the immense joy I feel as I pass the Stations of the Cross. [The rocky, steep path that winds its way to the top of the mountain has the fourteen Stations of the Cross strategically placed along the way. The most treacherous part of the climb is between the tenth and eleventh stations.]

Q. How do you manage since your surgery? Is it difficult for you?

A. I climb with love and patience.

Q. Why patience?

A. It takes patience to suffer, it takes patience to forgive myself for my weaknesses.

Q. You have traveled extensively since these apparitions began. Do you still enjoy Medjugorje?

A. Very much. This village where the Blessed Mother comes every day means a great deal to me. It used to be a humble little village. Now you can see construction everywhere. But much of the ground is still [August 1990] under cultivation.

Q. Do you like to work in the fields, Marija?

A. Yes. It gives me joy to handle the gifts of God that grow out of the earth.

Q. Marija, will all this area [the village of Medjugorje] become a shrine one day?

A. It is very much a shrine now. God has given immense graces to this village and to those who come here to honor the Blessed Mother.

Q. There is often great suffering on earth. Many people experience personal tragedy. You have had much suffering, especially physical suffering, since you donated your kidney to your brother. Does Our Lady ever speak about these matters?

A. In situations where there appears to be no solution, consecrate the misfortune to the Blessed Mother and to the Sacred Heart of

Jesus. God honors whatever we offer. In offering the Blessed Mother anything, through her Son Jesus, she changes it and makes it holy.

Q. What about people who have no faith, no belief in God or in things sacred?

A. When people are spiritually sick, the Blessed Mother says to treat them as if they are spiritually sick and *do everything* for them. Pray, fast, sacrifice, consecrate them.

Q. Does it matter how we pray or fast or sacrifice?

A. If you do things out of love, you cannot offend the Blessed Mother.

Q. What is the Blessed Mother saying to you these days?

A. She says, *do not wait for a sign* to be converted. The Blessed Mother does not need people who are capable. She needs people who say yes to her messages now. Form prayer groups. The Blessed Mother speaks often of youth and families. She has need for her priests, and ministers of the Gospel, to guide and help youth and families so that they may make good choices in their lives.

PRAYER AND DEVOTION

Q. Can you tell us something about prayer groups?

A. Yes. The first condition for any effective prayer group is to put away all fear from your heart forever.

Q. Why is fear so dangerous?

A. Fear comes from Satan. Those who trust the Lord do not experience fear. Trust the Lord that everything that comes to you is a gift. Trust that the Eternal Father watches over us every minute.

Q. Marija, do we have anything to worry about concerning the secrets, the prophesied chastisements?

A. I do not speak of the Second Coming of Christ, of catastrophes, destruction, or evil. With prayer and fasting, even war can be eliminated. The Blessed Mother says prayer and fasting can change even the natural law. The Blessed Mother has asked the whole world to pray for the youth. The young people in the world are in serious need of our prayers and sacrifices.

Q. What should the youth do?

A. They need to understand what the gift of their life really is. They should obey the Ten Commandments that God has given to us and lead a Christian way of life. We know that the end of our lives is not the end. Death is the beginning of our life in Heaven. We should use life on earth to prepare for heaven.

Q. How do we prepare for heaven while we are still here on earth?

A. Pray to recognize God's will for us here on earth and live it. Surrender to God as much as possible from day to day.

Q. Has the Blessed Mother ever touched you, kissed you, or held you in any way?

A. Yes. Often she hugs and kisses me.

Q. On December 31, 1982, the custom began at Saint James to celebrate the evening Mass in Medjugorje for peace in the world. Do you believe this Mass has made a difference in the world?

A. The Blessed Mother says it has. Look at the events in the world since that time. We can see the intervention of God's grace in many world situations.

Q. You yourself have been an intermediary between President Reagan and President Gorbachev—wasn't the date December 8, 1987?

A. I have tried to serve the Blessed Mother faithfully. She longs to see all her beloved children live in peace.[2]

SIGNS

Q. Marija, can you tell me some details about the Blessed Mother? You know her so well.

A. The Blessed Mother told us [the visionaries] that she was an ordinary woman of her times. She too experienced human suffering, problems, and difficulties. She too had much to endure for the faith. She understands our lives and needs even better than our own families do. She asks us to turn to her for assistance in every little need and every big need. She wants to be our true mother.

Q. Why?

A. In this way she honors Jesus, who asked her to be our true mother.

Q. Mirjana has told me that the Blessed Mother is warning all people on earth that Satan has immense power right now. This is the time prophesied from the beginning when the whole of mankind will be put to the test. Do you know anything about that?

A. Yes. The Blessed Mother says we must all undergo trials and tests of faithfulness to God. She says for those who pray and fast, Satan has no power. He has no strength when we are God's children.

Q. Why not?

A. Because we are clothed in God's strength.

Q. Are you saying that it is through prayer and fasting that we have the ability to resist the temptations and traps of the devil?

A. That's the way.

Q. You mentioned once before that it is prayer and fasting that give us discernment to distinguish between good and evil.

A. Mankind—each person—has an innate ability to distinguish between good and evil, but often, through incorrect choices, people lose or diminish their ability to make a distinction. When that happens, Satan gains opportunity in a soul's life with God.

Q. Is anyone spared this "testing time" with Satan?

A. No one. Not even Jesus was spared.

Q. Marija, Mirjana told me that one of the reasons Satan is so aggressive right now is that he has little time left since his power will be broken when the first secret happens. Will life be more pleasant after the first secret occurs?

A. We shall see.

Q. You and the other visionaries have indicated that there will be advanced signs [signs preceding the great sign] in many places in the world to warn the world. When will these advanced signs begin?

A. There are signs in many places in the world now. Many people see luminary signs. Many experience personal healings, both physical and spiritual, and also psychological. Many have private signs. People have come here from all over the world. Often they have or have had extraordinary signs in their lives.

Q. Will all people on earth believe in God, in the Blessed Mother when the permanent sign occurs?

A. The Blessed Mother has said that those who are still alive when the permanent sign comes will witness many conversions among the people because of the sign, but she also says blessed are those who do not see but who believe.

Q. Mirjana told me that there will still be some unbelievers even when the permanent sign comes.

A. The Blessed Mother has said there will always be Judases.

Q. Vicka told me that there is great urgency in the Blessed Mother's call to immediate conversion. She said that for those who only marginally believe, who choose to wait for the great sign to believe, it will be too late. Do you know why it will be too late for them?

A. This is a time of great grace and mercy. Now is the time to listen to these messages and to change our lives. Those who do will never be able to thank God enough.

THE BLESSED MOTHER'S LIFE

Q. The Blessed Mother has been telling you much about her own life on earth, hasn't she?

A. Yes. She tells me about her life, and she sometimes shows me details.

Q. Can you share some of these details?

A. Not yet.

Q. When?

A. When the Blessed Mother says.

Q. Do you know when the Blessed Mother will permit you to give the details you have regarding her hidden life as the mother of Jesus of Nazareth?

A. I will disclose those details when the Blessed Mother permits.

Q. Has hearing details of the life of the Blessed Virgin helped you with the trials and crosses in your own life?

A. Oh yes. Very much. So many of my sufferings are quite small in comparison to the hardship endured by the Blessed Mother.

Q. Do you know why the Blessed Mother suffered so much when she lived on earth?

A. It is part of the mystery of Jesus' passion and death on the cross. The Blessed Mother was always rich in the presence of God. She knew God better than any of us can. She was always filled with love and joy and peace even in the midst of great suffering.

Q. Do you know why the Blessed Mother knew and knows God better than we can?

A. Yes. It is sin that blinds us to God's presence in our lives in the world. The Blessed Mother was always free from the least sin. Her will was and is a clear mirror of the will of God.

Q. That means she always did God's will—not her own, doesn't it?

A. Yes, for the Blessed Mother, her own will was and is always God's most perfect will.

Q. How serious are the effects of sin?

A. Sin wounds us gravely. It separates us from God, who is our source of love and goodness and abundance and joy.

Q. How does this happen?

A. Sin darkens our capacity to choose wisely.

Q. Do many people live in darkness today?

A. The Blessed Mother says a cloud of darkness has enveloped the whole planet.

Q. What can be done?

A. Heed the messages of Medjugorje: prayer, fasting, reconciliation, peace, and conversion are a call from the Mother of God to all people on earth to restore God's kingdom of light and love and peace and joy to all people on earth.

Q. Is this happening?

A. Yes. Many people of all faiths and beliefs and races and nationalities are hearing the call of the Blessed Mother. They are responding.

Q. Will the whole world hear of these messages?

A. Yes.

Q. How?

A. Through God's faithful children who are spreading these messages to the farthest reaches of the globe.

Q. How do you know that, Marija?

A. The Blessed Mother said that God planted a tiny seed in the hearts of His faithful children. Through faithfulness to God's will, and prayer and fasting, the tiny seed has become a great shade tree in the hearts of the faithful ones, where the sick and the starving can find shade, rest, and nourishment for their journey to paradise.

Q. How beautiful, Marija. Who are the faithful ones?

A. Those who hear the messages and respond.

Q. Vicka told me that our Blessed Mother said her faithful children will spread these words of God's chosen visionaries—you six children of Medjugorje—to the entire world.

A. That is already happening. Much more will come. Those who hear the messages of Medjugorje and respond will rejoice even in this life.

Q. Why?

A. Because they will be permitted to taste the joys of heaven even here on earth as they struggle to do God's perfect will.

Q. Will they have less suffering than others?

A. They will experience a different kind of suffering. The Blessed Mother promises that she herself will bless and help any child of hers who calls to her. Just as Jesus used her strength during His crucifixion, so we too may use her strength during our times of suffering.

Q. Why is the Blessed Mother so capable of helping all God's children?

A. She knows God the best of any of His creatures.

Q. Even better than Jesus?

A. Jesus is not only a man. He is also God. The Holy Trinity trusted Mary, the Virgin of Nazareth, so much that Jesus was entrusted to her as a dependent fetus, a helpless, naked, persecuted infant, a young refugee child. The education, care, and development of Jesus, the Son of God, was entrusted to Mary, His mother. Now God our Father has sent her to our world, to our times, to our lives, that she may form and develop a faithful following who are prepared for her Son.

Q. Are you speaking of the Second Coming of Christ?

A. I never speak of the Second Coming of Christ. Christ is alive. He is risen. He is among us.

Q. Is this apparition of Medjugorje a preface of the Second Coming of Christ?

A. I do not speak at all in that way.

PILGRIMS AND PRAYERS

Q. Marija, you have been receiving many pilgrims. There seems to be a large number of Moslems and Jews who are coming here these days from the Middle East, as well as Indians and Africans, and Chinese and Filipinos. Many of these people are not even Christians.

A. They come because they love God. Many come here from all over the world to honor the Eternal Father.

Q. Why is Medjugorje fast becoming a place of honor and worship for the Eternal Father? Do all people who come here honor Him?

A. All people are created by God our Father. In the deepest chasm of all our hearts, there is a love and longing for God our Father.

Q. Why?

A. The Eternal Father *is* the deepest longing of all human hearts. Here in Medjugorje that longing finds expression.

Above: *The town of Medjugorje. Courtesy of Larry Galloway.* Below: *Vineyards near St. James Church. Photo courtesy of Sister Agnes McCormick.*

A *Medjugorje woman in traditional garb. Photo courtesy of Sister Agnes McCormick.*

Above: *Pilgrims from around the world flock to St. James Church. Courtesy of Larry Galloway.* Below: *Before the civil war, pilgrims purchase religious goods from outdoor stands. Photo courtesy of Jerry Sherlock.*

Cross Mountain is where the visionaries say the Blessed Virgin prays daily. Courtesy

of Larry Galloway.

Top: *Crosses placed by pilgrims at spots on Apparition Hill where the Blessed Virgin has appeared. Courtesy of Larry Galloway.* Above: *Pilgrims mount Apparition Hill in search of healing powers. Photo courtesy of Ted Connell.*

Pilgrims come from all over the world in search of Mary's messages. Courtesy of Larry Galloway.

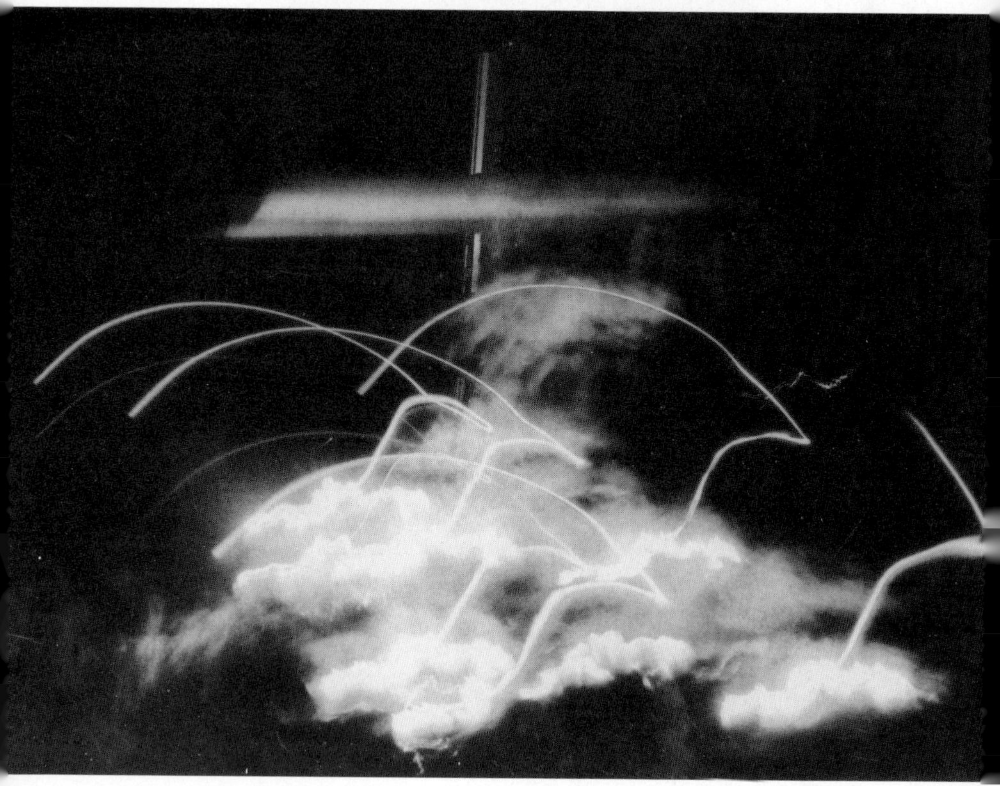

Top: *A station of the cross on Cross Mountain. Photo courtesy of Derek Minno.*
Above: *Easter Sunday, 1989. Lights appear around a cross at Medjugorje. Courtesy of R. J. Hughes.*

Above: *Ivanka with her daughter, Kristina. Notice streams of light on right. Author photo.*
Left: *Vicka is known for her joyous smile. Photo courtesy of Martin and Nancy Gullen.*

Above: *Mirjana with her daughter, Maria. Photo courtesy of* Ed Connell. Below: *Marija (center) greets pilgrims in Birmingham, Alabama. Photo courtesy of Father Richard Foley, S.J.*

Above: *Ivan and Jakov greet pilgrims. Photo courtesy of Will Connell.* Below: *Ivan. Photo courtesy of Ted Connell.*

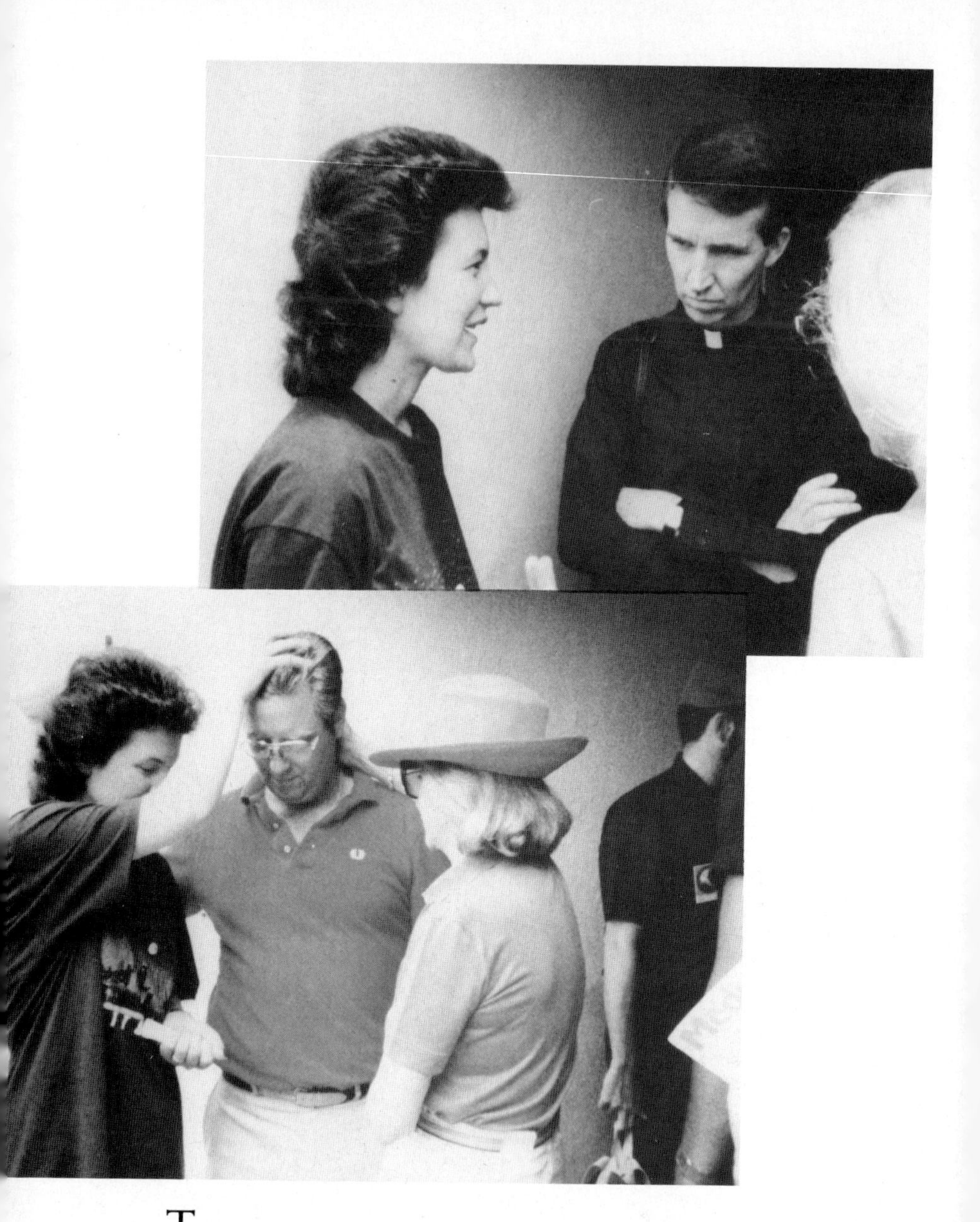

Top: *Vicka and all the visionaries have been subjected to the intense scrutiny of the Roman Catholic Church. Photo courtesy of Will Connell.* Above: *Vicka prays over pilgrims. Many visitors have experienced miraculous cures. Photo courtesy of Betsy Connell Minno.*

Above: *Malona Hapsburg, the Archduchess who exchanged a life of pleasure and wealth for a renewed faith in God after visiting Medjugorje. Photo courtesy of Betsy Connell Minno.*
Below: *Marija in bedroom where daily apparitions occurred in Birmingham, Alabama. Photo courtesy of Father Richard Foley, S.J.*

Above: *"The Blessed mother is my* real *Mother. I am so happy when I am around her that I feel I am already in heaven." Mirjana and author, Janice Connell. Photo courtesy of Rob Walsh.* Below: *Vicka and Janice Connell. Photo courtesy of Ed Connell.*

Below: *The author interviews Jakov and Ivan through a translator, on left. Photo courtesy of Tom and Posie Courtney.* Bottom: *Father Jozo, the village priest who was tortured, with Janice Connell on retreat. March 1989. Photo courtesy of Lee Bowers.*

Above: *Father Jozo blesses the pilgrims. Courtesy of Larry Galloway.* Below: *The messages of the Blessed Virgin are spread throughout the world via numerous documentaries. Photo courtesy of Ed Connell.*

Q. Why is there so much controversy surrounding this apparition?

A. It is the human condition. It is the battle of darkness and light.

Q. But why do so many people want to go to confession here? People from all over the world line up to receive sacramental confession, some having been away from the Church for thirty or forty years, some not even belonging to any Church.

A. The Blessed Mother says that there is great grace for those who come here. Among those graces is the great gift from the Eternal Father of the bread of sorrow for sins, which all pray for so frequently here in the Lord's Prayer.

Q. I thought the daily bread we pray for in the Lord's Prayer is the Eucharist, our spiritual food, and bread for our bodies.

A. We do pray for the Eucharist, the bread of eternal life, and for our daily human nourishment; but it is the bread of sorrow for sin that is the fruit of prayer with the heart. Repentance prepares the human heart to receive the Lord.

Q. In what way?

A. Prayer with the heart opens our hearts. When our hearts are open we can see God with our hearts, we can hear God with our hearts.

Those who see and hear God with their hearts taste God's love. Those who taste God's love are never again satisfied with anything less than God's love. Sin separates a heart from God's love. The gift of the bread of sorrow for sin restores a heart to the presence of God's love.

Q. Is that why sacramental confession is so extraordinary here? [People assert that they are freed from heavy spiritual and psychological burdens after partaking of sacramental confession at Medjugorje.]

A. Yes. It is a gift to us from the Eternal Father through Jesus and with Jesus and in Jesus.

Q. Is this gift for all people on earth?

A. No one is excluded from our Eternal Father's love.

Q. Do you have a special prayer you pray to the Eternal Father?

A. Jesus taught us all the Lord's Prayer. That prayer is dear to the Blessed Mother.

Q. How do you know?

A. She always prays that prayer and the Glory Be with us. I also love the Magnificat as the Blessed Mother prayed it, and I love the Apostles' Creed.

Q. Many heads of state and relatives of heads of state have come here as simple, unnoticed pilgrims, as well as bishops and cardinals and leaders of other faiths.

A. We are all beloved children of the Eternal Father, the least on the planet and the greatest.

Q. Do you know why we have so many poor people, Marija?

A. We have the poor because many do not share. As people become more aware of God our Father through prayer and fasting, it becomes easier to share.

Q. Why?

A. As we become aware of God's love for us, of His humility, of His servantship, we become open to His love for us and all our brothers and sisters on this planet, and we want to respond to His scorching love for us.

Q. Why do you call it "scorching love"?

A. Because the love of the Eternal Father for each creature of His, and especially for us His children, is so immense that the mere awareness of it ignites a flame in our hearts.

Q. A flame in our hearts?

A. Yes. The flame of love becomes so intense that it extinguishes all fear, all fatigue, all self-love.

Q. Marija, how do you experience this burning love for God here among the pilgrims you see daily?

A. From day to day I try to keep my thoughts directed toward heaven. I try to let nothing on earth hold my attention these days but uniting myself with all God's children who come here to me, and offering my heart, filled with all these children of God, to our Heavenly Father in the name of Jesus, our brother.

Q. Can you tell me a little about Jesus our brother?

A. Yes. He is with us. He carries us. He makes all things with God possible for us. Because I am with His Blessed Mother so much, she has taught me a love for Him that is both powerful and glorious. Powerful because my longing for Him is so great. Glorious because I trust all in Him.

Q. Have you offered your life to Jesus?

A. I have offered my life completely, without limitation, without exception, totally to the Blessed Mother in order that God's plan being manifested here at Medjugorje may be realized in the world.

Q. Why did you choose to give your life to the Blessed Mother?

A. Because I know that she is the mother of eternal life. Jesus gave her to me, and to all people on earth. She knows better than I how to please God, how to serve Jesus. Since I belong to her, I trust she will clothe me in her beauty, dress me in her virtue, bring me to live in her house with Jesus forever.

MARIJA'S PEACE

Q. Marija, you live a fairly ordinary-looking life. Actually, without these apparitions and the pilgrims, your life would appear rather dreary, and filled with drudgery. In the 1990s, there are many young people with far less education and experience than you who lead a much easier life. You tend the sheep, you do the wash and hang the clothes out to dry. You work in the fields and cook and clean; you stand in the heat and cold and serve the pilgrims every day. The conditions here are somewhat primitive. Your family has its share of ups and downs—and yet you seem so serene.

A. I have great peace.

Q. How do you achieve this great peace?

A. Through prayer.

Q. How is your health since you donated your kidney to your mortally ill brother, Andrea?

A. I get tired more quickly now, but when I see little Marija [Andrea's daughter, who was born in 1989 after the kidney transplant] and think about the baby [born in 1990], I feel so happy that I was able to give him the kidney. My joy far outweighs my fatigue.

Q. Marija, do you have any trials you want to share?

A. Yes [laughter]. I want to pass my driver's test so that I can drive a car!

Q. How often have you failed the test?

A. Several times.

Q. Do you pray about it?

A. I pray about everything!

Q. Will you eventually pass the test?

A. One day, I hope.

Q. Marija, will you share some things about your experience with the Blessed Mother?

A. She is so truly beautiful. The more I am with her, the more I appreciate her beauty. She likes to bless us all. She often extends her arms and prays over us, or over certain pilgrims.

Q. Do you see her do that?

A. Yes. You know these blessings we receive from the Blessed Mother are not for us alone. We are meant to be a conduit of God's love to others. As His love and blessings flow upon us, we receive them and pass them on to others. In that way as the love and blessings flow through us to others, they fill us too.

Q. So, in essence, Marija, we are a third-party beneficiary of God's love, in that God uses each of us to bless the other—and as we bless the other—we too are blessed?

A. Yes. The Blessed Mother said she rejoices because we come here in such great numbers and because we dedicate our prayers and sacrifices to her. She thanks us for every prayer and sacrifice we make. She says she loves us—each one—and she wishes us to be filled with her love—which is God's love—and her blessings—which are God's blessings; and she wishes us to fill our personal worlds with His love and these blessings.

Q. Once you described that in prayer you saw an image of a flower closed and wilting as if it were dying. Then you said you saw a drop of water fall upon the wilted flower and, as the water touched this flower, it spontaneously opened up, beautiful and blooming. Do you remember that image?

A. Yes. I asked the Blessed Mother what it meant, and she told me the flower symbolized the human soul. It blooms and has great beauty in and through the grace of God, but it wilts and dies when a person sins. The drop of water is God's grace. Though a person wilts with sin, a person's soul is beautiful and new again through repentance and sacramental confession.

Q. What about those who do not have confession or know about it?

A. God acts in each person's soul. Each person created by God has access to God in the silence of his heart.

Q. Is that why we are called here to pray with our hearts?

A. Yes.

Q. Marija, how do we pray with our hearts?

A. We need to make the commitment to faithfully give time to God every day as a gift on our part. God so honors us, His children, that when we sincerely give time to Him as our gift to Him, He blesses the time and the intention, and He manifests Himself to us more and more. Little by little, in this way, by an act of the will, each of us can come close to God by prayer with the heart. All prayer of the heart begins with a serious act of the will by us. Then God takes over.

Q. What is a serious act of will?

A. A commitment that we make and honor.

Q. What do we do when prayer isn't fun?

A. Persevere. Realize who we are and who God is, then trust Him totally. Trust His love, trust His patience, trust His mercy.

CHAPTER 10

I V A N

She comes to encourage us.

Ivan Dragicevic has matured into a quiet man given to solitude even in the midst of a crowd. Gracious, tall, good-looking with dark hair, penetrating brown eyes, and a serious demeanor, he has a gentleness that allows him to be available day after day to all who approach him. The questions are often tediously the same. Now Ivan travels around the world. Much sought after, he has been the guest of heads of state and even of hospitals for the incurably ill. Ivan is the same to all. He is neither impressed nor unimpressed. He is simply a quiet man with a message to deliver.

Whom does he serve? The most powerful woman in creation. What does he say of her? "She is love. Pure love." Ivan is the leader of a young people's prayer group that meets weekly on Apparition Hill, or Cross Mountain. Ivan readily admits it is really the Blessed Mother who is the leader of his prayer group. She has asked him to write a book, with her help, about the disease of materialism, which he says is destroying the beauty of God's people and God's world. When asked how soon the book will be available, Ivan responds: "As soon as the Blessed Mother says." The Blessed Mother has told Ivan many things about the future. A veteran, Ivan served his one-year compulsory military service. He likes basketball, and for exercise, he tosses a ball into a hoop in his front yard.

Ivan lives with his mother, father, and two younger brothers. The home is neat, clean, and there are always flowers growing in summer. Ivan wears a suit these days, or a blazer and slacks, dress shirt, and tie. Looking at him and remembering whom he sees everyday, a person could easily conclude that some things the Blessed Mother cares about are taste, cleanliness, order, and beauty.

From time to time Ivan has shown some humor and playfulness in spite of the burden he bears to have such a serious mission at such a young age. He has a deep prayer life. He says he arises each morning at five o'clock so that his private time with God will be protected from interruption. He says that each day he pleads with God to give him the light to see God's will and the strength to obey perfectly. He says that those who live right in the center of God's will each moment can experience heaven even while on earth. He admits that it is often difficult to know God's will, especially when prayer life diminishes. He knows that it is only through prayer that a man is capable of life, and that without prayer a man lives in an abyss of useless suffering.

Life without God is hell, he says. Only prayer and fasting will free the world from Satan. When a person is free from Satan, he lives in a kingdom of love.

Ivan says, "These apparitions have made a big difference in my life—the difference between heaven and earth. For example, the way I now live, I arrange my schedule so that even during the day I find time for prayer. Before there was no meaning in my life. Now I'm completely filled with contentment."

A compilation of several edited interviews with Ivan follows:

Q. Ivan, does it make you happy to be a part of this great visitation of the Mother of God?

A. God chose me. Everyday I try to be faithful.

Q. Does the Blessed Mother speak about this?

A. She tells me, and all of us, to try throughout our lives to be faithful to God, to work toward sanctity. She asks us all to be simple.

PRAYER AND FASTING

Q. How does the Blessed Mother want us to pray?

A. She asks us to seek prayer with our hearts.

Q. Do you do that, Ivan?

A. It is difficult. I have many distractions. I am not perfect, I am just a man like all the others. I am weak. I fall often.

Q. Does that bother you?

A. Yes. I am trying hard every day to become a saint.

Q. Does the Blessed Mother help you?

A. She helps all of us. We all need to find what is blocking us from being a saint.

Q. Is there some advice you can share that you have learned about prayer from the Blessed Mother?

A. Yes. She teaches me the importance of concentration. I try to concentrate on prayer. She says to be determined to pray, especially the rosary, to read the Bible, to have pious conversations, to fast on bread and water strictly on Wednesdays and Fridays.

Q. Do you find fasting easy, Ivan?

A. I personally find fasting very difficult. It is a decision. It takes determination. Another problem is that sometimes we excuse ourselves and we all decide we are sick and we can't fast, or we are so busy that we need to eat to get through. These are strong temptations not to fast.

Q. What do you do about the strong temptations?

A. When I rely on myself, I fail.

Q. Do you have a solution?

A. The Blessed Mother does help me. She has taught me to pray when I am experiencing strong temptation. Then I rely on God's strength and I seem to manage well. When I rely on myself, I fail.

Q. Why does the Blessed Mother want us to fast?

A. She has asked for this since the beginning. She calls us to change our hearts, to change our habits, to become saints. The Blessed Mother wants us to denounce our personal sins. For more than ten years she has been asking us for prayer.

Q. Tell me about your method of prayer with your heart.

A. Prayer with the heart is a process.

Q. What is that process?

A. First I must decide to pray, then I must concentrate on the prayer.

Q. What do you experience when you pray with your heart?

A. Peace. Real peace. God's peace.

Q. Do you have peace in your family?

A. If there is no peace in one member of the family, it reflects throughout the entire family. Satan does not sleep. Prayer must become our weapon. Every prayer can chase Satan away.

THE FIRST DAYS OF THE APPARITION

Q. Can you recall your first days of the apparition?

A. Yes. Most clearly. The Blessed Mother appeared first on June 24, 1981. The first ten days of the apparition were very intense. There was much tension and many crosses. The priests, the people, and the government were all against us.

Q. How close to the Blessed Mother were you on June 24, 1981?

A. At the first apparition, the Blessed Virgin was approximately three hundred meters away.

Q. Were you certain it was the Blessed Mother?

A. Not the first day.

Q. What about the second day?

A. She was right in front of me.

Q. She was that close to you?

A. Yes. Everything was very clear to me the second day.

Q. How did you feel the second day when you saw the Blessed Mother so clearly?

A. It was a great shock the first couple of nights. Try to put yourself in my place, then you will understand.

Q. What was it like for those first few weeks?

A. The Blessed Mother asked us to open our hearts to the Holy Spirit so we could receive mercy.

Q. Did the Blessed Mother look beautiful?

A. The Blessed Mother *is* beautiful.

Q. Can you describe her beauty?

A. Her beauty is difficult to describe with words. We have told painters what she looks like, but no one has been able to paint her. It is sad that none of us is a painter!

Q. Can you describe her appearance?

A. She is surrounded by immense light. She comes, sometimes, with angels. Often there is a shining cross behind her or beside her.

Q. Does she look young or old?

A. Her face is timeless. She is neither young nor old. Her age is eternal.

Q. How do you know that?

A. I just know. I see her every day.

Q. Do you notice her clothes?

A. Though she wears the same for most days, I really don't notice her clothes.

Q. Have you noticed her clothes of gold or turquoise described by Vicka?

A. The Blessed Mother's love is very great. I haven't focused on her clothes, though she does wear a beautiful gold dress for her feasts. She normally wears a gray dress and a white veil. She has blue eyes, rosy cheeks, black hair. She stands on a cloud. She has a crown of stars.

IVAN'S DAILY LIFE

Q. Were you devoted to the Blessed Mother before the apparitions began?

A. Our family prayed the daily rosary. It was just rote to me then; purely mechanical. It was just something we did.

Q. Did you know the other visionaries well?

A. We were only neighbors. We had never prayed together. We lived in the same neighborhood and each of us prayed the rosary at home with our families. Except for those two similarities, we have nothing else in common.

Q. Did you attend daily Mass?

A. No. Going to Mass was just a duty. I had no knowledge of the immense value of the Mass.

Q. What do you think of the Mass now?

A. The Blessed Mother has said attending a Mass with our hearts is the greatest privilege a person has.

Q. Ivan, do you still recall how the early days of the apparition affected you personally?

A. Yes. Very clearly. It was such an important event in my life that I felt I had to go to the seminary and become a Franciscan.

Q. How was your time in the seminary?

A. It was a time of trial and some suffering, but I was filled with joy because the Blessed Mother appeared to me every day.

Q. Do you have any advice for seminarians since you yourself were one of them?

A. Yes. I hope they are not there because of their parents, but because of strong prayer that has allowed them to respond to their own calling.

Q. Ivan, were you at the seminary because of pressure from your family?

A. I don't wish to disclose my personal life.

Q. Do you have any other advice for seminarians?

A. When crisis comes, pray for strong faith and turn to strong, tested, faithful priests for help.

ON PRIESTS

Q. That is good advice, not only for seminarians, but for everyone. Does the Blessed Mother speak about priests?

A. All these years she has prayed for priests and I have prayed with her. She asks all of us to pray for priests and ministers of the Gospel, to help those who bring the words and ways of God to the people with our support and encouragement.

Q. When Jesus was scourged His skin surface was covered with open wounds. A filthy cloak was placed around Jesus' shoulders, over the open wounds. This introduced infection into the bloodstream of Jesus. One of His tortures during the passion was a terrible thirst from the loss of blood and the high fever. You say the Blessed Mother prays about infection in the Church today due to weak faith?

A. Yes. People are dying of spiritual thirst. These days people come here from all around the world seeking God and they find Him here.

Q. Why do they find God here, Ivan?

A. Whenever the Blessed Mother is sent on apparition, there is immense light, immense grace for those who choose to participate.

Q. Do you have any regrets that you left the seminary?

A. I could not learn the Latin. I could not learn the philosophy and theology. I am a simple man. The work was more than I could do.

Q. Do you think it was God's will that you leave the seminary?

A. I tried. I prayed. I did my best. It was not enough. If God had wanted me to be a priest, He would have provided me with the intellect and the grace to succeed.

Q. Were you sad to leave?

A. Failure is never easy to bear.

Q. Is it better now?

A. Yes. I see more clearly now.

SECRETS, SIGNS, AND PRAYERS

Q. Can you tell me something about the secrets you know?

A. No.

Q. What about the signs promised here at Medjugorje and throughout the world?

A. I choose not to say anything about the signs.

Q. How many secrets do you have?

A. Nine.

Q. What about the tenth secret?

A. I don't know when I'll get the tenth secret.

Q. Will your daily apparitions cease when you receive the tenth secret?

A. We'll see.

Q. What name does the Blessed Mother call you?

A. "My dear child."

Q. Why did the Blessed Mother choose you?

A. I often ask myself that.

Q. Do others come into the room with you when you have your daily apparition?

A. Other people are present.

Q. Do all those in the room with you during an apparition see the Blessed Mother too?

A. Nobody has told me that. Some say they see some lights.

Q. What do you experience during these daily apparitions?

A. Many things have happened to me during these ten years. The Blessed Mother comes from heaven. Whenever we are in her physical presence we experience many things. I would like all people on earth to see her. Then people would not need to ask me so many questions.

Q. It must be quite a trial to be interrogated by so many. Ivan, will all people on earth see the Blessed Mother?

A. If you pray you will know.

Q. When you are having your prayer group up on the mountain on Monday and Friday evenings, can you describe what happens?

A. We pray. We sing. All share. We are always very happy because we know the Blessed Mother will be visiting us.

Last night on Apparition Hill [August 3, 1990], she appeared joyful. She was quite cheerful as she greeted us. It pleased her very much that so many had come in spite of the hardship, to celebrate her birthday [August 5]. She greeted us, and all in the village, and all her children in the world with the words, "Praised be Jesus, my dear children." After that she prayed over us with her arms extended. She blessed us all. I recommended all of us and all the intentions we brought tonight.

She said, "*Dear children, tonight your mother is calling you to pray during this time more than usual and to join together in your hearts with all the youth in the world in prayer. Especially my dear children, your mother wants you to renew family prayer.*"

Then the Blessed Mother and I prayed one Our Father and one Glory Be. The Blessed Mother continued praying over the crowd with her arms extended. She then departed in the sign of an illuminated cross.

Q. Ivan, please describe what you see during your daily apparition.

A. I see her the same way I see a normal person. I talk to her. She is my real mother.

Q. What does that mean?

A. She is my real human source of love.

Q. Is that what mothers are meant to be?

A. Mothers are the source of love in a physical sense but many mothers don't realize that today.

Q. Why not?

A. Many are so needy for love themselves that they seek love from others, or from work, or from pleasure instead of from God. When God is permitted to fill a mother's heart, then a mother can fill a child's heart. Children suffer when their mothers are not in a close relationship with God.

Q. What about fathers?

A. They are asked by God to be a source of strength, and support and protection for their wife and children.

Q. Isn't that the role Saint Joseph had with Jesus and Mary?

A. Yes. Few realize the power of Saint Joseph.

Q. What is that power?

A. The gratitude of Jesus and Mary.

Q. Tell me more about your daily apparitions of the Blessed Mother.

A. Sometimes the Blessed Mother is sad. This makes me sad.

Q. What is it like to be consoled by the Mother of God?

A. It is a source of great encouragement.

Q. Do you know why the Blessed Mother is often sad?

A. Yes, it is because of our sinful ways. She knows how much the sin hurts us, how far away from God it takes us. She has great love for us. She desires that we reach the place God has prepared for us in heaven. She sees how wounded we are by each bad choice we make. She sees how each sin deprives us of our life with God.

Q. Has God prepared a place in heaven for each of us?

A. Yes, the Blessed Mother prays for each person on this earth by name. She asks her faithful children to pray and fast and do penance for her children who are lost, who don't know or care about heaven. They don't know what they are throwing away. That is why the Blessed Mother wants us to pray, so that all can come home to heaven.

SIN AND LOVE

Q. Do you know anything about sin?

A. Sin makes us blind to God, deaf to God. It deprives us of eternal love.

Q. What is eternal love?

A. God's love.

Q. Do you feel you must be good to please the Blessed Mother?

A. She loves me just as I am. She knows how weak I am. She always encourages me to try harder to please God. She says He is so happy when we do the least thing to please Him. She says if we knew how much He loves us we would never sin. Most of us have a hard time letting God love us. Many are so wounded by sin that they aren't even aware of God.

Q. You speak of sin "wounding" a person. Is that why the Eucharist is referred to as "armor" here at Medjugorje?

A. Yes. It is through the Eucharist that we receive the armor to resist sin. Jesus said, "*I am the way and the truth and the life.*" We are taught that.

Q. The Eucharist is the body and blood, soul and divinity of Jesus. What does the Blessed Mother say about the Eucharist?

A. The Blessed Mother always encourages us to visit her divine Son, Jesus, truly present in the blessed sacrament. She says she is always there with her Son. She asks us to make the Mass the center of our lives and to receive the Eucharist daily when possible.

Q. Does she use those exact words—"truly present"—Ivan?

A. We know Jesus is truly present in the Eucharist. That is our faith.

Q. How do we become aware of God?

A. By prayer.

Q. Can prayer awaken us to the true presence of Jesus in the Eucharist?

A. Those who pray, fast, and read Scripture learn of Jesus. Those who understand the words of Jesus understand the Eucharist. All prayer is pleasing to God. It is Satan who always tells us our prayer is not good enough, that we are not good enough. The least prayer is very much. The Blessed Mother says God hears all prayer. God loves each child of His no matter what He has done. He always forgives.

Q. Ivan, what do you and the Blessed Mother talk about most these days, after ten years?

A. She is extremely concerned about the youth of the world and about family life in general. Look at the world situation for the young. See what the world offers youth? Many get tricked and lost in drugs, alcohol, and immorality. There is a moral decline among some of the young. They suffer much. It is worse than war. It ruins their lives.

Q. Why is all this happening, Ivan?

A. Satan is present in these situations. Look at his influence in family life. The Blessed Mother says you can see his power in the high divorce rate worldwide.

Q. Is Satan responsible for divorce?

A. Of course. Divorce is the product of sin. Sin is the result of strong temptation. Sin is the result of weakness. At least one party in a marriage has to sin to destroy a sacramental union. Wherever there is sin, there is Satan.

Q. How does Satan get involved in marriages?

A. Many ways. One of his favorite ploys is to divide a husband and wife, then go after the children one by one.

Q. That sounds like the age-old divide-and-conquer theory of war, Ivan.

A. Satan is very smart. He has a large intellect. He knows all our weaknesses.

Q. Can you give us an example of his influence in the family, Ivan?

A. Yes. Look at the responsibility of parents. Often they are so interested in material things, peer pressure among friends, or personal gratification in each other to the exclusion of children both born and unborn. God has placed upon parents the responsibility to help and guide the young. The parents' first job is to provide a loving environment of respect for the children to grow up in. Often there is little or no love between a husband and a wife. Often there is little respect. When that happens, the spirit of the children is sickened. Then Satan has immense power in the family. Where there is little love and respect, he has much strength. Where there is great love of luxury, or ease, or prestige, or professional accomplishment, Satan has much power.

Q. What does he do with that power, Ivan?

A. He wants to destroy love and peace. When he destroys the home, he gains eternal power over many lives.

Q. You often speak of the disease of materialism. What is that disease? What are the symptoms?

A. Materialism is a sickness. Things become more important than they really are. There is a kind of awareness blindness and people attach great importance to certain people or objects, like cars, houses, professional positions, or social positions. These become proportionally bigger and bigger until they eat up a person's whole sense of awareness. When that happens, love and peace and joy are no longer possible. Whole segments of the population of this planet are suffering from this illness. People's bellies have grown bloated with things as they die of hunger.

Q. Why?

A. Because the deepest longing of the human heart is God, not things.

Q. Marija told me that, Ivan. Things don't take us to heaven, but they can keep us from getting there, can't they?

A. Very true. The solution to this illness is prayer with the heart, and fasting.

Q. Ivan, doesn't the Blessed Mother say sacramental confession is a remedy for the materialism of the West?

A. Yes. She has said that monthly confession will heal the West.

Q. Why?

A. Because of the power of the grace of the sacrament of reconciliation.

Q. Ivan, you have seen heaven, haven't you?

A. Yes.

Q. Will you describe it?

A. I can't describe heaven because it is difficult to describe. It really is something you must experience.

Q. Do you know whether you will go to heaven when you die?

A. We must work to deserve heaven. People do not always do the work required, myself included.

PRAYERS AND PEACE

Q. Ivan, you lead a prayer group, don't you?

A. I am in a prayer group. The Blessed Mother is the leader of my prayer group.

Q. Why did you found the prayer group?

A. It was the Blessed Mother's wish.

Q. What is the purpose of your prayer group?

A. We pray for the intentions of the Blessed Mother and dedicate our sacrifices and fasts to her.

Q. Does the Blessed Mother really direct your group?

A. Yes. Very completely. She gives us directions on what to do and how to accomplish certain things.

Q. What are some of the things your prayer group has done?

A. We pray for world peace. We pray for the sick and the abandoned—born and unborn, the hungry, the homeless, the poor, the lonely. We do corporal works of mercy, too.

Q. How often do you meet?

A. On Monday evenings on Podbrdo [Apparition Hill] and Friday evenings on Krizevac [Cross Mountain].

Q. Ivan, many pilgrims have experienced extraordinary favors by climbing those mountains during your prayer group meeting. Does the Blessed Mother always appear?

A. Yes. And she prays for all those who come and she blesses all present.

Q. Ivan, does the Blessed Mother want prayer groups?

A. She insists that all people on earth be in prayer groups.

Q. Why?

A. She knows what lies ahead.

Q. Ivan, often there is much division and sometimes even infighting in prayer groups.

A. That shows Satan's hatred for prayer groups. Where there is much temptation, be warned. Take the dissension as a warning for the future. If Satan works so hard now to destroy, you can be sure he is setting a course for a future victory for himself.

Q. What does he want?

A. Human souls. Prayer groups are a protection from the triumph of Satan. Whenever there is dissension, pray more and fast often.

Q. What kind of prayer, Ivan?

A. For me, in extreme cases, daily Mass, Eucharistic adoration, three rosaries.

Q. That wouldn't leave much time to sleep.

A. The devil never sleeps.

Q. What kind of fasting?

A. Bread and water only, three days a week, until the dissension stops.

Q. Why prayer *and* fasting? Why not just prayer?

A. Prayer without fasting is like a soldier with one leg. He is easily defeated.

Q. Do you know anything about the war? [Date of the question: January 30, 1991, during the Persian Gulf War.]

A. We are on the path of peace.

Q. Ivan, do you know anything about the collapse of the "Iron Curtain"?

A. *In seeing the changes occurring there we must conclude that our prayers and fasting have been effective.* But the Blessed Mother pleads with all of us to continue to pray and fast. The changes there are not finished. We must pray and fast that the changes stabilize.

Q. Do you know anything about the conversion of Russia?

A. The real question is not when *Russia* will convert. *We* need conversion; the call of the Blessed Mother here in Medjugorje is to change our hearts. She asks for a change in our person and a change in society.

MESSAGES

Q. When do you have apparitions now, Ivan?

A. Every day. I see the Blessed Mother at twenty minutes before six. I talk to her and she talks to me.

Q. Do you ever get messages from the Blessed Mother for the Holy Father?

A. The Blessed Mother gives messages for the Holy Father through Vicka.

Q. Why has the Blessed Mother come to Medjugorje?

A. She has been sent by God to strengthen faith and prayer in the Church. If we, the people of God, are strong, the Church is strong. If we are weak, the Church is weak. The Blessed Mother is our real mother. She loves each of us as only our real mother can.

A wise person will accept what she is telling us. The most important thing in our lives must be the messages. These are peace, conversion, fasting and penance, faith and love. The Blessed Mother explains in each of her messages the need for God's people to live the Gospel. Her messages are the Gospel of her divine Son Jesus, our brother.

Q. How does peace come about, Ivan?

A. The Blessed Mother is the Queen of Peace. She can bring us to the road of peace so that we can find within ourselves the peace and happiness we desire. She is calling all people on earth to peace in the world.

Q. What about non-Christians?

A. She is the mother of all people on earth. She is calling all her children.

Q. How will this happen, Ivan?

A. Through the renewal of family prayer.

Q. That sounds so simple, Ivan.

A. If each family would pray and fast as a family, there would be peace in the world. If parents would pray, bless, and sacrifice more for their children, the children would thrive. If children would pray for their parents, especially the safety of their parents' marriage, and love and obey their parents, family life would be a source of great love and peace on the earth. God's abundance would fill the homes. Where there is no prayer and sacrifice, God is absent. A place without God is a place of great danger and pain. Family prayer and penance will bring peace in people, peace in the Church, and peace in the world.

Q. How can each person help?

A. The only way we can help is through family prayer. God respects the family so much that when Jesus took human nature in the womb of Mary, He chose to live in a family. The family is greatly threatened now by the disease of materialism. We work, therefore we have no time to pray together. This is a great excuse, but it really is a great lie and most people are living this lie.

The Blessed Mother has promised that for families who pray together there will be harmony and unity. It must begin when children are babies. It is a process. By the time children are in their twenties it is very hard to erase bad habits they have acquired.

Q. What about parental authority? Many young people rebel against their parents' ways. Does the Blessed Mother speak about that?

A. The authority of parents is a regime of love. What kind of freedom do we give youth? Where is Satan? Do parents really help Satan by neglecting their duties? Their authority? Parents must restrict their own freedom in the service of their children, just as children must obey and love their parents. Sacrificial love brings great blessings for parents and children.

Q. It has been said: Love begets love; selfishness begets selfishness; sin begets sin. What about the elderly?

A. The Blessed Mother says three generations in one household is most pleasing to God.

Q. Do you have any advice from the Blessed Mother?

A. She wants us to be carriers of her messages to others. We need fewer words and more actions.

THE COMMISSION

Q. Ivan, do you have any information about the commission established by Rome to study and decide the authenticity of these apparitions in Medjugorje?

A. The commission is investigating everything. Each month a bishop from the commission comes to Medjugorje to say the Mass and speak to the pilgrims. The medical section of the first and second commissions have finished their work.

Q. What is their conclusion?

A. Both commissions have concluded that all six of us [the visionaries] are healthy. But we knew that before they started. We submitted to their investigations because we wanted to prove to the world that we are normal.

Q. Were the tests difficult?

A. They worked on us for five years. I had one hundred forty tests. Thirteen doctors came to Medjugorje to thank us for our cooperation after they concluded their investigations. There is not one hair on my head that they did not test. When they were thanking us, I asked them, "Now can we investigate you?"

Q. What did they say?

A. They didn't respond.

CHAPTER 11

THE LOCUTIONISTS: JELENA AND MARIJANA

If God can clothe in such splendor the grass of the field, which blooms today and is thrown on the fire tomorrow, will he not provide much more for you, O weak in faith!

Apart from the six visionaries, there are two locutionists (people to whom God speaks internally) who have experienced special gifts at Medjugorje. In December 1982, nine-year-old Jelena Vasilj began to hear Our Lady speak to her. This phenomenon is known as an "inner locution." The same gift was given to Marijana Vasilj (no relation to Jelena) in March of 1983. These two youngsters have another type of apparition, an "interior" one in which they "see with the heart." Our Lady, by this means, teaches them the treasures of spiritual life that their lives might be a means of conversion for others.

In May of 1983, Our Lady asked Jelena to advise a priest that she desired a youth prayer group in the parish of Saint James. Approximately fifty-six boys and girls responded to the invitation from the Blessed Mother. Our Lady asked that they pray three hours a day, fast twice a week on bread and water, and attend Mass every day. She said, "*Do not be surprised that I ask this. You are not able to fulfill your duties because you pray too little.*"[1]

The locutionists interiorly see Jesus and angels as well as the Blessed Virgin Mary. It is said that countless others from around the world who have journeyed to Medjugorje or have responded to the Medjugorje messages have also received similar graces.

The Virgin said, "*I want a prayer group here. I will lead the group and give rules of sanctification to it. Through these rules all others in the world can consecrate themselves. I will give you one month to choose this group, but tell them the condition I lay down. First of all, they have to renounce everything, putting themselves totally at God's disposition; renounce all fear because if they are abandoned to God there is no place for fear. All difficulties they encounter will be for their spiritual growth and for the glory of God.*"

Jelena Vasilj, who was the first of these locutionists, is tall, strong, intelligent, and quick-witted. She has an evident sense of humor. Born on May 14, 1972, the second of six children, she lives with her family in a house situated midway along the road between Mount Krizevac and Saint James Church.[2] Her family would be considered devout. Her father built a chapel integral to the house, behind the courtyard, before the apparitions began. There are two long wooden benches in this chapel, a statue of the Blessed Virgin, a large picture of the Sacred Heart of Jesus, and some small candles scattered about. Here the family gathers daily for family prayer, led by Jelena's father. In addition, Jelena's prayer group assembles here twice a week, at the request of the Blessed Virgin herself. Some miraculous events have occurred in that chapel.

Experts who have interviewed Jelena, prayed with Jelena, and know her well, have referred to her as a "prophetess in line with the New Testament prophets and prophetesses."[3]

She has visions of Jesus and Mary from time to time during her prayer group meetings and at other times too. She "hears" Jesus and Mary, who give messages to the group through her.[4] She has also heard the voice of Satan. Her spiritual director, Father Slavko Barbaric, who is also the spiritual director of the six visionaries, asked her how she could distinguish between the voices.[5] She responded: "Very easily. When the Blessed Mother or the Lord Jesus speaks, there is an ease about it; no time pressure. I am free and totally at peace. However, when Satan starts to speak I become nervous, agitated. I feel pressure and urgency. I feel I have no time and must act immediately."[6]

One day Jelena asked the Blessed Mother if she, too, could know the ten secrets. The Blessed Mother responded, "I did not appear to you as to the other six because my plan is different. To them I entrusted messages and secrets. Forgive me if I cannot tell you the secrets that I have entrusted to them; it concerns a grace that is for them, but not for you. I appeared to you for the purpose of helping you to progress in spiritual life and through your intermediary I want to lead people to holiness."[7]

Experts have concluded that Jelena's spiritual journey epitomizes the spiritual possibilities of all people on earth in their search for God.[8] She heard about the apparitions occurring in her village and she responded generously to the requests of the Blessed Mother. She is one year younger than the visionary Jacov, and during the early years of her remarkable spiritual gifts, she attended the same school as Jacov, although they live in different parts of the village and have different friends and quite different family lives. Jelena heard from the visionaries' own mouths what the Blessed Mother said. She responded with the fervent heart of a loving, longing child.

Jelena's amazing story unfolds in the following interview, edited from a series of interviews conducted in August of 1990 in Medjugorje.

Q. Jelena, how old are you?
A. Eighteen.
Q. Do you speak English?

A. A little.

Q. Have you studied it in school?

A. No.

Q. Are you finished with school yet?

A. Unfortunately not.

Q. How much more school do you have?

A. If everything is as I plan, one more year.

Q. When you finish what will you do?

A. Right now I have no idea.

Q. Are you and Marijana the only ones in Medjugorje who have the unusual relationship with Our Lady?

A. As far as I know, yes. In this way.

Q. Father Slavko is your spiritual director, isn't he?

A. Yes, together with Father Tomislav Vlašić.

Q. In 1985 he did an analysis of the experience you and Marijana share.[9] What are the messages the Blessed Mother gives to you and your prayer group?

A. There are many. They include prayer, fasting, and conversion. Our Lady wants us to read Matthew 6:24–34 every Thursday before the Blessed Sacrament.

MATTHEW 6:24–34

No man can serve two masters. He will either hate one and love the other or be attentive to one and despise the other. You cannot give yourself to God and money. I warn you, then: do not worry about your livelihood, what you are to eat or drink or use for clothing. Is not life more than food? Is not the body more valuable than clothes? Look at the birds in the sky. They do not sow or reap, they gather nothing into barns; yet your heavenly Father feeds them. Are not you more important than they? Which of you by worrying can add a minute to his lifespan? As for clothes, why be concerned? Learn a lesson from the way the wildflowers grow. They do not work; they do not spin. Yet I assure you, not even Solomon in all his splendor was arrayed like one of these. If God can clothe in such splendor the grass of the field, which blooms today and is thrown on the fire tomorrow, will he not provide much more for you, O weak in faith! Stop worrying, then, over questions like, "What are we to eat, or what are we to wear?" The unbelievers are always running after these things. Your heavenly Father knows all that you need. Seek first His kingship over you, His way of holiness, and all those things will be given you besides. Enough then of worrying about tomorrow. Let tomorrow take care of itself. Today has troubles enough of its own.

Q. Do you always read Matthew 6:24–34 before the Blessed Sacrament on Thursdays as the Blessed Mother has asked you to do?

A. When we cannot get to church we read the passages at home as a family on Thursday.

Q. Does the Blessed Mother speak to you about church?

A. She wants Holy Mass to be the main gift of our day. She has taught us that Jesus gives Himself to us during the Mass. She says if we go to Mass with lukewarmness, we will return home with an empty heart.

Q. How do you receive Jesus?

A. Through deep prayer, which awakens immense desire for His presence.

Q. If your prayer life slackens, does your desire for God diminish?

A. Yes.

Q. Why does the Blessed Mother want you to absorb the teaching of her Son, Jesus, so thoroughly?

A. It helps unmask one of Satan's big lies.

Q. What lie, Jelena?

A. Tomorrow.

Q. Tomorrow? How interesting. Do you mean that one of Satan's big lies is the illusion of tomorrow?

A. Yes.

Q. The human mind and appetities are capable of many illusions, aren't they?

A. The Blessed Mother and Jesus help us to know that it is prayer and fasting that free the human mind from its illusions.

FAITH

Q. Since the beginning it has always been through faith in God's word that mankind is free from the tyranny of the evil one.

A. Yes. Faith is part of our life here in Medjugorje. What pain people must suffer who have no faith!

Q. Jelena, without faith in God's word, much of life makes no sense. What happens if people get too busy to pray in your family?

A. We have found that things do not go well for us. We become tired, or irritable. We lose our energy. We waste time. When these things happen we know we are not praying enough.

Q. Doesn't prayer take up a lot of time?

A. It's only when we don't pray that we have no time.

Q. Does that mean when you pray as a family your activities are covered by God's graces and that is why things go smoothly?

A. That could be. I don't know.

Q. Jelena, today is Our Lady's birthday [August 5]. Do you make any special preparations?

A. Our Lady has asked us to give her three days of celebration. She asked us not to work on those days but to pray and fast as a gift to her.

Q. Do you do that?

A. Of course. It is a great joy to do some little thing for our Blessed Mother that we know she wants.

Q. You do love her very much, don't you?

A. Oh yes! [Jelena has a twinkle in her eyes. Joy exudes from her.]

Q. Our Lady has said: *"If you would abandon yourselves to me you will not even feel the passage from this life to the next life. You will begin to live the life of heaven on earth."* Do you ever experience heaven on earth, Jelena?

A. [Look of surprise.] I'm not able to answer but I *am* happy. I feel great joy. The more I surrender my own goals and desires to God's will for me, the more filled with peace I am.

Q. How do you keep this state of mind?

A. I don't think it's a state of mind.

Q. What is it?

A. It is the fruit of prayer. It affects my whole person. When I am tuned into God through prayer, I forget all that is behind me. I focus only on God's immense love in the immediate present.

Q. Have you changed your life?

A. Every day. I try to change my heart so that I desire nothing contrary to God's will.

Q. How do you do this?

A. I think about Jesus a lot. I ask Him to help me.

Q. How do you know Jesus?

A. Through His words. He is my shepherd.

Q. How do you relate to the Good Shepherd parable in this modern world?

A. I try to be a good sheep who follows my shepherd. Our Lady has said that we must pray unceasingly to Jesus to fill our hearts with love.

Q. You have many sheep here in the village, so you understand this parable of the Good Shepherd.

A. [Giggle.] If a sheep here tried to be the shepherd, it wouldn't get very far.

Q. Would it be dinner?

A. [Laughter.] Maybe.

THE FIRST DAYS OF LOCUTIONS

Q. Jelena, can you remember the first time you heard an interior voice?

A. Yes. I can never forget that first day. It was December 15, 1982.

Q. Where were you?

A. I was in school. I was bored and wondered what time it was. I heard someone say "twenty minutes past ten."

Q. Why was this voice unusual?

A. Because it came from within—it answered a question I was asking myself, and no one knew about the question but me.

Q. Had this ever happened before?

A. No. But I didn't realize at that time that it was something supernatural.

Q. Were you confused?

A. I'm not sure the word is *confused*. I heard the voice again. This time, as I began to raise my hand to answer a question the teacher was asking, the same voice said, "Do not raise your hand. You will not be called on." Then I started laughing. It was then that I realized that something different or extraordinary was happening. I told a few of my friends.

Q. What was their reaction?

A. They thought I was weird.

Q. Were you afraid?

A. Maybe.

Q. What did you do?

A. I told my dad. He said that sometimes God gives people a gift to hear voices. That made me happy and grateful.

Q. Did you hear the voice again?

A. Yes. I was working in the field picking tobacco. I was praying in my heart as I had heard from Marija [the visionary]. The deeper I prayed, the more a real feeling of joy came over me. There the same voice said to me, "Are you happy?" This time my heart was filled with such joy that I said, "Oh, yes!" And I thanked God so much.

Q. Were you fasting at that time?

A. Yes. I was really trying to do what the Blessed Mother was asking of us. My whole family was.

Q. How were you fasting?

A. On bread and water only on Wednesdays and Fridays.

Q. Did you ever hear the voice again?

A. Yes. For days I listened to the voice. It was always pulling me deeper into prayer.

Q. Were you still able to communicate with your family during those days?

A. Yes. Certainly. And I told my friends, too. We shared what I was hearing. We were all learning about how to find God in the world through prayer.

Q. What did you do?

A. We went to confession.

Q. Why?

A. My dad phoned Father Slavko. He talked to us. He explained to us what was happening to me. He suggested some things, including confession.

Q. How old were you then?

A. Ten.

Q. Did anything else happen that you remember?

A. Yes. I can never forget the date. December 23, 1982. It was Advent. My mother and I were praying. We were thinking about Mary and Joseph traveling to Bethlehem to register for the census. We were thinking about the Blessed Mother, who was carrying the infant Jesus, who is really God, who is really the Second Person of the Blessed Trinity in her womb. The angels knew who Mary was carrying and suddenly I saw an angel!

Q. Did the angel speak?

A. Yes. He told me God sent him to speak to me. He asked us to pray more intently. He asked us to fast more generously. He told us never to be afraid.

Q. How did you react to this?

A. I had never been so happy in my life. The happiness was very deep, penetrating.

Q. What did the angel look like?

A. He was smaller than I. He looked maybe six years old. He had short, curly, golden hair. He had huge wings. He was barefooted and his hands were folded in prayer. He was totally surrounded by intense golden light.

Q. How long did you see the angel?

A. Several minutes.

Q. Did your mother see the angel, too?

A. No. Just me. But she knew something from God was happening.

Q. How do you know?

A. She told me. She said while I was seeing the angel she was experiencing God's nearness.

Q. Did you ever see that angel again?

A. Yes, on December 29 [1982]. I was praying the rosary. I felt his presence. This time I spoke to him and said, "Can I ever see the Blessed Mother?" He communicated to me that I would be close to the Blessed Mother. At that moment I did not understand that I would really be in contact with her, but suddenly she was truly with me. She is so beautiful that you must forget everything else and stare.

Q. Did you speak to her?

A. I just looked at her in amazement and awe. I was too happy. I could hardly believe that she was there—but I really had no thoughts. I just stared at her and gazed and gazed and gazed.

Q. What does the Blessed Mother look like?

A. Her face is shining with love. Her smile is love. Her eyes are filled with love. She is dressed all in white. Her hands are joined in prayer. She carries a brown rosary.

Q. You speak in the present tense. Do you always see her that way?

A. The memory of that day is engraved in my heart. I never forget. It is always there.

Q. Did Our Lady speak to you?

A. Yes. I recognized the feeling of her presence, not exactly her voice. It was the angel's voice I had been hearing since December fifteenth at school, but somehow I can distinguish between the Blessed Mother's voice and the angel's voice.

Q. Do you know why the Blessed Mother appeared to you?

A. I never asked her. She gave me a gift.

Q. What was the gift?

A. She gave me the rosary.

Q. Do you have the rosary?

A. Yes.

Q. Can others see it?

A. No. I didn't know that at first. When I showed the rosary to my mother and my friends they said they could not see it. Then I realized the rosary is a gift to me only from the Blessed Mother.

Q. How often do you see the Blessed Mother?

A. When I am in very deep prayer.

Q. Do you see others?

A. The Blessed Mother gives me many gifts. In deep prayer I have had many experiences with her. I have seen Jesus, the angels, Saint Joseph.

THE POPE

Q. Have you seen the Holy Father, the Pope?

A. Yes. But I was not in prayer when I saw the Holy Father. I went to Rome to see him in person.

Q. Can you describe your visit?

A. I was with a priest, and some others.

Q. Was it a personal interview?

A. The Holy Father spoke to my father personally. He said he would pray for Medjugorje.

Q. When was your visit with the Holy Father?

A. Summer of 1987.

Q. Does the Blessed Mother say anything to you about the Pope?

A. Yes. She tells us to pray much for him.

PRAYING WITH THE EYES AND EARS OF FAITH

Q. You have mentioned that you see the Blessed Mother when you are in very deep prayer. Vicka has explained that she has been taught by the Blessed Mother to pray with the eyes and ears of faith.[10] In that way she, too, can see and hear the Blessed Mother during those times when the apparitions cease for her for short intervals. Is your experience similar to Vicka's?

A. I see the Blessed Mother and Jesus with the eyes of the heart.

Q. Can you describe this vision with the eyes of the heart?

A. At the very beginning I could see the Blessed Mother dressed all in white with a brown rosary in her left hand, and a crown of twelve stars. She stands on a cloud. I saw her like this frequently in the late days of 1982 and in 1983.

Q. What about now?

A. Now I hear her voice internally and I see her in the sense that I experience her presence.

A. Do you have these visions and locutions from the Blessed Mother only during your prayer group?

A. I hear her and experience her presence during the prayer group and when I pray personally.

Q. Does the Blessed Mother ever awaken you from sleep to pray for things around the world?

A. I sleep so soundly that it would be very hard to awaken me.

Q. Is it always during prayer that you hear the Blessed Mother?

A. Yes.

Q. Do you still hear the voice of an angel?

A. Yes.

Q. Do you ever hear the voice of the devil?

A. I have heard his voice internally.

Q. Like an inner locution?

A. Yes.

Q. How can you distinguish between the voice of the devil and the Blessed Mother?

A. The most significant difference is peace. In the presence of the Blessed Mother, there is only peace. Anything connected with her presence is totally peaceful.

When Satan is involved, or he speaks, it is totally the opposite. I become very nervous when he speaks. I feel agitated. I become upset.

Q. What does his voice sound like?

A. An inner locution does not mean I hear an actual voice. I experience the presence of Satan. I feel I am in the presence of the enemy.

Q. Does Satan bother you now, Jelena?

A. I am tempted by Satan just like everybody else.

Q. Can you sense Satan's presence when you are around people who are of possible evil or unwholesome dispositions?

A. My situation is like other people in that regard.

Q. How does your commitment to prayer, to your prayer groups, the time they take, impact your school life and your social life?

A. I don't understand the question.

Q. How do you integrate a normal high school life with such a profound prayer life?

A. I try to keep things in order. I prioritize my time. Home, school, work, but I admit sometimes it is difficult to keep everything in the proper order that I would like. But we are managing quite well so far.

Q. Does the Blessed Mother give you advice about these matters?

A. That is exactly what she is doing.

Q. So it is really with the guidance of the Blessed Mother that you manage a normal teenage life in the world with a deep contemplative prayer life?

A. The Blessed Mother knows what is best for her children. She is the mother of our eternal life. Not just my eternal life, but the eternal life of all people on earth. She is guarding us so that we can live a life of great happiness.

Q. Can you share some practical advice that the Blessed Mother gives you? How does she guide your life? How do you live the life the Blessed Mother seeks for her faithful children?

A. First of all, the Blessed Mother says young people are inexperienced. Little things can bother them and take them off the path to heaven, so they should accept the messages the Blessed Mother gives at face value.

Q. What does that mean?

A. It means when she says to fast on bread and water on Wednesdays and Fridays they should do that because the Blessed Mother knows better than we do what is good for us. When she tells us to pray the rosary she knows how valuable that prayer is for our eternal life.

Q. Why?

A. Certain things, like a disciplined will, and trust in God, are necessary. The most important thing is to make God's will first in our lives, and to trust God no matter what happens.

Q. Is that what the Blessed Mother wants?

A. She always teaches us to accept God's will graciously.

Q. Jelena, do you have any social life? Do you go out with boys?

A. Yes. Of course. I am not afraid of boys.

Q. Does the Blessed Mother speak to you about dating?

A. That is the first time I have ever been asked that question by anyone!

Q. People would be interested in the Blessed Mother's opinions about the "social scene," if she has ever voiced such an opinion.

A. The Blessed Mother certainly knows kids my age go out. She knows that and she always asks that we behave well.

Q. Does the Blessed Mother mind if you dance?

A. [Giggles and laughter.] We do dance here in Medjugorje, but social life is quite different here than in Western Europe or in the United States. To have a "date" here in Medjugorje is different than the "dating scene" in the United States.

Q. In what way?

A. There is no occasion here to go out every night. And there is always much work to be done. Here everyone works, even the little children and the old people. Everyone is busy, everyone has responsibilities.

Q. Do you ever go out just to relax, to have fun?

A. Sure.

Q. Do you find yourself praying internally in your heart, when you are out socially?

A. Sometimes. Well, maybe all the time. But we are normal. A date is a date!

Q. How do you pray when you are out?

A. [Shy giggle.] It's hard to forget God!

Q. Would you say that the Blessed Mother has influenced your thinking so that you are aware of God all the time?

A. Don't misunderstand. I am not obsessed with God. Rather, I would say I am connected in my thoughts with God. I experience God in a normal, peaceful way.

Q. So your life is definitely not the equivalent of the life of a contemplative nun. You live very much in the world, don't you?

A. I am a daughter. I am a student. The Blessed Mother has not yet mentioned convent life to us. My own opinion is that if you go to a convent and you are not enriched with deep insight, then you are not satisfied with the life in a convent, and it is not a real life.

Q. What do you mean, "it is not a real life"?

A. God means for his children to be happy. That is why the Blessed Mother is teaching us to pray, to experience God in the world, to experience His love, His ways, His plan for our life.

Q. Does God have a plan for each person on earth?

A. Oh, yes! Each person on earth is a deeply loved child of God. Those who know God's will for them know that. Those who live out God's will for them are happy.

Q. Have you decided what you want to do with your life?

A. I am still thinking about it.

Q. Do you think you will go on to the university?

A. Everything depends on this next year. [Jelena matriculated at Franciscan University in Steubenville, Ohio, during the 1991–92 school year.]

Q. Are you a good student?

A. My professors are enthusiastic about me.

Q. Does the Blessed Mother encourage you to study hard?

A. The Blessed Mother never mentions anything about schoolwork.

Q. Is your prayer group fun or is it very serious?

A. Everything has a time. Sometimes at the prayer group we laugh and have fun.

Q. Some people think a prayer group is a time of long faces and some sort of affected "piety."

A. They have a wrong picture of prayer and piety.

Q. What kind of picture should they have?

A. God is our life. God is not here just for priests or nuns or pious people. God is here for all of us. We accept God as our life, our reason for existence.

Q. Is it really important to fast only on bread and water?

A. The Blessed Mother said that is the best way. But we have to do it with love or it isn't worth anything.

Q. That is an interesting point. God doesn't want a world of hungry grouches, does He?

A. [Laughter.] Our Blessed Mother tells us that everything has to come from our hearts with love. But we are not to use that as an excuse not to fast! [More laughter.]

Q. If you do not pray and fast, do you still see and hear the Blessed Mother?

A. No.

Q. That's very interesting. Is it the prayer and fasting that causes you to see and hear the Blessed Mother?

A. It is not the cause. Rather prayer and fasting are the means that permit a person to become aware of the heavenly reality that is all around us.

Q. If a person truly prays and seriously fasts will that person see Jesus, the Blessed Mother, and the angels as you do, and hear them?

A. Scripture tells us whoever seeks God finds Him.

Q. Is your answer yes?

A. Yes.

Q. Do you ever sin?

A. Yes.

Q. What do you do about that?

A. Trust God's mercy.

Q. Do you ever have disagreements in your family?

A. We don't fight.

Q. Then you are not normal!

A. [Laughter.] My brothers and sisters are still young. If there is a disagreement over a toy or a chore to be done, we are friends again in ten minutes.

Q. What about clothes? Does the Blessed Mother speak to you about fashion?

A. As far as I can remember, Marija [the visionary] told me she was wearing a nightgown once during an apparition. She said the Blessed Mother asked her to always be dressed appropriately when the Blessed Mother appears.

Q. Do you know why?

A. It gives great pleasure to the angelic court when we honor the Queen of the Angels. It is a sign of love and affection. The Blessed Mother and her Son appreciate all our efforts to welcome them. All of paradise rejoices when we honor the Mother of God by our choices.

Q. Has the Blessed Mother or Jesus ever spoken to you about clothes or hairdos?

A. Long ago she did mention to us that for certain situations we should be dressed properly.

Q. What does that mean?

A. Well, she doesn't want us ever to be overdressed or underdressed at church. We should not draw attention to ourselves. We should always be dressed respectfully.

Q. Jelena, is there anything particular that the Blessed Mother stresses?

A. Yes. The Blessed Mother asks the youth of the world to study. She says to use these remaining years well. Each one of us needs to be conscious of our relationships in high school and college. She wants us to realize those things we may do, and those things that are forbidden. She wants us to learn the Gospel. Then we will always *know* what we have to do.

Q. Is the Blessed Mother preparing you for something special in Medjugorje in these remaining years?

A. Something very special is already happening here.

Q. Will something more happen?

A. We will see.

Q. Do you know anything about the permanent sign?

A. Only what the visionaries say; that it will be here on Apparition Hill, that it will be permanent, and you know nothing of the earth is permanent; that it will be indestructible—you know nothing of the earth is indestructible; and it will be beautiful.

Q. Does that mean the permanent sign will be something of heaven?

A. I don't know.

Q. Do you know anything about the chastisements that the visionaries speak about?

A. The Blessed Mother never mentions things of the future to us.

Q. Do you know anything about the Second Coming of Christ?

A. No.

Q. Do the extraordinary gifts you have received have anything to do with the visionaries' gifts?

A. All the messages the Blessed Mother is giving are meant for all people on earth because she is the mother of all people on earth and she brings these gifts for all. She never loves one person more than another.

SIGNS AND CHASTISEMENTS

Q. Jelena, do you know why the Blessed Mother has come here to Medjugorje?

A. She is here as the mother of all people on earth. She says: *"Peace will not reign in the world until people accept Jesus, until they live His words, the Gospel."*

She says: *"Dear children, this is the reason for my presence among you for such a long time, to lead you on the path of Jesus.*

"I want you to be saved, and through you the whole world to be saved."

Q. Many people now live without faith. Some don't even want to hear Jesus' words, but they do want peace and satisfaction.

A. Prayer and fasting are the only ways to peace.

Q. Jelena, all creation honors God. Human beings alone among His creatures have freedom to choose God or ignore Him. Does Our Lady speak about that?

A. Yes. The only way to recognize God in the world is through the heart. A heart filled with love recognizes God in everything. That is why the Blessed Mother asks us to pray, fast, and do penance. In that way we can know God. When we know God we have life and we are one with all life.

Q. Jelena, what do you do during your prayer group meetings?

A. We sing hymns, we pray. Marijana [Jelena's friend] and I often receive locutions, which we share with the group.

Q. What is the difference between these interior locutions you hear and prophesy?

A. I receive these locutions because Jesus is guiding the groups through these locutions. I am only a messenger.

Q. How does the Blessed Mother participate?

A. Wherever Jesus is, His mother is also. She is our mother, the mother of our eternal life. She teaches us those things we need to know to be like Jesus.

Q. Did the Blessed Mother ask you to begin these prayer groups?

A. Yes. She wants everyone in the world to be in a prayer group.

Q. Why?

A. These are difficult times. There is much evil in the world. It is through the prayer groups that people are and will be safe.

Q. Is this only for Christians?

A. No. The prayer groups are for all people on earth.

Q. What do people need to do to start a prayer group?

A. Our Blessed Mother has said emphatically that the first condition for any prayer group is to eliminate all fear from your heart forever.

Q. That is hard to overcome. There is so much fear in the world right now.

A. Fear does not come from God. God is love.

Q. What about the gift of the Holy Spirit, which is fear of God. Also, isn't "fear the beginning of wisdom"?

A. Fear of God is the awe of a creature for the Creator. It is rooted in love. God sustains and nurtures His children when they allow Him to do so.

Q. How do we preclude God from sustaining and nurturing us?

A. By wandering away from His will for us.

Q. Jelena, on May 25, 1983, the Blessed Mother told you of her strong desire that a prayer group, totally abandoned to Jesus, be formed. Is it really true that she herself dictated the rules for this group to you?

A. The Blessed Mother has a strong desire that all her children on earth observe some guidelines for a happy and successful life here on earth, and in heaven forever.

Q. Can you mention these guidelines?

A. Yes, the leader of a prayer group is important, but not in the ways of the world.

Q. Jelena, tell us some qualities that help you to be an effective leader of your prayer groups.

A. A leader of a prayer group does not necessarily have the same qualities as a leader in the world has. It is necessary to pray and discern the Lord's choice for the prayer group leader. That person should be most humble, most abandoned to the spirit of God. It is actually the Lord Himself who is the true leader, so the one who will be the messenger needs to be as transparent as possible so that the spirit of God may flow through that person.

Q. What about non-Christians, Jelena?

A. The Blessed Mother has said: *"Tell everyone that it is you who are divided on earth. The Moslems and the Orthodox for the same reason as Catholics, are equal before my Son and me. You are all my children. Certainly all religions are not equal,—'All men are equal before God.' It does not suffice to belong to the Catholic Church to be saved. It is necessary to respect and obey the Commandments of God in following one's conscience. Those who are not Catholics are no less creatures made in the image of God and destined ultimately to live in the house of God our Father. Salvation is available to everyone without exception. My Son Jesus redeemed all people on earth.*

Only those who refuse God deliberately are condemned by their own choice. To him who has been given little, little will be asked for. To whomever has been given much (Catholics, Christians, who know) very much will be required. It is God alone, in His infinite justice, who determines the degree of responsibility and renders judgment."

SECRETS AND CONVERSIONS

Q. Jelena, that message from the Blessed Mother through you gives us much to ponder. Can you tell me anything about the message the Blessed Mother gave you on April 25, 1983. *"Be converted! It will be too late when the sign comes. Beforehand, several warnings will be given to the world. Have people hurry to be converted. I need your prayers and your penance."* Why will it be too late to convert when the permanent sign comes?

A. The visionaries know.

Q. What do you know?

A. Only what the visionaries have told me.

Q. Has the Blessed Mother told you anything at all about the events preceding the permanent sign?

A. The Blessed Mother said, "*Hurry to be converted. Do not wait for the great sign. For the unbelievers, it will then be too late to be converted. For you who have the faith, this time constitutes a great opportunity for you to be converted, and to deepen your faith.*"

Q. The visionaries have told me many things about the secrets they know, but never the secrets.[12] Do you know the secrets?

A. No.

Q. Do you know anything you can share?

A. People here in Medjugorje do not think about the secrets much. We know there will be warnings to the world before the visible sign is given to humanity because the Blessed Mother has said that.

Q. It seems many will die between now and that time, for Mirjana said repeatedly that those who are still alive when the permanent sign comes will have little time for conversion.[13] Do you know anything at all about events that are to happen that may cause suffering?

A. The worst suffering is to live without God.

Q. Is that why the Blessed Mother is calling all people on earth to conversion?

A. She is the Queen of Peace and the Mother of our eternal life.

Every thing or person that is not of God, or for God, or with God passes away.

Q. Some people have said that there are many things and places on this earth that would be better off passing away. [Laughter.]

A. The Blessed Mother said: "*The sign will come and you must* not *worry about it.*" She has said that the only thing she wants is that we all be converted as quickly as possible. She has asked that we—not just me, but all her faithful children—make this message known to all people on earth as quickly as possible. She has said, "*No pain, no suffering is too great for me in order to reach you. I will pray to my Son not to punish the world, but I beseech you, be converted!*

"*You cannot imagine what is going to happen, nor what the Eternal Father will send to the earth. That is why you must be converted! Renounce everything. Do penance. Express my acknowledgment to all my children who have prayed and fasted. I carry all this to my divine Son in order to obtain an alleviation of His justice against the sins of mankind. I thank the people who have prayed and fasted. Persevere and help me to convert the world.*"[14]

Q. That is quite a serious message, Jelena. Do you think all the prayer, fasting, and penance that has come out of Medjugorje, including the visits of millions of pilgrims of all faiths, from all over the world, has made a difference?

A. Our Blessed Mother always thanks her children for responding to her call.

Q. Do you think the collapse of the Berlin Wall and the renunciation of Marxism have been a fruit of Medjugorje?

A. There is much prayer still needed for this part of the world.

Q. Has the Blessed Mother spoken about the political conditions in the world?

A. She always calls us to peace through prayer, penance, and fasting.

Q. Jelena, Father Petar Ljubicic, who will announce the secrets entrusted to the visionary Mirjana, is now acting as spiritual director for your prayer group, and he has said to the pilgrims this week that you have been singled out by God to receive special gifts, which are these inner locutions and inner visions. He has explained that your group is being taught how to relate to God. He said the Blessed Mother shows you how to sit during meditation, what positions of the body to use, how to achieve inner concentration, and how to obtain peace. Can you comment?

A. We come to know through prayer that God is love. The Blessed Mother and her divine Son, Jesus, lead us to a oneness with God even now.

Q. You mentioned earlier that the leader of a prayer group must be one chosen by the Lord. What other conditions do you know are significant for a prayer group?

A. The Blessed Mother asks that all people on earth be in a prayer group. It doesn't have to be a big group or even a formal group. Jesus promised that wherever two or more are joined in His name, He is present, and we know that when He is present His mother is present also because she told us that. The family is the first prayer group, and actually the best prayer group.

RULES FROM THE BLESSED MOTHER

Q. Could you give us the rules the Blessed Mother gave you?

A. These are: Renounce all passions and inordinate desires. Avoid frequent television, particularly evil programs, excessive sports, the unreasonable enjoyment of food and drink, alcohol and tobacco.

Q. That is very interesting, especially since alcohol is produced here, and tobacco is also grown here.

A. The Blessed Mother wants us to be very careful, very moderate about the use of alcohol and tobacco.

Q. What other conditions did she dictate to you?

A. Abandon yourselves to God without any restrictions.

Definitely eliminate all anguish. Whoever abandons himself to God does not have room in his heart for anxiety. Difficulties will persist but they will serve for spiritual growth and will give glory to God.

Love your enemies. Banish from your heart hatred, bitterness, preconceived judgments. Pray for your enemies and call the divine blessings over them.

Fast twice a week on bread and water. Reunite the group at least once a week.

Devote three hours, at least, to daily prayer with half an hour in the morning and half an hour in the evening. Include the Holy Mass and the rosary in this time. Set aside moments of prayer during each day. Always receive Holy Communion when circumstances permit. Pray with great meditation. Allow yourself to be led by the grace of God. Do not concern yourself too much with the things of this world, but entrust all that in prayer to our Heavenly Father. If a person is preoccupied, he will be unable to pray well because internal serenity is lacking. God will contribute to lead to a successful conclusion the things of this earth if a person strives to do his utmost in working on his own. It is necessary to extend the spirit of prayer to all daily work.

Be prudent because the devil tempts all those who have made a resolution to consecrate themselves to God. He will suggest to them that they are praying too much and fasting too much, that they should be like young people who seek pleasures. Do not listen to Satan; do not obey him. When you are strengthened in your faith, the devil will no longer be able to seduce you.

Pray intensely for the bishop and those responsible for the Church.[15]

Q. Jelena, that is quite a list. Is it difficult for you to remember all those details?

A. No. We have been living that plan since the Blessed Mother gave it to us. She wants all people on earth to follow that plan.

Q. What about those who have no bishop to pray for?

A. All people have leaders to pray for.

Q. How do you suggest that we pray in response to the Blessed Mother's call?

A. The Blessed Mother says: *"Do not think about wars, chastisements, evil. It is when you concentrate on these things that you are on the way to entering into them. Your responsibility is to accept divine peace, to live it."* All people on earth need to pray and be prayed for. That includes the leaders and those who follow. We are all God's children. His plan is that we all live in peace, His peace.

Q. How many prayer groups do you lead?

A. We have three prayer groups, but I am part of one.

Q. How often do they meet?

A. Three nights a week. Tuesday, Thursday, and Saturday.

Q. How long do the prayer groups last?

A. They average one and a half hours.

Q. Do you pray the rosaries every day?

A. The Blessed Mother asks that. Some days I don't get all three sets of mysteries said, but I always try.

Q. Do you go to daily Mass?

A. When I go to school in Mostar I cannot get to daily Mass because of the bus schedule. Every other day I go to Mass.

THE SUFFERING OF JESUS

Q. What do you know about the Eucharist?

A. The Eucharist is the most precious gift we have received from the Lord.

Q. In what way?

A. Jesus saved all of us when He accepted death on the cross. We personally receive Him every time we receive the Eucharist. At that moment, we join ourselves to Him in all His sufferings.

Q. That sounds mystical.

A. We, today, by our choice, by our preparation, can join Jesus, be physically one with Him on the cross. Don't you see what a great gift that is? He took all sin upon Himself. He paid the price. And we can be one with Him, where we are, in time and place now, in the Eucharist.

Q. In what way do we share His sufferings?

A. The Blessed Mother has shown me many of the misfortunes of my brothers and sisters throughout the world. God is our Father. Jesus is our brother. The pain of one of us is the pain of all of us.

Q. What are some of these misfortunes you have shared?

A. The Blessed Mother showed me Africa and many blacks who live there. I saw a mother holding her child. They lived in a house made of straw. They were hungry. No one had any food. Not the neighbors, not anyone. The child was dying from starvation and the mother was crying. The neighbors were crying, too, because no one had any way to help. They were asking, "Is there anyone, anywhere who can give us water or a little bread?"

The Blessed Mother said, "*See how they live? Is there no one to love these brothers and sisters of yours?*" The Blessed Mother then showed me Asia. There was a war going on. I saw men killing each other. People were terrified. They were screaming. Everyone was in a panic. It was horrible. Then the Blessed Mother showed me America. There was much luxury, there was much beauty. I saw some young people who were sneaking drugs and injecting them. They thought they were happy, but the Blessed Mother said they are very sick when they do that. They are suffering just as the others I saw.

Q. What does the Blessed Mother say about these misfortunes?

A. She says those who pray bring blessings upon those who suffer and upon themselves.

Q. How does sacramental confession fit into your personal preparation for reception of the Eucharist?

A. The Blessed Mother constantly asks all people to go to sacramental confession at least once a month. She encourages us to go more often, every time the need arises.

Q. How often do you go?

A. Frequently.

Q. More often than once per month?

A. Yes.

Q. Tell me more about young people and their parents.

A. The Blessed Mother says that God intended love and respect between parents and children. Then the relationship will be happy.

Q. How do the parents and children achieve this love and respect?

A. By watching and emulating the love and respect between the mother and father.

Q. But if there is no love and respect between husband and wife, this can poison future generations.

A. Without prayers, fasting, and sacrificial love by both mother and father, family harmony is impossible.

Q. What does the Blessed Mother say about family life where only one member prays, fasts, and sacrifices?

A. One is enough. The lost family is one where no one prays, no one fasts, and no one sacrifices. The more members of a family who pray, fast, and sacrifice, the more peace and happiness the family experiences.

REACHING TOWARD GOD AND JESUS

Q. How close are you to Jesus? Vicka has said that Our Lady has helped her to know Jesus is God, and every person and thing exists before His face. Every creature, all created things exist because of God. He sustains and nurtures all life. He looks at us day and night. He knows us so well that we don't even need to ask for anything. He knows our hearts.[16]

A. For me, I believe, it is good to ask for things we think we need. God is our Father. Because He is our Father, He listens to His children.

Q. Has Our Lady helped you to know God better?

A. Yes. She said:

Dear children, this is my advice. I would like you to conquer some fault each day.

If your fault is to get angry at everything, try each day to get angry less.

If your fault is not to be able to study, try to study.

If your fault is not to be able to obey, or if you cannot stand those who do not please you, try on a given day to speak with them.

If your fault is not to be able to stand an arrogant person, you should try to approach that person.

If you desire that person to be humble, be humble yourselves. Show that humility is worth more than pride.

Each day, try to go beyond, and to reject every vice from your heart.

Find out which are the vices that you most need to reject.

Try truly to desire to spend your life in real love. Strive as much as possible.[17]

Q. That is truly a beautiful way of life and a hard way of life.

A. The Blessed Mother wants us to live a beautiful life in union with God. She says such a life is never hard. It is a joy. She wants us to have a pure heart.

Q. Jelena, what is a pure heart?

A. A heart free from any desires that are contrary to God's will for us.

Q. Is that difficult to accomplish?

A. It takes awareness every minute.

Q. What kind of awareness?

A. That God is God and I am His creature.

Q. How does the Blessed Mother's apparitions here in Medjugorje affect you?

A. The Blessed Mother's apparitions here are for the whole world. What she has done for me she wants for all people, everyone on earth. It is possible for all people on earth. She said: "*Know that I love you. Know that you are mine. I do not wish to do anything more for anyone, that I do not wish to do for you. All of you, all people on earth, come to me. Remain with me and I will be your mother always. Come. I wish to have all of you in my heart.*"[18]

JELENA'S PRAYERS FROM THE BLESSED MOTHER

Q. Jelena, the Blessed Mother has dictated some prayers to you, hasn't she?

A. Yes.

Q. Do you think prayers composed by the Blessed Mother would be more powerful than those by others?

A. The Blessed Mother knows Jesus better than any other human. We know from Scripture that Jesus turned water into wine at her suggestion. She tells us God hears all prayer. All prayer is pleasing to God.

Q. Will you tell us the prayers, Jelena?

A. They are:

CONSECRATION TO THE IMMACULATE HEART OF MARY

O Immaculate Heart of Mary, ardent with your goodness, show your love toward us.
May the flame of your heart, O Mary, descend on all mankind.
We love you so.
Impress true love in our hearts so that we have a continuous desire for you.
O Mary, humble and meek of heart, remember us when we are in sin.
You know that all men sin.
Give us, by means of your Immaculate Heart, spiritual health.
Let us always see the goodness of your maternal heart and may we be converted by means of the flame of your heart.
Amen.

CONSECRATION TO THE SACRED HEART OF JESUS

Jesus, we know that You are merciful and that You have offered Your Heart for us.
It is crowned with thorns and with our sins.
We know that you implore us constantly so that we do not go astray.
Jesus, remember us when we are in sin. By means of Your Heart make all men love one another.

Make hate disappear from amongst men.
Show us Your love.
We all love You and want You to protect us with Your shepherd's Heart and free us from every sin.
Jesus, enter into every heart!
Knock at the door of our hearts.
Be patient and never desist.
We are still closed because we have not understood Your love.
Knock continuously.
O Good Jesus, make us open our hearts to You at least in the moment we remember Your Passion suffered for us.
Amen.

PRAYER FOR THE SICK

O my God, this sick person here before You has come to ask You what he desires, and what he believes to be the most important thing for himself.
Grant, O God, that these words enter into his heart:
It is important to be healthy in the soul!
Lord, may Your holy will be done unto him in everything!
If You will that he be healed may he be given health.
But if Your will is different may he continue to bear his cross.
I pray to You also for us who intercede for him; purify our hearts so as to make us worthy for Your holy mercy to be given through us.
Protect him and relieve his sufferings, may Your holy will be done unto him.
Through him may Your holy name be revealed; help him to bear his cross with courage.

Q. Jelena, do you ever get special messages from the Blessed Mother or from the Lord Jesus about the future?

A. The Blessed Mother says we make a mistake when we always look to the future, because people then think of wars, punishment, evil. The Blessed Mother says if you think that way, about wars, punishment, chastisements, evil, you are on the road toward them. Our task is to accept divine peace, to live it and to spread it. There is only one attitude about the future for a child of God: the hope of salvation.

Marijana Vasilj is pensive. She has haunting dark eyes and lovely long dark hair. She is small and delicate by Croatian standards. She was chosen by the Blessed Mother to lead, with Jelena, the three young people's prayer groups. Unlike Jelena, who exudes spontaneity and effervescence, Marijana is quiet and withdrawn. When asked, "Do you have a message to share?" she smiled graciously. Though she was present for all the interviews I conducted with Jelena, she rarely spoke. She served meals, she scrubbed and cleaned. No one knew that she had special gifts. Her own family is committed to service. They work, they smile, and they bless. Marijana does not stand out in any way unless one is fortunate enough to catch a glimpse of her eyes when she is unaware. Therein is a hint of the mystery she carries.

Here is her message, given in her own words, "with a heart full of love and gratitude."

"Our Blessed Mother thanks all of us for all the sacrifices and prayer and work that we have done, are doing, and will continue to do. She asks us to pray more."

A brief interview with Marijana follows.

Q. Marijana, do you see the Blessed Mother, too?

A. Yes, with my heart.

Q. Do you hear her voice?

A. Yes.

Q. Is that why you are so quiet?

A. [Deep blush.] If I speak, I cannot listen.

Q. What does the Blessed Mother say to you?

A. Many things. She is always happy when I give her sacrifices.

Q. What kind of sacrifices?

A. Mostly bread-and-water fasts.

Q. Have you given up sweets?

A. Yes.

Q. Does the Blessed Mother like that?

A. Yes. The Blessed Mother asks us to give up those things we really like for the love of God.

Q. Do you ever watch television?

A. Sometimes.

Q. What is your favorite program?

A. I like to watch sports.

Q. What is your favorite sport?
A. Soccer.
Q. Do you plan to go to the university?
A. No.
Q. Do you know what you want to do for the rest of your life?
A. I want to be faithful to God.
Q. Do you think you will enter a convent or get married?
A. [Laughter.] I don't know!
Q. Do you have a boyfriend? [Much laughter in the group.]
A. There is no one to go out with.

FIRST DAYS OF THE LOCUTIONS

Q. How did you become involved in these extraordinary mystical phenomena?

A. I began praying with Jelena when she told me about hearing the voice in school.

Q. How old were you?

A. Nine.

Q. How much did you pray?

A. At least an hour every day. Sometimes Jelena and I didn't like each other very much. We had disagreements. But the Blessed Mother told me she loves me very much. She wanted us to be friends. One day Jelena came to my house and said the Blessed Mother wanted to give me a great gift.

Q. What is that gift?

A. The Blessed Mother gave me a crucifix.

Q. What kind of crucifix?

A. It is very simple. Only when I pray much can I see this crucifix. It helps me concentrate.

Q. Can others see this crucifix, too?

A. No. It is a gift from the Blessed Mother only for me.

Q. Can you see the Blessed Mother always?

A. No. Only when I am in very deep prayer.

Q. What does the Blessed Mother look like when you see her?

A. She is dressed all in white with a rosary in her left hand and a crown of twelve stars.

Q. Do you still get locutions?

A. Yes. During prayer groups and during personal prayer.

Q. Do your prayer groups have a purpose?

A. Yes. Our prayer groups are meant to be a great sign of love to the world.

Q. Has the Blessed Mother ever asked you to pray especially for anyone?

A. Yes. She asked us to pray especially for those people who will be coming here in these days and those who have come here in the past.

Q. Do you know why she wants your prayer groups to pray for these pilgrims?

A. Yes. The Blessed Mother says people search for God in a deep way in this place. They work to experience His presence here and to understand His words. She asks us, "*Dear children, you should become a light for the people. Pray that you can recognize Christ in each person.*"

PART III

NONE OF MY CHILDREN IS EVER LOST

You can always find Me in the less fortunate.

CHAPTER 12

AND THE PILGRIMS AFTER THEM

Man's choices are the ladder to paradise.

In the early days of the apparitions of Medjugorje, the stories abounded that the Blessed Mother promised to give a gift to all those who would come there from around the world. She indicated that this "gift" was meant for each pilgrim to present to her divine Son at the personal judgment. When questioned, the visionaries indicated that the "gift" was holiness. All those who came to Medjugorje were invited to drink from the wellspring of holiness. When the people returned home, their lives were somehow different. Others noticed the changes. Perhaps the strongest validation of the authenticity of the apparitions at Medjugorje was the transformed lives of those who have been there on pilgrimage, for Scripture tells us you know a tree by its fruit.

Much insight, much light routinely seem to accompany the people who return. They are on fire with the urge to evangelize, to start prayer groups, to fast, and to return to Medjugorje. The underlying reason seems to be an unexplainable peace they have experienced there. One man said, "Once you have tasted that peace, nothing else satisfies."

Another effect of a journey to Medjugorje is the desire to seek and obey God's will. Returning pilgrims speak of God's mercy from generation to generation for those who seek His will. They tell of a newfound love for the Eternal Father. They say they have experienced His love for all His children at Medjugorje, especially those who seek to please Him. They say things, and they do things too. Medjugorje Centers have been founded all over the world. Many operate from kitchen tables. Others, like the centers in Australia and Asia, are so advanced that they come with their own TV studio to spread the messages of the Mother of God to all people on earth. There is a telephone line in most major cities of the world to phone for the monthly message Marija receives from the Blessed Mother for the world.

It is obvious that genuine sinners come to Medjugorje as well as the faithful. Many people who have been away from organized religion for fifty years or more are drawn to the holy mountains. Their attitude is open. One old man in his eighties arrived knowing he had only a few weeks to live. He was trying one last time to find the great God of Abraham, Isaac, and Jacob before he died. How was his trip? He said, "I heard the Lord." When asked what he heard, the man was moved to tears.

"I asked Him why He bothered with me, after so many years that I denied His existence. The Lord told me, '*You are the child of My great covenant with My people. All my children are sinners. To repent is to choose Me, to choose My ways. Your peace is only in My will.*' I asked Him, 'Father, how do I obey you now?' and He told me, '*Pray more, My son. Pray with great confidence in My mercy. My mercy is your garment now and for all eternity.*' I thought of His justice and I was afraid. Then He said, '*My justice is joyful. See how it corrects? See how it cleanses? Do not seek Me in places. Seek Me in your heart.*' "

"Did you ask Him about churches?" someone asked.

The old man sighed. "Yes. I haven't been in a church since I was a kid. I didn't even go to the church when my mother and father died. The Lord told me, '*The church is your home on earth. Wherever My church is, so is your home.*' "

One of the people listening said, "Did you see a burning bush, too?" No one laughed.

The old man was weeping now. "I asked Him, 'Father, how do I find you?' He said, '*In your heart, My son.*' I asked Him if it was too late for me and He said it was never too late. '*Keep your heart pure, My son. Do not fill your heart with sensual longing. A pure heart is My dwelling place. That Tabernacle of the Most High is your sanctuary from all the cares of the temporal world.*'

"I asked: 'Dear Father, what must I do so that only you dwell there?' He said: '*Hold all things of the earth with great love for Me, dear child. Consecrate every moment of your life to Me. Consecrate your use of every moment in time. Consecrate your use of everything you experience to My will. Consecrate every encounter with every creature to My will. Then every use of all things will be for Me, and with Me, and in Me. Then you, too, dear child of Mine, will be a servant of humanity with Me and for Me and in Me. Then total peace will be yours. The tears will flow for love of Me. Those tears will water My souls who long for Me. Those tears free my wounded children. Those tears melt hearts of stone grown cold with neglect and nonlove. Love My Son. Love My world. Love My lost children. Love My wounded children. Love My broken children. Bring their hearts to Me by your compassion. Never fear, My child. Find Me in the peace of your heart. Do you see now why your heart is your center for peace?*' "

Everyone was weeping now. Someone said, "Heaven is right here, isn't it?" No one answered.

* * *

The Blessed Mother says, through her visionaries, that all people on earth, like this unlikely pilgrim with only a scant few weeks to live, have a role to play in the unfolding of God's great plan for the salvation of the world—a plan that is being manifested at Medjugorje. She tells us each child of the Eternal Father on the planet earth has gifts of great beauty before His eyes. She says God made Lucifer very beautiful too. But she warns us that he took his gifts for himself. All God's gifts, she reminds us, are for our use in *His* kingdom. Should we take our gifts for ourselves alone, as Lucifer did, they become anchors lodged in hell. Should we use His gifts for the glory of His kingdom, they become stepping-stones to paradise. All is God's but mankind's freedom.

The Blessed Mother is a tender mother who loves her children. Through her visionaries she explains simply how to use our freedom.

> *Always surrender to His will, dear children. Surrender implies trust. Trust implies love. All God's children are worthy of paradise. I am the Queen of Peace. I bring peace to my children who turn to me. I am the mother of all people.*

The Blessed Mother points her children lovingly to the words of her Son. She patiently explains that she is the mother of life; that she protects those children who allow her protection. She promises, "*None of my children is ever lost!*" She pleads with all people on earth to allow her to be their mother—the mother of their eternal life. She asks for prayer, fasting, penance, which lead to conversion, which permit forgiveness of all wrongs. The result is peace. Real peace, first in each heart, then in each family, and ultimately in the whole world. How? It takes faith. Real faith.

The Blessed Mother says all God's children are worthy of love. To receive love, to experience love, however, she explains that God's people must choose to be faithful. When His children wander from His will by unfaithfulness, they do not experience His love. They have no peace. Those who live in God's will know love and peace well. Though they may suffer for a while, they continuously experience His peace and they are filled with love. There is peace and love in God's will, she promises. The Blessed Mother, the Virgin filled with grace, has brought great light to a darkened planet. She asks that all people on earth avail themselves of the privilege of consecration to her Immaculate Heart. This is a way of entrusting ourselves and our future to the mother of Jesus Christ, in response to His invitation from the cross. "Son (all children of the Eternal Father), behold your mother." John 19:26. "*Consecrate the entire world to my Immaculate Heart,*" she invites. How? Each by an act of his or her free will, who so chooses.

Will it work? Will it bring peace? Approximately twenty million people have responded. Are these the times of the triumph of the Immaculate Heart, which was prophesied by the Blessed Virgin at Fatima? What is the alternative?

The urgent cry of the Blessed Mother at Medjugorje to her children of the earth to turn their eyes and their goals toward the kingdom of heaven is a thread woven through other Marian apparitions. She points her children to the reality of the unseen world of God and His covenant with His people that is as ancient as recorded history. She asks her children to accept God's divine presence and protection with love and surrender to His ways.

The visionaries of Medjugorje constantly tell anyone who will listen to them that God exists and sees all things. They say His celestial court is very much a part of the world in which we live. They tell us to turn to God's angels because the angels find immense joy in serving God's children of the earth. The Blessed Mother, also known as the Queen of the Angels, invites all people on earth, in the name of God, to give the angels projects, to assign them tasks, to see and experience their presence in human lives. She asks all families to turn to His angelic court. God intends for life on earth to be sweet for his children, she tells us.

God created His children out of His love to live in truth. But He made them free. Those who live in truth use His gifts for His glory. The manifestations of divine presence invite all people on earth to praise Him when we experience pleasure; to praise Him when we experience pain; to praise Him in all circumstances; to trust that He makes all things well for those who love Him and serve Him faithfully. He does provide for all His children in all situations of their lives. Those who obey Him will have peace. Those words are the message of Medjugorje.

The visionaries, especially Vicka, exhort the crowds who flock to hear them speak: "You must pray for strong faith." Weak faith has introduced infection into God's church. "Pray for courage in adversity," say the visionaries. "Pray when you begin to experience difficulties." Then you will experience true peace. Always turn to God for comfort. Turn to Him for all your needs. He never refuses His children. "God loves all His children of the planet earth uniquely and fully," the visionaries say. No one is excluded from this love. He always blesses those who come to Him.

The Blessed Mother has allowed her visionaries to experience, with her, the passion of her divine Son. *"See how much He loves you!"* the Blessed Mother tells them. *"Remember His passion,"* she says. *"Always think of His passion with joy. See how He loves all His Father's children. There is no occasion that He does not bless. He knows His Father. His Father loves all His children. Nothing is too difficult for His Father to forgive. His Father is love. Jesus' life on earth is an exercise in the love of His Father for all His children."*

The Blessed Mother says over and over that all people on earth are the children of the Eternal Father. She calls to all people on earth to meditate often on what it means to be a child of the Eternal Father. She reminds the world that Jesus' grace is powerful. His grace is power to walk as a child of our Father.

The central theme of the apparitions at Medjugorje is a call to all people, not just Christians, to walk with Jesus and in Jesus and through Jesus to paradise. *"Jesus redeemed all,"* says the Blessed Mother. But not all people yet accept redemption. The kingdom of hatred and of death is the lot of those who choose to ignore God, to use His water, and His sun, and the fruits of His earth, and His children, and ignore Him, or even curse Him. He waits patiently for His children to choose Him. He sends rain and sun on the just and the unjust. The good Father, He awaits His sons and daughters. But they must choose Him. How? The apparitions at Medjugorje bring a peace plan to the planet earth. Eternal peace. Medjugorje is the Fatima peace plan in action.

MY LOVE FOR YOU IS ETERNAL
Man's freedom ends a death.
The purpose of man's life is to cooperate with God's will.
There is much merit for those who cooperate with God's will.
All things of the earth pass away but God's words.
Jesus is the Word made flesh.
His path is the will of the Father for all His children.
His path is the road to heaven.

The Blessed Mother warns: Never deviate from the path of Jesus.
If a man does not pray, if a man does not fast, he will be helpless to distinguish between the path of life and the path of death.
The Blessed Mother asks all people on earth to love God, to trust God.
She says:
Jesus is the way, the truth, and the light for all God's children's journey to paradise. Jesus is life. All else is death. Those who live in His love never die. Accept His love, she pleads.

As for ambition, accomplishments, riches and power, fashion and trends, those who follow these are like living corpses adorned for the world to see. Why? The beauty of a soul is determined by the obedience of the will of each soul to God's will. Nothing else has lasting consequences. All passes away but God's will. God has given each of His children projects (each is free to obey God's will or to disobey).

That which is not His will has no life.
God allows mankind the great gift of freedom to choose His ways. He gives mankind the light to see His ways.
Man's choices are the ladder to paradise.
God's love for each child of His is beyond the capacity of man to comprehend now, the Blessed Mother says, though His faithful ones who pray experience His love in "every little thing."

God's love burns a path to paradise in man's psyche.
The fire of His love consumes inordinate desires.
The fire of His love purifies.

The ashes Vicka saw in purgatory symbolize the debris of the purification process of the soul that belongs to God. Nothing can live in a soul but love for God.

God is pure love. God is.
All else is deception.
God's way is sweet. God's way is gentle.
God's way is peaceful. God's way is joy-filled.
Mankind on his own without God's presence is incapable of love.
Without His presence, the human heart is a pit of suffering.

Through prayer and fasting God's children come to His waiting arms.
Every prayer frees the bonds of His captive children.
Every renounced appetite softens hearts of stone.
Peace is God's gift.
Like water it rolls off stone.
When the soil of God's children's hearts is rich and fertile through prayer and fasting, He shall plant anew the tree of eternal life in their hearts.
God longs for His lost children's hearts.
God pines for their love.
God agonizes over their suffering.

The simplest prayer resounds in the canyons of paradise awakening in man the longing for Me.
He who loves resides in Me and I in Him.
When My children wander from My will they do not experience My love. They have no peace.
You can always find Me in the less fortunate.
I am hidden there waiting to love you and affirm you as you relieve My misery.
I left My blessing on those who crucified Me so that it would come back to you when you are scorned and mocked.
Be like Me. Rejoice in My love. Only bless My creation. Then you will be blessed.

AND THE PILGRIMS AFTER THEM: THREE TRUE STORIES

He left the priesthood. It was not easy to do in Italy. It was a terrible life for him. People were indifferent. Nobody listened. Nobody cared. His biggest assignment was to raise money for the diocese. Then he found work. And he found a pretty woman. She had a prestigious job and an alcoholic mother. It was a comfortable relationship, at times. Marriage, though, was out of the question. She could never accept being married to an ex-priest, because her mother had raised her as an observant Jew. He made do with her. He tried not to remember. At the seminary, he had learned from John of the Cross how to purge his memory.

She got pregnant. He didn't know about it until it was too late.

After that things between them were different. He saw his weakness and dependence every time he came near her. An ugly loathing began to seethe in his chest. He began to run. Every day. Twice a day. Three times a day. Nothing tasted good anymore. Not food, booze, sex, even being with people. Not even the sun and sky and mountains he had always loved.

One day, she signed him up for a pilgrimage to Medjugorje. After all, it wasn't much of a trip from Italy. Maybe he would go.

He parked his rental car in the village by Saint James Church. He needed the car because the noisy people on the tour bus drove him crazy. Too many pious old ladies, he reasoned. As he locked the door of his rental car, a hefty Croatian nun grabbed him and dragged him into the rectory. "The apparition is about to begin," someone said. He found himself in a small room, stuffed in among perhaps thirty others. They were praying the rosary. They were singing the *Ave* at the end of each decade, each ten beads of the rosary. But he didn't have a rosary so he kept his hands folded. All those memories.

Then the three young people bolted forward. The ecstasy began. It was marked by silence. Everyone stared. The visionaries' eyes didn't move. They were rooted on an unseen object, high on the wall. Marija Pavlovic's dark brown eyes were piercing the emptiness he saw. Jacov Colo's eyes were melting into the void, and Ivan Dragicevic's eyes seemed languid. What were they seeing? Then he heard a sorrowful voice. *"You give me much pain, my son."*

He heard himself mumble, "I am a bad priest, dear Mother."

"You have forgotten the love of your childhood, my son. You have lost the faith of your childhood. Look at your consecrated hands. See the blood that rolls from them? It is the blood of my beloved Jesus, your brother, you shed. So many die eternal death because you serve death, not life, with your hands. Repent, my dearest son. Come back to me before it is too late."

The tears were spilling down his chest now. "I don't know how to repent, dear Mother. I can't go back." Then he saw his whole life flash before his eyes. The time before he was born. Yes. He saw that he was selfish, still now. He heard his mother's tears, but he wouldn't move to ease the pressure. And his childhood. All those days he thought no one saw him. He loved hidden pleasure even as a little one. The years raced by. He saw all the people he had neglected, all the gifts God had for him that he ran from. And he fell to the ground in terror.

"Was that God's plan for me?" he choked out of his agony. And it was too much. The deep hole of despair was familiar—now there was no place to hide. "All that is unseen will be seen," he remembered. There was no place to go. The scenes began to torment him. He felt anger, then violent rebellion. He didn't ask to be born. He didn't like his life. He didn't like the path God chose for him. He wouldn't follow it. He felt the rage inside him, and it was a comfort. It was his life. His freedom. He would be in charge no matter what the cost. And the anger became his friend and ally. He "saw" himself rise up cursing and seething.

As he tried to strike out, suddenly, as if enchanted, he was frozen in place. There she was! Powerful, terrifying was the presence. The light allowed him to see her face, her eyes. The love in those eyes burned away the rage. He thought he smelled the "scorched despair" as it fell away from him. She spoke and the words had the effect of a lullaby from long ago: *"You loved my Son once. You served my Son once. I can't give you heaven, but I can give you time. Choose."* The tenderness in her voice caressed the contorted circumstances of his life and he felt peace. Real peace.

"Who are you?" he managed, though he already knew.

"I am your real mother," she said. *"I have loved you before God made the world. I shall always love you. You belong to me if you want me."*

The next thing he remembered was waking up in the rectory where several Franciscan friars were busy talking.

"Oh, you awake? You all right?"

He went to confession. He had time.

Melona Hapsburg is young and tall. Royalty watchers are often impressed with her title. She is an archduchess of the Austro-Hungarian Empire, but there is no longer an empire. A jet-setter, she traveled with European royalty and the so-called beautiful people.

At twenty-five, she found herself in the village of Medjugorje. She had fame, beauty, wealth, and "friends." But she was afraid. She said she believed evil and bitterness were much stronger than the sweet, religious stories of good. She hoped there was a God, but she wasn't sure. Love? She didn't know what that was. She had everything, but she had no life. There were just different types of despair as she tried to survive. There were fashionable clothes, and exciting trips and stimulating jobs, and a lot of harassment. She said she tried each day just to get through that day. She said she traveled and partied just to "feel nice for the moment." "That life is a lie. It is death," she said.

Studying both in Paris and London, Melona also traveled by ship around the Mediterranean. She went from one quest to another looking for more things, places, and people. How did she feel? In Melona's words: "Empty. Totally empty."

Medjugorje was another quest. Her words: "I had this incredible experience on the mountain [Cross Mountain]. I was too stunned. I felt I couldn't breathe. And then I wanted to breathe, and breathe and breathe. It was like all the poison left me. For the first time in my life I could breathe pure air; really clean air.

"I just opened up. I can't begin to explain. I began to pray the rosary. I saw my life change. I experienced the stupidity of my life. Then I had a spiritual heart attack. The pain of my stupidity, my ridiculous choices, was so intense that I choked on the memories. I heard myself cry out, 'God, do you exist? Please answer me now before I die and become extinguished.' Then I felt a quiet longing begin to well up in me, and the longing became an insatiable urge to find God. I tried to get up, but my body wouldn't move. The rosary was in my hands and the words were in my mouth. My heart began to experience love. Real love, eternal love. God's love. I lay there for I don't know how long, bathed in the fountain of God's love. It might sound strange but that's what happened. It was like His love pierced my heart and broke it. All I could do was respond to the love God was pouring into me. And I committed myself to Him. Completely. I gave Him a blank check.

"Has my life changed? Totally. Now I live very modestly at Medjugorje. It is my joy to serve the pilgrims who come here. I have not one ounce of fear. The more I give my life to Him, the more I do for Him, the more peace I have. But then I know I can do *nothing* for Him. And so my illusions die quietly. The most I can do is accept His love. It seems so incredible, so undeserved, it hurts. I am learning to accept His love. He has given everything.

"What did I find in Medjugorje? Everything. I learned that God is real. God is alive. The same God who always is. His love is everything. He gives us everything. You have to give up every tear, every pain, every discipline, everything you say and do.

"But you give up nothing and find everything."[1]

* * *

The Olympic gold medals Alan (not his real name) won when he was young many years before lent a certain irony to the gossip that still surrounded him and his family. It was 1985. In the town where he lived, everybody knew everything, or so they thought, for it was a small community with a country club whose small membership roster reads like the Social Register.

Though all his children were now grown, Alan's youngest child, Brad, would soon be leaving for his freshman year at the Ivy League school where his older siblings had studied. Tall, nearly six feet five inches, Brad did not yet have the polish of the Harvard man he was to become. Brad's tennis partner had just returned from Medjugorje with stories of a dancing sun, of visions and physical healings. According to the friend, the blind were seeing, the lame were walking, and there were rainbows when there was no rain. "Please tell my dad," he pleaded, suddenly displaying a sorrow that was so poignant it almost could be tasted. The other three, exhausted from the tennis match, understood. Brad's Sunday school teacher had taught them, too, when they were just beginning their weekly tennis lessons on that very court seven summers earlier. She told Brad to pray for his parents' marriage. He did, and so did his friends.

"Dad always talks about religion," sighed Brad. "Maybe if he hears that the Blessed Mother is appearing in Yugoslavia it will make a difference!" And Alan did hear, for it is a small town and there are no coincidences. People at the club were listening, and Brad's tennis partner wasn't the kind who fabricates stories of miracles.

Eleanor, Alan's estranged wife, was athletic but melancholy. She wanted the divorce, for, as she said, some pain is so great that finality is, in itself, a relief. For her, a relationship with Alan was a life of cold silence. He never talked (around her). He never laughed (around her). He never shared, not money, or friendship, or time.

Decisive, Alan insisted that his family accompany him to Yugoslavia before any divorce settlements were signed because Alan discovered he didn't believe in divorce. Brad and his friends prayed. Alan's passion suddenly became everyone's interest.

Thanksgiving break that year saw the family in Medjugorje. The "children" set a "family record" climbing Cross Mountain. Alan carved the ascent "time" into a rock to mark the feat. Always the

Olympian, he kept his stopwatch in his pocket at all times. "Discipline! That's what makes winners," was his motto at Medjugorje, too.

They did it all: the mountains, the Masses, the treks to the visionaries' houses to listen to them. They even went to sacramental confession. After all, Alan reasoned, there are supposedly "special graces" for confessing at Medjugorje. Not one to miss an opportunity, he strongly "suggested" the whole family get their share of graces, including his wife, though she was not even Catholic. Alan was accustomed to giving orders. When he did, he generally expected people to obey.

The last night in Medjugorje, a strange thing happened. The entire family was invited to Marija Pavlovic's home. There was no translator present as they gathered around her dining room table. Each fired questions at her. Humble but never timid, Marija fielded questions with such gentleness that the family began to notice a softening in their own voices. Her English was "quite lovely," they later remembered. Eleanor, familiar with verbal abuse and experiencing the pain of an unappreciated wife and mother, asked Marija about divorce.

"The Blessed Mother says every act of ours must be motivated by love. Great prayer and discernment are necessary to understand the true motives for divorce," Marija responded.

Uncomfortable, Alan boomed: "Have you actually seen heaven, hell, and purgatory?"

"Yes," said Marija, to the amazement of her listeners. "We choose heaven, hell, or purgatory for ourselves," she continued. "The Blessed Mother explained to me that at death we are the same person we are in life, though we no longer have the use of our body. It returns to the earth. We receive the light at death to see the plan God has had for us from the beginning. We then understand how we have chosen to comply with His divine plan. In the light of truth we know where we belong, where we fit, and we choose heaven, hell, or purgatory."

Eleanor asked, "Marija, do you know what God's divine plan is?"

Marija chuckled as she said: "I am the fruit of God's love. Everyone knows that God made us to know Him, to love Him, and to serve Him in this world so that we can be happy in His kingdom of love and peace and joy forever."

"Why do we have to serve?" asked Brad.

"God serves us. To live in His house with Him, we need to be like Him," replied Marija.

Surprised, Alan inquired, almost timidly: "Do you know what God is like?"

Marija looked at Alan. "The Blessed Mother has taught us to pray. She asks all people on earth to pray with their hearts. Those who pray with their hearts know that God asks us to love one another as He loves us, to serve one another as He serves us, to help one another as He loves us. He is the God of peace and love and joy. Those characteristics flow from His Heart. He created mankind to be like Him. He has made all people on earth beautiful. He has given us His own life. He asks us to choose Him while the sun shines. When the darkness comes He will not be found. He asks us to come to Him in peace, to come to Him in joy, to come to Him in love. He sees all hearts. He alone judges. The Blessed Mother asks all people to read Scripture."

Scripture teaches us His ways, mused Alan. In the silence of Marija's stare he experienced the words:

Love one another as I love you.
Forgive one another as I forgive you.
Sing to one another as I sing to you.
Dress one another as I dress you.
Feed one another as I feed you.
Educate one another as I educate you.
Free one another as I free you.

Gentle is My way. Peaceful is My way.
Humble is My Heart. Humble is My path. Humble is My love.
Come to My Heart, dear little ones of My covenant.
Bless and forgive one another.

I alone am the Lord. I alone redeem. I alone save.
My Heart is gentle.
All power resides in My Heart alone. All love resides in My Heart alone.
My Heart is humble. My Heart is pure.

My power sees all things, permits all things, and brings the glory of

the Resurrection to those who turn to My Heart, My love, My peace, My humility.
Have confidence in My love for you, My dear little children of the covenant of My love.

Eleanor came away dazed, A Protestant of Huguenot descent, she was deeply touched by Marija's gentleness. For a fleeting second, her husband displayed a softness that awakened in her memories of long ago when they were both young and briefly knew great love together.

Later, when the family returned home, they learned that Marija had no command at that time of the English language. They came to treasure their photos with her, and their memories of that visit, and the language miracle they had experienced.

The following summer, Eleanor and Alan, though still separated, returned with a group of pilgrims to Medjugorje. Early one morning, Alan climbed Cross Mountain alone. At the tenth Station of the Cross he suddenly cried out, "Lord Jesus Christ, Son of the Living God, some of us need You more than others!" He knew that his marriage had died, his financial empire was crumbling, and his children were gone. What a waste his life was, he thought, as he relived those glittering moments when he won the gold for the United States. He and his trainer had prayed the Memorare of the Blessed Virgin Mary before each event. "Maybe that's why I am here now," he reassured himself. There, between the sky and the rocks, he fell down upon the earth and wept like a five-year-old who has become a refugee—for that's what he was. He belonged nowhere, to no one.

Eleanor's minister had said that only a miracle could save their nearly thirty-year-old marriage. So Alan asked for a miracle. He sensed that there was a joy, a vibrancy, an "unknowing" that could make marriage an exquisite harmony of sharing. Suddenly he knew he needed to be "empty." But he had worked so hard to be full! The loneliness of his childhood and the bleakness of his home life unmasked a fear in the pit of his gut that caused him to shudder. "I can't let go," he reasoned. "I don't trust anyone but myself! God? Do You really exist? Do You even know me? Do You care about me?"

He lay there on Cross Mountain as the darkness covered the valley below. He had a decision to make and he knew it. Fear or faith. He had to choose only one. As the sun came up he heard himself surrender. Faith! "You *are* there, God, because *I choose* to believe! Help my unbelief. Create in me the capacity to love and to be loved." There on Cross Mountain he knew how Thomas the Apostle must have felt, for he found himself now wanting to touch the wounds of a Risen Savior. "Unless I place my fingers in His wounds . . ." He longed for some sign. Then the words of long ago flooded his memory.

> *Remember O most gracious and loving Virgin Mary that never was it known that anyone who fled to your protection, implored your help, or sought your intercession was left unaided. Inspired by this confidence, I fly unto you, O Virgin of virgins, my Mother. To you do I come, before you I stand sinful and sorrowful. O Mother of the Word Incarnate, do not despise my petition but in your mercy hear and answer me. Amen.*

He was sweating now and he was very cold. That was the prayer he and his trainer had said before he won his three gold medals in the Summer Olympics several decades ago. Would that prayer now bring him the golden years all men dream of?

Such is the test of faith. He was empty now. There between the sky and the rocks he finally knew. Man has nothing but faith in the unseen God. All else is illusion. All else is death.

"Lord, give me eyes to see You in the world, ears to hear You in the world, and a heart that beats for You alone."

He had heard Jacov speak those words taught to him by the Blessed Mother, and he prayed them constantly from that moment.

When he returned home, he told the men in the locker room of the club: "I want to do God's will, not mine. I need to learn to serve others." The change was slow. Everyone noticed his wife now, for she was joyful. She had always been loving. He was looking for love, and now he saw it in her.

Today Alan and Eleanor say they have never been happier, not even in the beginning. He chose the gold. It's called faith.

NOTE: Except for the story of Melona Hapsburg disclosed to the author at Medjugorje, some of the events used in these stories have been adapted, combined, synthesized, and rearranged to protect the privacy of the pilgrims whose experiences are herein recorded.

CHAPTER 13

CURES AND LUMINARY PHENOMENA

Suffering is a test of a soul's faithfulness.

Approximately fifteen to twenty million people from everywhere on earth have, within a dozen years, made their way to the remote little village of Medjugorje in southwestern Yugoslavia. In that isolated little village, untold thousands of people of all races, religions, and nationalities claim to have witnessed miraculous lights and sights.

Hundreds, possibly thousands, report cures of everything from cancer to strokes. And the stories proliferate. Many are so grateful to be healed that they quietly resume their lives, unwilling to undergo the rigorous scrutiny imposed by the Roman Catholic Church upon alleged beneficiaries of miraculous healings.

On July 25, 1982, in one of her first messages, the Blessed Mother said:

> *For the cure of the sick it is important to say the following prayers: The Creed, and seven times each: the Our Father, the Hail Mary, and the Glory Be to the Father, and to fast on bread and water. It is good to impose one's hands on the sick and to pray. It is good to anoint the sick with holy oil. All priests do not have the gift of healing. In order to receive this gift, the priest (or minister of the Gospel) must pray with perseverance and believe firmly.*[1]

The visionary Vicka promises that miraculous healings will happen spontaneously all over the world when the promised "permanent sign" occurs at Medjugorje.[2] The visionaries have spoken of "signs" prefacing the "great sign" at Medjugorje.[3] Cures and luminary phenomena, popularly referred to by Medjugorje devotees as the "Miracle of the Sun," are happening all over the world. "Cures" of everything from blindness to broken marriages are claimed. These "signs of God's graciousness," as they are called, are becoming so prolific that a synonym for the Blessed Virgin at Medjugorje could be "Queen of Hope."

HEALING AND THE POWER OF THE ROSARY

The Blessed Mother stresses with great urgency the power of the rosary, especially when it is prayed as a family. She says the rosary is so powerful that a family joined together at her knee, praying in this way, pierces the very heart of God. The Blessed Mother has reminded the pilgrims frequently to study the fifteen promises made by her to Saint Dominic, to whom she was sent in the early thirteenth century with the first rosary, when times were dark and fraught with moral weakness. Those promises are:

1. To all those who will recite my rosary devoutly, I promise my special protection and very great graces.
2. Those who will persevere in the recitation of my rosary shall receive some signal grace.
3. The rosary shall be a very powerful armor against hell; it shall destroy vice, deliver from sin, and shall dispel heresy.
4. The rosary shall make virtue and good works flourish, and shall obtain for souls the most abundant divine mercies; it shall substitute in hearts love of God for love of the world, elevate them to desire heavenly and eternal goods. Oh, that souls would sanctify themselves by this means!
5. Those who trust themselves to me through the rosary, shall not perish.
6. Those who recite my rosary piously, considering its mysteries, shall not be overwhelmed by misfortune, nor die a bad death. The sinner shall be converted; the just shall grow in grace and become worthy of eternal life.
7. Those truly devoted to my rosary shall not die without the consolations of the Church, or without grace.
8. Those who will recite my rosary shall find during their life and their death the light of God, the fullness of His grace, and shall share in the merits of the blessed.
9. I will deliver very promptly from purgatory the souls devoted to my rosary.
10. The true children of my rosary shall enjoy great joy in heaven.
11. What you ask through my rosary, you shall obtain.
12. Those who propagate my rosary shall obtain through me aid in all their necessities.
13. I have obtained from my Son that all those who pray the rosary shall have for their brethren in life and death the saints in heaven.

14. Those who recite my rosary faithfully are all my beloved children, who are the brothers and sisters of Jesus Christ.
15. Devotion to my rosary is a special sign of predestination.

An insightful statement made by the Blessed Virgin and relayed by Vicka is the following: *The rosary is the chain that binds generations to Eternal Life.*

Many who come to Medjugorje, or hear about Medjugorje and know the Mother of God is indeed calling them, remember that they too are a child of the rosary, though some must trace that heritage back as far as the thirteenth or fourteenth century. The visionaries say the Mother of God is calling her children for the last times.

Millions of rosaries of pilgrims, and those who are not pilgrims, often turn a golden or copper color.[4] Medals, too, and even statues have turned this color. What does this "sign" mean? No one really knows, but the Blessed Mother has promised many signs, both in Medjugorje and in other parts of the world, before the great sign on Apparition Hill.[5] She said these signs are designed to strengthen people's faith until the Permanent Sign comes.[6]

THE SECOND COMING

God prepared the world through Mary
for the first coming of Christ.
Possibly He is preparing the world now,
through Mary for the Second Coming.
Could it be the Eucharistic reign of Christ?

Luminary phenomena continue to be experienced by multitudes of ordinary pilgrims of all faiths who come to Medjugorje from all over the world. Often cameras record the unexplainable solar occurrences. The "Miracle of the Sun" has become an important part of the apparitions of Medjugorje because of the large number of pilgrims who claim to experience this subjective wonder.

The cross on Mount Krizevac has become a powerful "sign" to millions of pilgrims. Some, who see this high cross of concrete disappear before their eyes, have testified that they see this cross mysteriously spin. Often the cross becomes a column of light more intense than a neon cross, though there is no electricity whatsoever on the mountain.

Sometimes a shining female silhouette, a human form, resting on a flat globe, is seen. This form resembles the Miraculous Medal, which depicts the Virgin standing upon a globe of the earth. Video exists that allows study of this "sign" at Medjugorje.

In November 1981, when the visionaries asked Our Lady who the shining silhouette on Mount Krizevac was, Our Lady replied, "*Why do you ask me, my angels? Did you not see me?*"[7]

Large numbers of pilgrims claim to see the Blessed Virgin at Medjugorje. Often, they describe the beauty of her face, the mistlike vision of her at prayer before the cross on the mountain, or a sudden encounter with the beautiful Lady from Heaven at any number of places in the village. Many photographs are circulating that purport to validate those claims.

Is the "Miracle of the Sun" really the pregnant Virgin, the Theotokos, the God-bearer hovering over the planet with the pulsating Light of Christ awakening all people on earth? Who has eyes to see? Is the Blessed Mother at Medjugorje a synonym for Our Lady of the Eucharist? Is the "Miracle of the Sun" the sign of the Eucharist?

SUFFERING, DEATH, AND PURGATORY

Suffering is a lesson that is being taught at Medjugorje, especially by example through the lives of Vicka and Marija, though each of the visionaries has varying degrees of obvious suffering.

Their relationship with suffering shows the ironic lesson the Blessed Mother teaches, which is that suffering is often a blessed gift of our Father. Suffering is a test of a soul's faithfulness. There is no suffering a soul experiences that our Father does not experience too. The Blessed Mother teaches that patient suffering brings peace. Patient suffering brings happiness. Patient suffering brings freedom.

The Blessed Mother has even spoken about reincarnation. She said on July 24, 1982, to Marija:

> *We go to heaven in full conscience: that which we have now. At the moment of death, we are conscious of the separation of the body and soul. It is false to teach people that we are reborn many times and that we pass to different bodies. One is born only once. The body, drawn from the earth, decomposes after death. It never comes back to life again. Man receives a transfigured body.*

Whoever has done very much evil during his life can go straight to heaven if he confesses, is sorry for what he has done, and receives Communion at the end of his life.

The visionaries have also all seen purgatory, a place the visionaries are hard-pressed to describe, though Vicka refers to the ashes in purgatory, which she saw everywhere as the debris of a heart that does not beat for God alone. Mirjana has described the situation of the souls in purgatory as ascending and descending levels of suffering. Those closest to heaven suffer the least. Those souls who know how to pray and enjoy praying apparently have it the easiest in purgatory. For those, the suffering is the least. For those who don't pray, have no joy in prayer, apparently the suffering is the most difficult.[8]

Marija has said that a soul at death is given the "light" to see its whole life, from the moment it is breathed out of the Heart of God into its mother's womb until the moment when its freedom of choice is ended at biological death. Marija says that in such a "light," a soul can see the fruit of every choice and decision the soul has ever made. She says at that moment, the soul knows where it belongs.[9] The soul happily enters heaven if its choices have been totally compatible with God's will.

The soul, however, gratefully accepts purgatory, a place of some sort of reparation. Here a soul must wait until someone else among the people still on earth corrects, through God's graciousness, all the deliberate violations that soul has caused to God's loving plan for the universe and His beloved children who interacted, in His plan, with that soul. Marija has said that the Blessed Mother told her one hour in purgatory is more painful than the longest, hardest life on earth. Vicka has said that the Blessed Mother often visits the souls in purgatory to comfort them. She says they are absolutely helpless to help themselves. Vicka said that the Blessed Mother revealed to her great numbers of souls "*from religious on earth who just now do not believe there is a purgatory. These souls are quite abandoned by their families and their churches,*" the Blessed Mother told Vicka.

No one prays for them. They need prayers and penance so that they too can go to heaven. Please ask my faithful children to pray much for my beloved ones in purgatory who have no one to pray for them.

Ivan often speaks of the souls in purgatory who are quite abandoned. He says they can see their loved ones of the earth. The Blessed Mother asks all families to pray for their own dead by name. Many pilgrims from all faiths who have climbed Apparition Hill report that they have experienced a strong urge to pray for their deceased family members generationally back to Adam and Eve. One exuberant pilgrim was heard to exclaim, "I just cleared all my family out of purgatory," as she struggled down the mountain dragging her paralyzed foot along in its brace and leaning on her crutch.[10]

On January 10, 1983, the Blessed Mother said:

> *In purgatory there are different levels: the lowest is close to hell and the highest gradually draws near to heaven. It is not on All Souls Day, but at Christmas, that the greatest number of souls leaves purgatory. There are, in purgatory, souls who pray ardently to God, but for whom no relative or friend prays on earth. God allows them to benefit from the prayers of other people. It happens that God permits them to manifest themselves in different ways to their relatives on earth in order to remind people of the existence of purgatory and to solicit their prayers to come close to God, who is just, but good.*
>
> *The majority of people go to purgatory. Many go to hell. A small number go directly to heaven.*

CHAPTER 14

THE MESSAGES OF THE BLESSED MOTHER

Return with me to paradise.

The visionaries have received many messages; some for themselves; some for priests, bishops, and the Pope; some for visiting groups and individuals. Some are for the world. Here are messages given to Saint James Parish and the world, first weekly, then monthly from March 1, 1984 through April 1992. This is as complete a library of the Blessed Mother's messages from Medjugorje as currently exists. (Note: The Medjugorje Centers worldwide provide the monthly messages of the Blessed Virgin Mary within hours of their transmission to Marija Pavlovic.) Before March of 1984 these messages were personal and confined to the local populace. After that, they were directed to and intended for the entire world.

March 1, 1984 Dear children! I have chosen this parish in a special way and I wish to lead it. I am guarding it in love and I wish everyone to be mine. Thank you for your response this evening. I wish that you will always be here in greater numbers with me and my Son. Every Thursday, I will give a special message to you. Thank you for your response to my call.

March 8, 1984 Dear children! In this parish, start converting yourselves. In that way all those who come here will be able to convert. Thank you for your response to my call.

March 15, 1984 This evening, dear children, in a special way I am grateful to you for being here. Adore continually the most Blessed Sacrament. I am always present when the faithful are in adoration. Special graces are then being received. Thank you for your response to my call. [This day, like every Thursday evening, the faithful were worshiping the most Blessed Sacrament, but this evening it was noticed that many men remained in the church for adoration although they had worked hard in the fields.]

March 22, 1984 Dear children! This evening I am asking you in a special way during this Lent to honor the wounds of my Son, which He received from the sins of this parish. Unite with my prayers for this parish so that His suffering may become bearable. Thank you for your response to my call. Make an effort to come in greater numbers.

March 29, 1984 Dear children! This evening in a special way I am asking for your perseverance in trials. Ponder how the Almighty is still suffering, because of your sins. So when sufferings come, offer them as your sacrifice to God. Thank you for your response to my call.

April 5, 1984 Dear children! This evening I am especially asking you to venerate the Heart of my Son, Jesus. Make atonement for the wounds inflicted to the Heart of my Son. That Heart has been offended with all sorts of sin. Thank you for coming this evening.

April 12, 1984 Dear children! This evening I ask you to stop slandering and pray for the unity of the parish, because my Son and I have a special plan with this parish. Thank you for your response to my call.

April 19, 1984 Dear children! Sympathize with me. Pray, pray, pray!

April 26, 1984 [Although this was Thursday Our Lady gave no message. Therefore Marija came to the conclusion that probably Our Lady was going to give the Thursday messages only during Lent. However, on April 30, Marija asked Our Lady: "Dear Lady, why have you not given me the messages for the parish on Thursday?" Our Lady replied: "Even though I had a special message for the parish to awake the faith of every believer, I do not wish to force anyone to anything he doesn't feel or doesn't want. Only a very small number have accepted the messages on Thursdays. At the beginning there were more, but now it seems as if it has become something ordinary to them. And some have been asking recently for the message only out of curiosity, and not out of faith and devotion to my Son and me."]

May 10, 1984 [Many believers were struck by the last message of Our Lady. Many thought that Our Lady was not going to give the messages for the parish anymore.] But this evening she said this: "I am still speaking to you and I intend to continue. Just listen to my instructions."

May 17, 1984 Dear children! Today I am very happy because there are many who desire to devote themselves to me. I thank you! You have not made a mistake. My Son, Jesus Christ, wishes to bestow on you special graces through me. My Son is happy because of your dedication. Thank you who have responded to my call.

May 24, 1984 Dear children! I have told you already that I have chosen you in a special way, the way you are. I, your Mother, love you all. And in any moment when it is difficult for you don't be afraid. I love you even when you are far away from me and my Son. I ask you not to allow my heart to cry with tears of blood because of the souls who are being lost in sin. Therefore, dear children, pray, pray, pray! Thank you for your response to my call!

May 31, 1984 [This was the feast of Ascension. There were many people from abroad. Our Lady did not give any message. She said to Marija that she would give the message on Saturday to be announced to the people on Sunday.]

June 2, 1984 [It is Saturday and this is the novena of Pentecost.] Dear children! This evening I wish to say: In the days of this novena pray for the outpouring of the Holy Spirit upon all of your families and your Parish. Pray, and you shall not regret it. God shall give you the gifts and you shall glorify Him and them till the end of your life. Thank you for your response to my call.

June 9, 1984 [Last Thursday again Our Lady did not give any message for the parish. She promised she would give it this evening.] The message is: Dear children! Tomorrow night pray for the Spirit of truth. Especially you from the parish. The Spirit of truth is necessary for you in order to convey the messages just as I give them to you not adding anything, or taking anything away. Pray that the Holy Spirit inspires you with the spirit of prayer, that you pray more. I, as your Mother, say that you pray too little. Thank you for your response to my call.

June 21, 1984 Pray, pray, pray! Thank you for your response to my call.

July 5, 1984 Dear children! Today I wish to tell you: Always pray before your work and end your work with prayer. If you do that God will bless you and your work. These days you have been praying too little and working too much. Pray therefore. In prayer you will find rest. Thank you for your response to my call.

July 19, 1984 Dear children! These days you have been experiencing how Satan is working. I am always with you. Do not be afraid of temptations. God is always watching over you. I have given myself up to you and I sympathize with you even in the smallest temptations. Thank you for your response to my call.

July 12, 1984 Dear children! These days Satan is trying to thwart all my plans. Pray that his plan may not be fulfilled. I will pray to my Son, Jesus that He will give you the grace to experience His victory in Satan's temptations. Thank you for your response to my call.

July 26, 1984 Dear children! Today also I would like to call you to persistent prayer and penance. Especially let the young people of the parish be more active in their prayer. Thank you for your response to my call.

August 2, 1984 Dear children! Today I am happy and I thank you for your prayers. Pray more these days for the conversion of sinners. Thank you for your response to my call.

August 11, 1984 [Our Lady did not give a message last Thursday.] This is what she said to Marija this evening: "Dear children! Pray, because Satan is continually trying to thwart my plans. Pray with your heart and in prayer give yourselves up to Jesus."

August 14, 1984 [This apparition was unexpected. Ivan was praying in his house. After that he started getting ready to go to church for the evening service. Unexpectedly Our Lady appeared to him and asked him to relate this message to the people.] I ask the people to pray with me these days. Pray all the more. Fast strictly on Wednesday and Friday: say every day at least one rosary: joyful, sorrowful, and glorious mysteries."

[Our Lady asked the people to accept this message with a firm will. She asked this in a special way from the parishioners and believers of the surrounding places.]

August 16, 1984 Dear children! I beg all of you, especially those from this parish, to live my messages and relate them to whomever you meet. Thank you for your response to my call.

August 23, 1984 Pray, pray, pray! [Marija informed us that Our Lady had asked the people, especially the young, to keep order in the church during Mass.]

August 30, 1984 Dear children! The cross was in God's plan when you built it. Especially these days go on the hill and pray at the foot of the cross. I need your prayers. Thank you for your response to my call.

September 6, 1984 Dear children! Without prayer there is no peace. Therefore, I say to you, dear children, pray at the foot of the cross for peace. Thank you for your response to my call.

September 13, 1984 Dear children! I continually need your prayer. You wonder what all these prayers are for. Turn around, dear children, and you will see how much ground sin has gained in this world. Therefore, pray that Jesus conquers. Thank you for your response to my call.

September 20, 1984 Dear children! Today I ask you to start fasting from your heart. There are many people who fast but only because everyone else is fasting. It has become a custom that no one wants to stop. I ask the parish to fast out of gratitude to God for allowing me to remain this long in the parish. Dear children, fast and pray with your heart. Thank you for your response to my call.

September 27, 1984 Dear children! Your prayer has helped my plans to be fulfilled. Pray continually for their complete fulfillment. I beg the families of the parish to pray the family rosary. Thank you for your response to my call.

October 4, 1984 Dear children! Today I would like to tell you that your prayers delight me, but there are those in the parish who do not pray and my heart is sad. Pray therefore that I may bring all your sacrifices and prayers to the Lord. Thank you for your response to my call.

October 8, 1984 [This message was given to the parish through Jacov in his home. He did not go to church on that day because he was not well. This is the message:] Dear children! Let all the prayers you say in your homes in the evening be for the conversion of sinners, because the world is in great sin. Pray the rosary every evening.

October 11, 1984 Dear children! Thank you for offering all your pains to God, even now when He is testing you through the fruits that you are reaping. Realize, dear children, that He loves you and for that reason He tests you. Always present your burdens to God and do not worry. [The "testing" was a long rain in the middle of the reaping season, which caused great damage to the harvest.]

October 18, 1984 Dear children! Today I ask you to read the Bible in your homes every day and let it be in a visible place there, so that it always encourages you to read and pray. Thank you for your response to my call.

October 25, 1984 Dear children! Pray during this month. God gave this month to me. I give it to you. Pray and ask for the graces of God. I will pray that He gives them to you. Thank you for your response to my call.

November 1, 1984 Dear children! Today I call you to renewal of family prayer in your homes. The field work is over. Now let all of you be devoted to prayer. Let prayer take the first place in your families. Thank you for your response to my call.

November 8, 1984 Dear children! You are not aware of the messages that God is sending to you through me. He is giving you great graces and you are not grasping them. Pray to the Holy Spirit for enlightenment. If you only knew the greatness of the graces God was giving you, you would pray without ceasing. Thank you for your response to my call.

November 15, 1984 You are a chosen people and God gave you great graces. You are not aware of every message I am giving you. Now I only wish to say: Pray, pray, pray! I do not know what else to tell you because I love you and wish that in prayer you come to know my love and the love of God. Thank you for your response to my call.

November 22, 1984 Dear children! These days live all the main messages and continue to root them into your hearts this week. Thank you for your response to my call.

November 29, 1984 Dear children! You do not know how to love and you do not know how to listen with love to the words I am giving you. Be aware, my beloved, that I am your mother and that I have come to the earth to teach you how to listen out of love, how to pray out of love, and not out of compulsion of the cross you are carrying. Through the cross God is being glorified in every man. Thank you for your response to my call.

December 6, 1984 Dear children! These days I am calling you to family prayer. In God's name many times I have been giving you messages but you did not listen. This Christmas will be unforgettable for you only if you accept the messages I am giving you. Dear children, do not allow the day of joy to be a day of greatest sorrow for me. Thank you for your response to my call.

December 8, 1984 [This was the Feast of the Immaculate Conception. Vicka had been taken to the hospital the night before to have an operation on her appendix. Ivan, Jacov, and Ivanka were present.] I am very happy with your prayer. Continue on this way.

December 13, 1984 Dear children! You know that the day of joy is coming near, but without love you will attain nothing. Therefore, first of all start loving your family and everyone in the parish, then you will be able to love and accept all those who are coming here. Let this week be the week of learning to love. Thank you for your response to my call.

December 20, 1984 Today I am asking you to do something practical for Jesus Christ. On the day of joy I wish that every family of the parish bring a flower as a sign of abandonment to Jesus. I wish that every member of the family have one flower next to the crib so that Jesus can come and see your devotion to Him. Thank you for your response to my call.

December 27, 1984 Dear children! This Christmas Satan wanted in a special way to thwart God's plans. You dear children have discerned Satan even on Christmas Day. But your hearts God has conquered. Let your hearts be continually joyful.

January 3, 1985 Dear children! These days the Lord has granted you many graces. Let this week be a week of thanksgiving for all the graces God has granted you. Thank you for your response to my call.

January 10, 1985 Dear children! Today I want to thank you for all your sacrifices. Especially, I thank those who have become dear to my heart and have come here gladly. There are many parishioners who are not listening to the messages. But because of those who are in a special way close to my heart, because of them, I give messages to the parish. And I will continue giving them for I love you and wish you to spread them by your hearts.

January 17, 1985 In these days Satan is fighting deviously against this parish, and you, dear children, are asleep in prayer, and only some are going to Mass. Persevere in these days of temptation. Thank you for your response to my call.

January 24, 1985 Dear children! These days you have savored the sweetness of God through renewal in your parish. Satan is working even more violently to take away the joy from each of you. Through prayer you can totally disarm him and ensure your happiness. Thank you for your response to my call.

January 31, 1985 Dear children! Today I wish to tell you to open your hearts to God like flowers in spring yearning for the sun. I am your mother and I always want you to be closer to the Father, that

He will always give abundant gifts to your heart. Thank you for your response to my call.

February 7, 1985 Dear children! Satan is manifesting himself in this parish in a particular way these days. Pray dear children that God's plan is carried out and that every work of Satan is turned to the glory of God. I have remained this long to help you in your great trials. Thank you for your response to my call.

February 14, 1985 Dear children! Today is the day when I give you the message for the parish, but the whole parish is not accepting the messages and does not live them. I am sad, and I wish you, dear children, to listen to me and to live my messages. Every family must pray family prayer and read the Bible. Thank you for your response to my call.

February 21, 1985 Dear children! From day to day I have been appealing to you for renewal and prayer in the parish. But you are not accepting. Today I am appealing to you for the last time. This is the season of Lent, and you as a parish in Lent can be moved, for the sake of love, to my call. If you do not do that, I do not wish to give you the messages that God has permitted me to give. Thank you for your response to my call.

February 28, 1985 Dear children! Today I call you to live the Word this week. "I love God!" Dear children, with love you will achieve everything, and even what you think is impossible. God wants this parish to belong to Him completely. And I want that too. Thank you for your response to my call.

March 7, 1985 Dear children! Today I invite you to renew prayer in your families. Dear children, encourage the very young to pray and to go to the Holy Mass. Thank you for your response to my call.

March 14, 1985 Dear children! In your life you have all experienced light and darkness. God gives to each person knowledge of good and evil. I am calling you to the light, which you have to carry to all people who are in darkness. From day to day people who are in darkness come to your homes. Give them, dear children, the light. Thank you for your response to my call.

March 21, 1985 Dear children! I want to give you the messages and therefore, today also I call you to live and to accept my messages. Dear children, I love you and in a special way I have chosen this parish, which is more dear to me than others where I have gladly been when the Almighty sent me. Therefore, I call you, accept me, dear children for your well-being. Follow the messages. Thank you for your response to my call.

March 24, 1985 Dear children! Today I wish to call you to confession, even if you had confession a few days ago. I wish you to experience my feast day within yourselves. You cannot, unless you give yourselves to God completely. And so I am calling you to reconciliation with God! Thank you for your response to my call.

March 29, 1985 Dear children! Today I want to call you to pray, pray, pray! In prayer you will come to know the greatest joy and the way out of every situation that has no way out. Thank you for moving ahead in prayer. Every individual is dear to my heart. And I thank all of you who have rekindled prayer in your families. Thank you for your response to my call.

April 4, 1985—Holy Thursday Dear children! I thank you because you begin to think of the glory of God in your hearts. Today is the day when I wanted to stop giving messages because some individuals did not accept me. The parish has responded, and I wish to continue giving you the messages, like never before in history since the beginning of time. Thank you for your response to my call.

April 5, 1985—Good Friday You, the parishioners, have a great and heavy cross. But do not be afraid to carry it. My Son is with you and He will help you. Thank you for your response to my call.

April 11, 1985 Dear children! Today I wish to say to everyone in the parish to pray in a special way for the enlightenment of the Holy Spirit. From today God wants to try the parish in a special way in order that He might strengthen it in faith. Thank you for your response to my call.

April 18, 1985 Dear children! Today I thank you for every opening of your hearts. Joy overwhelms me for every heart that opens to God, especially in the parish. Rejoice with me. Pray all the prayers for opening the sinful hearts. I want this. God wants this through me. Thank you for your response to my call.

April 25, 1985 Dear children! Today I want to tell you to begin to work in your hearts as you work in the fields. Work and change your hearts so that the spirit of God will move into your hearts. Thank you for your response to my call.

May 2, 1985 Dear children! Today I invite you to prayer with the heart and not only by habit. Some are coming but do not experience prayer. Therefore I beg you as a mother, pray, that prayer prevails in your heart in every moment. Thank you for your response to my call.

May 9, 1985 Dear children! You do not know how many graces God is giving you, these days when the Holy Spirit is working in a special way. You do not want to advance, your hearts are turned toward earthly things, and you are occupied by them. Turn your hearts to prayer and ask that the Holy Spirit be poured upon you. Thank you for your response to my call.

May 16, 1985 Dear children! I am calling you to more attentive prayer, and more participation in the Mass. I wish you to experience God within yourselves at Mass. I wish to say to the youth, especially, be open to the Holy Spirit, because God wants to draw you to Himself these days when Satan is active. Thank you for your response to my call.

May 23, 1985 Dear children! Open your hearts to the Holy Spirit in a special way these days. The Holy Spirit is working in a special way through you. Open your hearts and give your lives to Jesus, so that He will work through your hearts and strengthen you. Thank you for your response to my call.

May 30, 1985 I am calling you again to prayer of the heart. Let prayer, dear children, be your everyday food. In a special way now when work in the fields is exhausting you, you cannot pray with your heart. Pray and then you will overcome every tiredness. Prayer will be your happiness and rest. Thank you for your response to my call.

June 6, 1985 Dear children! In these days many people of all nationalities will come to the parish; and now I am telling you to love. Love first of all the members of your own family and then you might be able to accept in love all those who are coming. Thank you for your response to my call.

June 13, 1985 Dear children! Until the anniversary day I am calling you, you in the parish, to pray more. Let your prayer be a sign of your surrender to God. Dear children, I know about your tiredness. But you don't know how to surrender yourselves to me. These days surrender yourselves to me completely. Thank you for your response to my call.

June 20, 1985 Dear children! I wish on this feast day for you to open your hearts to the Lord of all hearts. Give me all your feelings and all your problems. I wish to console you in all your temptations. I wish to fill you with the peace, joy, and love of God. Thank you for your response to my call.

June 25, 1985 Dear children! I ask you to ask everyone to pray the rosary. With the rosary you will overcome all the troubles that Satan is trying to inflict on the Catholic Church. [Our Lady gave this message to Marija Pavlovic when she asked, "Our Lady, what do you wish to say to priests?"] Let all priests pray the rosary. Give time to the rosary.

June 27, 1985 Dear children! Today I give you the message through which I am calling you to humility. These days you have felt great joy because of all the people who are coming, and you have spoken about your experiences with love. Now I call you to continue in humility and with an open heart to speak to all those who are coming. Thank you for your response to my call.

July 4, 1985 Dear children! Thank you for every sacrifice you have offered. Now I urge you to offer every sacrifice with love. I desire that you who are helpless begin with trust. The Lord will give you always if you trust. Thank you for your response to my call.

July 11, 1985 Dear children! I love this parish and I protect it with my mantle from every work of Satan. Pray that Satan flees from the parish and from every individual who comes to this parish. In that way you will be able to hear every call and answer it with your life. Thank you for your response to my call.

July 18, 1985 Dear children! Today I am begging you to put more blessed objects in your homes, and that every person should carry blessed objects on himself. Let everything be blessed so that Satan will tempt you less because you are armed against him. Thank you for your response to my call.

July 25, 1985 Dear children! I want to shepherd you but you do not want to obey my messages. Today I call you to obey my messages and then you will be able to live everything that God tells me to relate to you. Open yourselves to God and God will work through you and give you everything you need. Thank you for your response to my call.

August 1, 1985 Dear children! I wish to tell you that I have chosen this parish. I guard it in my hands as a little flower that doesn't want to die. I am begging you to give yourselves to me, so that I can offer you as a gift to God, fresh and without sin. Satan has taken one part of the plan and wants to possess it. Pray that he does not succeed because I desire to have you for myself so I can offer you to God. Thank you for your response to my call.

August 8, 1985 Dear children! Today I am calling you to pray against Satan in a special way. Satan wants to work more now that you know he is active. Dear children, dress up in clothes of armor against Satan; with rosaries in your hands you will conquer. Thank you for your response to my call.

August 15, 1985 Dear children! Today I bless you and wish to tell you I love you. I appeal to you in this moment to live my messages. Today I bless you with a solemn blessing, which God grants me. Thank you for your response to my call.

August 22, 1985 Dear children! Today I wish to tell you that God wants to send you tests, which you can overcome with prayer. God is testing you through your everyday work. Now pray that you may overcome every temptation peacefully. Come through every test from God more open to Him, and come to Him with love. Thank you for your response to my call.

September 5, 1985 Dear children! Today I thank you for all your prayers. Pray continuously and more so that Satan will be far from this place. Dear children, the plan of Satan has been destroyed. Pray that every plan of God will be realized in this parish. I thank especially the youth for the sacrifices that they have offered. Thank you for your response to my call.

September 12, 1985 Dear children! I wish to tell you these days to put the cross at the center of your life. Pray especially before the cross from which great graces are coming. Now, in your homes make a special consecration to the cross of the Lord. Promise that you will not offend Jesus and that you will not insult Him. Thank you for your response to my call.

September 19, 1985 Dear children! Today, I am calling you to live in humility all the messages I give you. Dear children, do not glorify yourselves when living the messages by saying: "I live the messages." If you carry the messages in your heart and live them everyone will realize this, so there is no need for words, which serve only those who do not hear. For you it is not necessary to speak. For you my dear children it is necessary to live and witness by your lives. Thank you for your response to my call.

September 26, 1985 Dear children! I thank you for all your prayers. I thank you for all your sacrifices. I wish to tell you, dear children, to renew the messages I am giving you. Especially live the fasting, because with fasting you will give me joy for the fulfillment of all

God's plan here in Medjugorje. Thank you for your response to my call.

October 3, 1985 Dear children! I want to say to you, be thankful to God for every grace that God gave you and for all the fruit. Be thankful to the Lord and praise Him. Dear children, learn to be thankful in little things and then you will be able to be thankful in great things. Thank you for your response to my call.

October 10, 1985 Dear children! Today I want to call you to live the messages in this parish. Especially I want to call the young people to this parish because this parish is beloved to me. Dear children, if you are living the messages you will live the seed of holiness. As a mother I want to call all of you to holiness, so that you may give it to others because you are like a mirror for the people. Thank you for your response to my call.

October 17, 1985 Dear children! Everything has its time. Today, I invite you to start working on your hearts. All the work in the fields is finished. You find time to clean the least important places but you left your hearts aside. Work more and with love, clean your hearts. Thank you for your response to my call.

October 24, 1985 Dear children! I want to dress you from day to day in holiness, goodness, obedience, and love of God so that from day to day you can be better prepared for your Lord. Dear children, listen to my messages and live them. I desire to lead you. Thank you for your response to my call.

October 31, 1985 Dear children! Today I wish to call you to work in the Church. I do love you equally. I want you to work as much as you can in the Church. I know, dear children, that you can work but you do not want to work because you feel that you are unworthy of the duties. You have to be courageous. With the little flowers you enrich the Church and Jesus so that we can all be happy. Thank you for your response to my call.

November 7, 1985 Dear children! I am calling you to love your neighbors, to love those people from whom evil is coming to you, and so, in the power of love, you will be able to judge the intentions of the heart. Pray and love, dear children. In the power of love you can do even those things that seem impossible to you. Thank you for your response to my call.

November 14, 1985 Dear children! I, your mother, love you and I wish to urge you to prayer. I am, dear children, tireless and I call you, even when you are far away from my heart. I feel pain for everyone who has gone astray. But I am a mother and I forgive easily, and I rejoice for every child who comes back to me! Thank you for your response to my call.

November 21, 1985 Dear children! I wish to tell you that this time is special for you who are from the parish. In the summer you say that you have a lot of work to do. Now that there is no work in the fields, work on yourselves personally. Come to the Mass because this time has been given to you. Dear children, there are many of those who come regularly in spite of bad weather because they love me and they wish to show their love in a special way. I ask you to show me your love by coming to the Mass and the Lord will reward you abundantly. Thank you for your response to my call.

November 28, 1985 Dear children! I want to give thanks to all for what they have done for me, especially the young ones. I beg you, dear children, to come to prayer consciously and in prayer you will know the majesty of God. Thank you for your response to my call.

December 5, 1985 Dear children! I call you to prepare yourselves for Christmas by penance, prayer, and works of charity. Don't look at the material, because then you will not be able to experience Christmas. Thank you for your response to my call.

December 12, 1985 Dear children! For Christmas I invite you to give glory to Jesus together with me. I will give Him to you in a special way on that day, and I invite you on that day to give glory and praise with me to Jesus at His birth. Dear children, pray more on that day and think more about Jesus. Thank you for your response to my call.

December 19, 1985 Dear children! I want to invite you to love your neighbor. If you love your neighbor you will experience Jesus' love more, especially on Christmas Day. God will give you a great gift if you abandon yourself to Him. I want to give to mothers, in particular on Christmas Day, my maternal blessing and I will bless the others with His blessing. Thank you for your response to my call.

December 26, 1985 Dear children! I want to thank all of you who have listened to my messages and who have lived on Christmas Day what I have told you. I want to guide you. Put aside your sins now. Go forward in love from now on. Abandon your heart to me. Thank you for your response to my call. [On Christmas Day, Mary appeared with the baby Jesus.]

January 2, 1986 Dear children! I invite you to decide completely for God. I beg you, dear children, to surrender yourselves completely and you will be able to live everything I say to you. It will not be difficult for you to surrender yourselves completely to God. Thank you for your response to my call.

January 9, 1986 Dear children! I invite you to prayer so that with your prayers you will help Jesus to realize all plans that are here. By offerings and sacrifices to Jesus everything will be fulfilled that is planned. Satan cannot do anything. Thank you for your response to my call.

January 16, 1986 Dear children! I invite you to pray. I need your prayers so much in order that God may be glorified through all of you. Dear children, I beg you to listen and to live your mother's call because I am calling you, by reason of my love, so that I can help you. Thank you for your response to my call.

January 23, 1986 Dear children! Again I invite you to prayer of the heart. If you pray from your heart, dear children, the ice-cold hearts of your brothers will be melted and every barrier will disappear. Conversion will be easily achieved by those who want it. You must intercede for this gift for your neighbors. Thank you for your response to my call.

January 30, 1986 Dear children! Today I invite all of you to pray in order that God's plan for you and all that God wills through you may be realized. Help others to be converted, especially those who are coming to Medjugorje. Dear children, do not allow Satan to reign in your hearts. Do not be an image of Satan, but be my image. I am calling you to pray so that you may be witnesses of my presence. God cannot fulfill His will without you. God gave everyone free will and it is up to you to be disposed. Thank you for your response to my call.

February 7, 1986 Dear children! This parish is elected by me and is special. It is different from others and I am giving great graces to all who are praying from their hearts. Dear children, I am giving you my messages first of all for the parish and then for all others. The messages are first of all for you, and then for others who will accept them. You will be responsible to me and to my Son Jesus. Thank you for your response to my call.

February 13, 1986 Dear children! This Lent is a special incentive for you to change. Start from this moment. Turn off the television and renounce other things that are useless. Dear children, I am calling you individually to convert. This time is for you. Thank you for your response to my call.

February 20, 1986 Dear children! The second message for Lenten days is that you renew your prayer before the cross. Dear children, I am giving you special graces and Jesus is giving you special gifts from the cross. Accept them and live them. Reflect on Jesus' passion and unite yourselves to Jesus in life. Thank you for your response to my call.

February 27, 1986 Dear children! Be humble. Live in humility. Thank you for your response to my call.

March 6, 1986 Dear children! Today I am calling you to open yourselves more to God so that He can work through you. For as much as you open yourselves you will receive the fruits from it. I wish to call you again to prayer. Thank you for your response to my call.

March 13, 1986 Dear children! Today I am calling you to live this Lent with your little sacrifices. Thank you for every sacrifice you have brought me. Dear children, live in such a way continuously and with love. Help me to bring offerings of your sacrifices to God for which He will reward you. Thank you for your response to my call.

March 20, 1986 Dear children! I am calling you to an active approach to prayer. You wish to live everything I am telling you, but you do not have results from your efforts because you do not pray. Dear children, I beg you to open yourselves and begin to pray. Prayer will be joy. If you begin, it will not be boring because you will pray out of pure joy. Thank you for your response to my call.

March 27, 1986 Dear children! I wish to thank you for your sacrifices and I invite you to the greater sacrifice, the sacrifice of love. Without love you are not able to accept me or my Son. Without love you cannot witness your experience to others. That is why I invite you, dear children, to begin to live the love in your hearts. Thank you for your response to my call.

April 3, 1986 Dear children! I wish to call you to live the Holy Mass. There are many of you who have experienced the beauty of the Mass but there are some who come unwillingly. I have chosen you, dear children, and Jesus is giving you His graces in the Holy Mass. Therefore, consciously live the Holy Mass. Let every coming to Holy Mass be joyful. Come with love and accept the Holy Mass. Thank you for your response to my call.

April 10, 1986 Dear children! I wish to call you to grow in love. A flower cannot grow without water. Neither can you grow without God's blessing. You should pray for blessings from day to day so that you can grow up normally and carry your activities with God. Thank you for your response to my call.

April 17, 1986 Dear children! Now you are preoccupied about material things and in the material you lose everything that God wants to give you. I am inviting you, dear children, to pray for the gifts of the Holy Spirit that you need now, in order that you may witness my presence here and in everything I am giving you. Dear children, abandon yourselves to me so that I can lead you totally. Do not be so preoccupied about the material things of this world. Thank you for your response to my call.

April 24, 1986 Dear children! Today I am calling you to prayer. You are forgetting that everyone is important, especially the elderly in the family. Incite them to pray. Let all the youth be an example by their lives and testify for Jesus. Dear children, I beg you to start transforming yourselves through prayer and then you will know what you have to do. Thank you for your response to my call.

May 1, 1986 Dear children! I ask you to begin to change your life in your families. Let your family be a harmonious flower, which I wish to give to Jesus. Dear children, every family should be active in prayer. It is my wish that the fruits of prayer will be seen one day in the family. Only in that way will I give you as petals to Jesus in fulfillment of God's plan. Thank you for your response to my call.

May 8, 1986 Dear children! You are responsible for the messages. The source of grace is here, but you, dear children, are the vehicles transmitting the gifts. Therefore, dear children, I am calling you to work responsibly. Everyone will be responsible according to his own measure. Dear children, I am calling you to give the gift to others with love and not to keep it for yourselves. Thank you for your response to my call.

May 15, 1986 Dear children! Today, I am calling you to give me your heart so I can change it to be like mine. You are asking yourselves, dear children, why you cannot respond to what I am asking from you. You cannot because you have not given me your heart so I can change it. You are seeking, but not acting. I call you to do everything I tell you. In that way I will be with you. Thank you for your response to my call.

May 22, 1986 Dear children! Today I will give you my love. You don't know, dear children, how great is my love and you don't know how to accept it. In many ways I wish to express it but you, dear children, do not recognize it. You don't comprehend my words with your heart and so you are not able to comprehend my love. Dear children, accept me in your life so you will be able to accept all I am saying to you and all I am calling you for. Thank you for your response to my call.

May 29, 1986 Dear children! Today I am calling you to a life of love toward God and your neighbor. Without love, dear children, you cannot do anything. Therefore, dear children, I am calling you to live in mutual love. Only in that way can you love me and accept everyone around you. Through coming to your parish, everyone will feel my love through you. Therefore, today I beg you to start with the burning love with which I love you. Thank you for your response to my call.

June 5, 1986 Dear children! Today I am calling you to decide if you wish to live the messages I am giving you. I wish you to be active in living and transmitting the messages. Especially, dear children, I desire you to be the reflections of Jesus, who enlightens an unfaithful world that is walking in darkness. I wish that all of you may be a light to all and witness to the light. Dear children, you are not called to darkness, you are called to light and to live the light in your lives. Thank you for your response to my call.

June 12, 1986 Dear children! Today I am begging you to pray the rosary with lively faith. Only this way can I help you. Pray, I cannot help you because you don't want to be moved. Dear children, I am calling you to pray the rosary. The rosary should be your commitment, prayed by you with joy and so you will understand why I am visiting you for such a long time. I want to teach you to pray. Thank you for your response to my call.

June 19, 1986 Dear children! In these days the Lord has allowed me to intercede for more graces for you. Therefore, dear children, I want to urge you once again to prayer. Pray constantly and in this way I will give you the joy that the Lord gives me. With these graces, dear children, I want your suffering to be for you a joy. I am your mother, and I want to help you. Thank you for your response to my call.

June 24–25, 1986—The Anniversary [On the anniversary Mary said that she was giving special blessings to all who had come and to all who were associated with Medjugorje. On the evening of June 24 Mary appeared on the mountaintop to Marija and Ivan, where a group of people had gathered. Marija said she recommended everyone to the Madonna. The Virgin blessed everyone and said, "Continue to pray here. Pray the rosary again." She (Mary) said that this Tabor is for everyone and that we should bring this Tabor experience to all our homes. With this Tabor experience we must bring peace and reconciliation. Marija said that Mary appeared with five angels and that she was very happy.]

June 26, 1986 Dear children! God allowed me to bring about this oasis of peace. I want to invite you to guard it and let the oasis remain pure. Always there are those who are destroying peace and prayer by their carelessness. I am calling you to witness and, by your life, preserve peace. Thank you for your response to my call.

July 3, 1986 Dear children! Today, I am calling you to prayer. Without prayer you cannot feel me, nor God, nor the graces I am giving you. Therefore, I call you always to begin and end each day with prayer. Dear children, I wish to lead you evermore in prayer, but you cannot grow because you don't want it. I invite you to let prayer have the first place. Thank you for your response to my call.

July 10, 1986 Dear children! Today I invite you to holiness. You cannot live without holiness. Consequently, overcome all sin with love. Overcome every difficulty you meet with love. Dear children, I beg you to live love within yourselves. Thank you for your response to my call.

July 17, 1986 Dear children! Today, I invite you to meditate on why I am with you for such a long time. I am the mediator between you and God. For that reason, I would like to invite you to live always, out of love, what God is expecting from you. Dear children, live all the messages that I give you in complete humility. Thank you for your response to my call.

July 24, 1986 Dear children! I am happy about all of you who are on the way of holiness, and I am begging you to help all those with your witness who don't know how to live in the way of holiness. For that reason, dear children, your families should be the place where holiness is born. Help everybody to live in a sanctified way, especially your own family. Thank you for your response to my call.

July 31, 1986 Dear children! Hatred creates division and does not see anybody or anything. I invite you always to carry unity and peace. Especially, dear children, act with love in the place where you live. Let love always be your only tool. With love turn everything to good that the devil wants to destroy and take to himself. Only this way will you be completely mine and I will be able to help you. Thank you for your response to my call.

August 7, 1986 Dear children! You know I promised you an oasis of peace here, but you are not aware that around every oasis is a desert where Satan is lurking; he wants to tempt each one of you. Dear children, only by prayer are you able to overcome every influence of Satan in your place. I am with you, but I can't take away your free will. Thank you for your response to my call.

August 14, 1986 Dear children! I am inviting you so that your prayer may be a joyful encounter with the Lord. I cannot guide you unless you yourself experience joy in prayer. I want to guide you in prayer more and more, from day to day, but I do not want to force you. Thank you for your response to my call.

August 21, 1986 Dear children, I am grateful for the love you are showing me. Dear children, you know that I am loving you without limit and that I am praying daily to the Lord so that He may help you to understand the love I am showing you. Therefore, dear children, pray and pray and pray. Thank you for your response to my call.

August 28, 1986 Dear children! I call you to be a picture to everyone and everything, especially in prayer and witnessing. Dear children, I cannot help the world without you. I want you to cooperate with me in everything, even in the smallest things by your prayer from your heart and by surrendering to me completely. Dear children, help me. In that way I will be able to teach you and to lead you on this road, which I began with you. Thank you for your response to my call.

September 4, 1986 Dear children! Today again I am calling you to prayer and fasting. You know, dear children, with your help I can do everything and force Satan not to seduce people to evil and to remove him from this place. Satan, dear children, watches for every individual. He wants particularly to bring confusion to every one of you. Dear children, I ask that your every day becomes prayer and complete surrender to God. Thank you for your response to my call.

September 11, 1986 Dear children! For these days when you celebrate the cross with joy, I wish your cross to be joyful. Dear children, pray that you can accept sickness and suffering with love like Jesus. Only in that way can I give you the graces of healing with the joy that Jesus allows. Thank you for your response to my call.

September 18, 1986 Dear children! Today again I am grateful for everything you have done for me in these days. I am thanking you in the name of Jesus, especially for the sacrifices you offered in the last week. Dear children, you are forgetting that I want sacrifices from you to help you and to banish Satan from you. Therefore, I am calling you again to offer sacrifices with a special reverence toward God. Thank you for your response to my call.

September 23, 1986 Dear children, through your own peace, I am calling you to help others to see and to start searching for peace. Dear children, you are at peace and therefore, you cannot comprehend the absence of peace. Again, I am calling you so that through prayer and your life you will help destroy everything evil in people and uncover the deception that Satan is using. Pray for truth to prevail in every heart. Thank you for your response to my call.

October 2, 1986 Dear children! Today again I invite you to prayer. You, dear children, do not realize the preciousness of prayer. Now is the time of prayer. Now, nothing else is important. Now, nobody is important except God. Dear children, dedicate yourselves to prayer with special love. Only in that way can God give you graces. Thank you for your response to my call.

October 9, 1986 Dear children! You know that I wish to guide you on the way of holiness, but I do not want to force you. I do not want you to be holy by force. I wish every one of you to help yourselves and me by your little sacrifices so that I can guide you to be more holy day by day. Therefore, dear children, I do not want to force you to live the messages; but rather this long time I am with you shows that I love you immeasurably and that I wish every single one of you to be holy. Thank you for your response to my call.

October 15, 1986 Dear children! Today, also, I want to show you how much I love you. I am sorry that I am not able to help each and every one of you to fathom my love. Therefore, dear children, I am calling you to prayer and complete surrender to God, because Satan wants to conquer you in everyday affairs. He wants to take the first place in your life. Pray, dear children, without ceasing. Thank you for your response to my call.

October 24, 1986 Dear children! Today I invite you to pray. I give you a special invitation, dear children, to pray for peace. Without your prayers, my dear children, I cannot help you to understand what my Lord has given me to give you. Therefore, dear children, pray that peace will be given to you by God. Thank you for your response to my call.

October 30, 1986 Dear children! Today also I want to call you to take seriously and live the messages that I am giving you. Dear children, because of you I have remained this long to help you to put into practice all the messages that I am giving you. Therefore, dear children, out of love for me live all the messages that I am giving you. Thank you for your response to my call.

November 6, 1986 Today, I would like to invite you to pray day by day for the souls in purgatory. Every soul needs prayer and grace to reach God and His love. With this, you too, dear children, will find new intercessors who will help you in life to know that all the things of this earth are not important to you. The only one you have to turn to is in heaven. For this reason, dear children, pray without interruption so that you might help yourselves and those whom prayer gives you. Thank you for your response to my call.

November 13, 1986 Dear children! Today, also, I call you to pray with your whole heart and to change your life day by day. Especially,

I am calling you, dear children, by your prayers and sacrifices. Begin to live in holiness, because I want every one of you who has been here at this spring of grace to come to heaven with a special gift for me, the gift of holiness. Therefore, dear children, pray daily and change your life in order that you may be holy. I will always be close to you. Thank you for your response to my call.

November 20, 1986 Dear children! Today, also, I am calling you to live and to pay attention with a special love to all the messages I am giving you. God does not want you lukewarm and indecisive, but totally committed to Him. You know that I love you and that I am burning out of love for you. Therefore, dear children, commit yourselves to love so that you will comprehend and burn with God's love from day to day. Decide for love, dear children, so that love may prevail in all of you, not human love, but God's love. Thank you for your response to my call.

November 27, 1986 Dear children! Today, also, I invite you to dedicate your life to me with love, in order that I can guide you with love. I love you, dear children, with a special love and I want to bring you to heaven to God. I want you to comprehend that this life is very short in comparison with that in heaven. Therefore, dear children, today decide anew for God. Only in that way can I show you how much you are beloved to me and how much I want all of you to be saved and to be with me in heaven. Thank you for your response to my call.

December 4, 1986 Dear children! Today, also, I invite you to prepare your hearts for these days when the Lord is about to purify you in a special way from all the sins of your past life. You, dear children, cannot do it by yourselves, and for that reason I am here to help you. Pray, dear children. Only in that way will you be able to recognize all the evil that dwells in you, and abandon it to the Lord so that He may purify your hearts completely. So, dear children, pray without ceasing and prepare your hearts in penance and fasting. Thank you for your response to my call.

December 11, 1986 Dear children! I invite you especially to pray during this season so that you may experience the joy of meeting the newborn Jesus. Dear children, I desire that you experience these days just as I experience them, with joy. I wish to guide you and show you the joy that I want to bring to all of you. Therefore, dear children, pray and surrender yourselves completely to me. Thank you for your response to my call.

December 18, 1986 Dear children! Once again today I want to invite you to pray. When you pray, dear children, you become more beautiful. You become like flowers, which after the snow show forth their beauty, and whose colors become indescribable. And so you, dear children, after prayer before God display everything that is beautiful so that you may become beloved by Him. Therefore, dear children, pray and open your inner self to the Lord so that He may make of you a harmonious and beautiful flower for heaven. Thank you for your response to my call.

December 25, 1986 Dear children! Today also I am grateful to my Lord for all He is giving me, especially for this gift of being with you again today. Dear children, these are the days in which the Father is giving special graces to all who open their hearts. I am blessing you. My desire, dear children, is that you may recognize God's graces and place everything at His disposal so that He may be glorified by you. My heart follows all your steps attentively. Thank you for your response to my call.

January 1, 1987 Dear children! Today I want to call you to live the messages I am giving you in the New Year. Dear children, you know that for your sake I have remained so long as to teach you how to walk on the road of holiness. Therefore, dear children, pray without ceasing and live the messages I am giving you. For I do it with great love toward God and you. Thank you for your response to my call.

January 8, 1987 Dear children! I want to thank you for every response to my call. I want to thank you for all the suffering and prayers you have offered to me. Dear children, I want to give you messages from now onward no longer every Thursday, but on the twenty-fifth of each month. The time has come when what our Lord wanted has been fulfilled. From now on I give you fewer messages but I will be with you. Therefore, dear children, I beg you to listen and to live my messages so I can guide you. Thank you for your response to my call.

January 25, 1987 Dear children! Today again, I want to call you to begin to live the new life from today onward. Dear children, I want you to comprehend that God has chosen each one of you in order to use you for the great plan of salvation of mankind. You cannot comprehend how great your role is in God's plan. Therefore, dear children, pray so that through prayer you may comprehend God's plan toward you. I am with you so that you can realize it completely. Thank you for your response to my call.

February 25, 1987 Dear children! Today I would like to envelop you with my mantle and lead you toward the road to resurrection. Dear children, I beg you to give our Lord your past and all the evil that has accumulated in your hearts. I want all of you to be happy and with sin no one can be happy. That is why, dear children, you must pray and in your prayers you will realize the path to happiness. Happiness will be in your heart and you will be the witness to that which I and my Son want for all of you. I bless you, dear children. Thank you for your response to my call.

March 25, 1987 Dear children! Today I thank you for your presence in this place where I give special graces. I call upon each one of you to start living the life that God wants from you and to start doing good deeds of love and generosity. I do not want you, dear children, to live the messages and commit the sins, which I do not like. Therefore, dear children, I want each of you to live the new life without destroying everything God creates in you. I give you my special blessing and I remain with you on your way to conversion. Thank you for your response to my call.

April 25, 1987 Dear children! Today I am inviting you to pray. You know, dear children, that God is granting special graces in prayer. Therefore, dear children, seek and pray in order that you may be able to understand all I am giving you in this place. I am calling you, dear children, to pray with your hearts. You know that without prayer you cannot comprehend all that God is planning through each one of you, and so, pray please. I want that, through every one of you, God's plan may be realized, and all that God has given you in your heart may increase. Therefore, pray that God's blessing may protect every one of you from all the evil that is threatening you. I am blessing you, dear children. Thank you for your response to my call.

May 25, 1987 Dear children! I invite every one of you to start living in God's love. Dear children, you are ready to commit sins and to put yourselves in the hands of Satan without reflecting. I call on every one of you to consciously decide yourselves for God and against Satan. I am your mother and therefore I want to lead all of you to perfect holiness. I want every one of you to be happy here on earth and every one of you to be with me in heaven. This is, dear children, the reason of my coming here and is my desire. Thank you for your response to my call.

June 25, 1987 Dear children! Today I thank you and want to invite you all to God's peace. I want to invite you to experience in your heart that peace that God gives. Today I want to bless all of you. I bless you with God's blessing. I beg you, dear children, to follow and to live my way. I love you dear children, and therefore, I continue to invite you. I thank you for all that you are doing for my intentions. I beg you to help me present you to God, and to save you and to lead you on the way of salvation. Thank you for your response to my call.

July 25, 1987 Dear children! I beseech you to take up the way of holiness and to begin today. I love you, and therefore, want you to be holy. I do not want Satan to block the way. Dear children, pray and accept all that God is offering you and realize that the way is going to be bitter, but at the same time God will reveal every sweetness to whoever begins to go in that way. And He will gladly answer every call. Do not attribute importance to petty things, but long for heaven and holiness. Thank you for your response to my call.

August 25, 1987 Dear children! Today also, I am inviting each one of you to decide to live in my messages. God has permitted me also, in this year that the Church has dedicated to me, to be able to speak to you and to spur you on to holiness. Dear children, seek from God the graces that He has given you through me. I am ready to intercede with God all that you seek so that your holiness may be complete. Therefore, dear children, do not forget to seek, because God has permitted me to obtain graces for you. Thank you for your response to my call.

September 25, 1987 Dear children! Today, I wish to invite you all to pray. Let prayer be life to you. Dear children, dedicate your time only to Jesus and He will give you everything that you are seeking. He will avail Himself to you completely. Dear children, Satan is strong and is waiting to test each one of you. Pray and that way he will neither be able to injure you nor block you on your way to holiness. Dear children, grow from day to day through prayer, always toward God. Thank you for your response to my call.

October 25, 1987 My dear children! Today, I wish to invite all of you to decide for paradise. The way is difficult for those who have not decided for God. Dear children, decide and believe that God is offering Himself to you in His fullness. You are invited and you need to answer the call of the Father, who is calling you through me. Pray, because in prayer each one of you will be able to achieve complete love. I am blessing you and I desire to help you so each one of you might be under my motherly mantle. Thank you for your response to my call.

November 25, 1987 Dear children! Today also I invite each one of you to decide again to surrender everything completely to me. Only that way will I be able to present each one of you to God. Dear children, you know that I love you immeasurably and that I desire each of you for myself. But God has given to all a freedom, which I lovingly respect and to which I humbly submit. I desire, dear children, that you help so that everything God has planned in this parish shall be realized. If you do not pray you will not be able to recognize my love and the plans God has for this parish and for each individual. Pray that Satan does not entice you with his pride and deceptive strength. I am with you and want you to believe me that I love you. Thank you for having responded to my call.

December 25, 1987 Dear children, rejoice with me. My heart is rejoicing because of Jesus and today I want to give Him to you. Dear children, I want each one of you to open your hearts to Jesus and I will give Him to you with love. Dear children, I want Him to change you, to teach you, and to protect you. Today I am praying in a special way for each one of you, and I am presenting you to God so He will manifest Himself in you. I am calling you to sincere prayer with the heart so that every prayer of yours may be an encounter with God. In your work and in your everyday life do put God in the first place. I invite you today with great seriousness to obey me and to do as I am inviting you. Thank you for responding to my call.

January 25, 1988 Dear children! Today, again I am calling you to complete conversion, which is difficult for those who have not chosen God. I am inviting you, dear children, to convert fully to God. God can give you everything that you seek from Him. But you seek God only when sicknesses, problems, and difficulties come to you and you think that God is far from you and is not listening and does not hear your prayers. No, dear children, that is not the truth. When you are far from God, you cannot receive graces because you do not seek them with a firm faith. Day by day, I am praying for you and I want to draw you evermore near to God, but I cannot if you don't want it. Therefore, dear children, put your life in God's hands. I bless you all. Thank you for responding to my call.

February 25, 1988 Dear children! Today again I am calling you to prayer and complete surrender to God. You know that I love you and am coming here out of love so I could show you the path of peace and salvation for your souls. I want you to obey me and not permit Satan to seduce you. Dear children, Satan is very strong and therefore I ask you to dedicate your prayers to me so that those who are under his influence may be saved. Give witness by your life; sacrifice your life for the salvation of the world. I am with you and am grateful to you, but in heaven you shall receive the Father's reward, which He has promised to you. Therefore, dear children, do not be afraid. If you pray Satan cannot injure you even a little, because you are God's children and He is watching over you. Pray and let the rosary always be in your hands as a sign to Satan that you belong to me. Thank you for responding to my call.

March 25, 1988 Dear children! Today, also, I am inviting you to complete surrender to God. Dear children, you are not conscious of how God loves you with such a great love, because He permits me to be with you so I can instruct you and help you to find the way of peace. This way, however, you cannot discover if you do not pray. Therefore, dear children, forsake everything and consecrate your time to God and then God will bestow gifts upon you and bless you. Little children, do not forget your life is fleeting like a spring flower, which today is wondrously beautiful and tomorrow has vanished. Therefore, pray in such a way that your prayer, your surrender to God, may become like a road sign. That way your witness will not only have value for yourself, but for all eternity. Thank you for having responded to my call.

April 25, 1988 Dear children! God wants to make you holy. Therefore, through me He is inviting you to complete surrender. Let Holy Mass be your life. Understand that church is God's palace, the place in which I gather you and want to show you the way to God. Come and pray. Neither look at others nor slander them, but rather, let your life be a testimony on the way of holiness. Churches deserve respect and are set apart as holy because God who became man dwells in them day and night. Therefore, little children, believe and pray that the Father increase your faith, and then ask for whatever you need. I am with you and I am rejoicing because of your conversion and I am protecting you with my motherly mantle. Thank you for having responded to my call.

May 25, 1988 Dear children! I am inviting you to a complete surrender to God. Pray, little children, that Satan may not carry you about like branches in the wind. Be strong in God. I desire that through you the whole world may get to know the God of joy. By your life bear witness for God's joy. Do not be anxious or worried. God Himself will help you and show you the way. I desire that you love all men with my love. Only in that way can love reign over the world. Little children, you are mine. I love you and I want you to surrender to me so that I can lead you to God. Never cease praying so that Satan cannot take advantage of you. Pray for the knowledge that you are mine. I bless you with blessings of joy. Thank you for responding to my call.

June 25, 1988 Dear children! Today I am calling you to that love that is loyal and pleasing to God. Little children, love bears everything bitter and difficult for the sake of Jesus, who is love. Therefore, dear children, pray that God comes to your aid, not however according to your desires, but according to His. Surrender yourselves to God so that He may heal you, console you, and forgive everything inside of you that is a hindrance on the way of love. In this way, God can move your life and you will grow in love. Dear children, glorify God with a hymn of love so that God's love may be able to grow in you day by day to its fullness. Thank you for having responded to my call.

July 25, 1988 Dear children! Today I am calling you to complete surrender to God. Everything you do and everything you possess give over to God so that He can take control in your life as the king of all that you possess. That way, through me, God can lead you into the depths of the spiritual life. Little children, do not be afraid because I am with you, even if you think there is no way out and that Satan is in control. I am bringing peace to you. I am your mother and the Queen of Peace. I am blessing you with the blessings of joy so that for you God may be everything in your life. Thank you for having responded to my call.

August 25, 1988 Dear children! Today I invite you all to rejoice in the life that God gives you. Little children, rejoice in God, the Creator, because He has created you so wonderfully. Pray that your life may be full of joy and thanksgiving, which flows out of your heart like a river of joy. Little children, give thanks unceasingly for all that you possess and for each little gift that God has given you so that a joyful blessing always comes down from God upon your life. Thank you for having responded to my call.

September 25, 1988 Dear children! Today I am inviting all of you without exception to the way of holiness in your life. God gave you the grace and the gift of holiness. Pray that you may comprehend it more and more, and in such a way you will be able by your life to be a witness for God. Dear children, I am blessing you and I intercede for you to God, so that your witness may be a complete one and a joy for God. Thank you for having responded to my call.

October 25, 1988 Dear children! My invitation that you live the messages that I am giving you is a daily one. Especially, little children, because I want to draw you closer to the Heart of Jesus. Therefore, little children, I am inviting you today to the prayer of consecration to Jesus, my dear Son, so that each of your hearts may be His. And then, I am inviting you to consecration of my Immaculate Heart. I want you to consecrate yourselves as persons, as families, and as parishes, so that all belongs to God through my hands. Therefore, dear little children, pray that you may comprehend the greatness of this message that I am giving you. I do not want anything for myself, rather, all for the salvation of your souls. Satan is strong and therefore, you, little children, by constant prayer, press tight against my motherly heart. Thank you for having responded to my call.

November 25, 1988 Dear children! I am inviting you to prayer so that in prayer you have an encounter with God. God is offering and giving Himself to you. But He seeks from you that you answer His call in your freedom. Therefore, little children, set a time during the day when you can pray in peace and in humility and meet with God the Creator. I am with you and I intercede with God for you. So be on watch that every encounter in prayer be a joyful meeting with God. Thank you for having responded to my call.

December 25, 1988 Dear children! I am inviting you to peace. Live peace in your heart and in your surroundings so that all men may recognize the peace, which does not come from you but from God. Little children, today is a great day. Rejoice with me. Celebrate the birth of Jesus with my peace, the peace with which I come as your mother, the Queen of Peace. Today, I am giving you my special blessing. Bring it to every creature so that each one may have peace. Thank you for having responded to my call.

January 25, 1989 Dear children! Today I am calling you to the way of holiness. Pray that you may comprehend the beauty and greatness of this way where God reveals Himself to you in a special way. Pray that you may be open to everything that God does through you and that, in your life, you may be able to give thanks to God and to rejoice over everything that He does through each individual. I give you my blessing. Thank you for having responded to my call.

February 25, 1989 Dear children! Today I invite you to prayer of the heart. Throughout this season of grace, I wish each of you to be united with Jesus, but without unceasing prayer you cannot experience the beauty and greatness of the grace that God is offering you. Therefore, little children, at all times fill your heart with even the smallest prayers. I am with you and unceasingly keep watch over every heart that is given to me. Thank you for having responded to my call.

March 25, 1989 Dear children! I am calling you to a complete surrender to God. I am calling you to great joy and peace, which only God can give. I am with you and I intercede for you every day before God. I call you, little children, to listen to me and to live the messages that I am giving you. Already for years, you are invited to holiness. But you are still far away. I am blessing you! Thank you for having responded to my call.

April 25, 1989 Dear children! I am calling you to a complete surrender to God. Let everything that you possess be in the hands of God. Only in that way shall you have joy in your heart. Little children, rejoice in everything you have. Give thanks to God because everything is God's gift to you. That way in your life you shall be able to give thanks for everything and discover God in everything, even in the smallest flower. Thank you for having responded to my call.

May 25, 1989 Dear children, I invite you now to be open to God. See, children, how nature is opening herself and is giving life and fruit. In this same way, I invite you to live with God and to surrender everything completely to Him. Children, I am with you and I want to introduce you continuously to the joy of life. I desire that everyone may discover the joy and love that can be found only in God and that only God can give. God doesn't want anything from you, only your surrender. Therefore, children, decide seriously for God because everything else passes away. Only God doesn't pass away. Pray to be able to discover the greatness and joy of life that God gives you. Thank you for having responded to my call.

June 25, 1989 Dear children! Today I call you to live the messages that I have been giving you during the past eight years. This is the time of grace and I desire the grace of God be great for every single one of you. I am blessing you and I love you with a special love. Thank you for having responded to my call.

July 25, 1989 Dear children! Today I am calling you to renew your heart. Open yourself to God and surrender to Him all your difficulties and crosses, so God may turn everything into joy. Little children, you cannot open yourself to God if you do not pray. Therefore, from today decide to consecrate a time in the day only for an encounter with God in silence. In that way you will be able, with God, to witness my presence here. Little children, I do not wish to force you, rather freely give God your time like children of God. Thank you for having responded to my call.

August 25, 1989. Dear children! I call you to prayer. By means of prayer, little children, you obtain joy and peace. Through prayer you are richer in the mercy of God. Therefore, little children, let prayer be the life of each one of you. Especially I call you to pray so that all of those who are far away from God may be converted. Then all hearts will be richer because God will rule in the hearts of all men. Therefore, little children, pray, pray, pray. Let prayer begin to rule in the whole world. Thank you for having responded to my call.

September 25, 1989 Dear children! Today I invite you to give thanks to God for all the gifts you have discovered in the course of your life, and even for the least gift you have perceived. I give thanks with you and want all of you to experience the joy of these gifts, and I want God to be everything for each one of you. And then, little children, you can grow continuously on the way of holiness. Thank you for having responded to my call.

October 25, 1989 Dear children! Today also I am inviting you to prayer. I am always inviting you, but you are still far away. Therefore, from today, decide seriously to dedicate time to God. I am with you and I wish to teach you to pray with the heart. In prayer with the heart you shall encounter God. Therefore, little children, pray, pray, pray! Thank you for having responded to my call.

November 25, 1989 Dear children! I am inviting you for years by these messages that I am giving you. Little children, by means of the messages I wish to make a very beautiful mosaic in your heart, so that I might be able to present each one of you to God like the original image. Therefore, little children, I desire that your decision be free before God, because He has given you freedom. Therefore, pray so that, free from any influence of Satan, you may decide only for God. I am praying for you before God and I am seeking your surrender to God. Thank you for having responded to my call.

December 25, 1989 Dear children! Today I am blessing you in a special way with my motherly blessing, and I am interceding for you before God that He will give you the gift of conversion of the heart. For years I am calling you and exhorting you to a deep spiritual life and simplicity. But you are so cold. Therefore, little children, I ask you to accept and to live the messages with seriousness so that your soul will not be sad when I will no longer be with you, and when I will no longer lead you like insecure children in their first steps. Therefore, little children, each day read the messages that I have given you and transform them into life. I love you and, therefore, I am calling you all to the way of salvation with God. Thank you for having responded to my call.

January 25, 1990 Dear children! Today I invite you to decide for God once again and to choose Him before everything and above everything, so that He may work miracles in your life and that day by day your life may become joy with Him. Therefore, little children, pray and do not permit Satan to work in your life through misunderstandings, not understanding and not accepting one another. Pray that you may be able to comprehend the greatness and the beauty of the gift of life. Thank you for having responded to my call.

February 25, 1990 Dear children! I invite you to surrender to God. In this season I especially want you to renounce all the things to which you are attached, but are hurting your spiritual life. Therefore, little children, decide completely for God and do not allow Satan to come into your life through those things that hurt both you and your spiritual life. Little children, God is offering Himself to you in fullness and you can discover and recognize Him only in prayer. Therefore, make a decision for prayer. Thank you for having responded to my call.

March 25, 1990 Dear children! I am with you even if you are not conscious of it. I want to protect you from everything that Satan offers you and through which he wants to destroy you. As I bore Jesus in my womb, so also, dear children, do I wish to bear you unto holiness. God wants to save you and sends you messages through man, nature, and so many things which can only help you to understand that you must change the direction of your life. Therefore, little children, understand also the greatness of the gift that God is giving you through me, so that I may protect you with my mantle and lead you to the joy of life. Thank you for having responded to my call.

April 25, 1990 Dear children! Today I invite you to accept with seriousness and to live the messages that I am giving you. I am with you and I desire, dear children, that each one of you be ever closer to my heart. Therefore, little children, pray and seek the will of God in your everyday life. I desire that each one of you discover the way of holiness and grow in it until eternity. I will pray for you and intercede for you before God that you understand the greatness of this gift that God is giving me that I can be with you. Thank you for having responded to my call.

May 25, 1990 Dear children! I invite you to decide with seriousness to live this novena [preceding the feast of Pentecost]. Consecrate the time to prayer and to sacrifice. I am with you, and I desire to help you to grow in renunciation and mortification that you may be able to understand the beauty of the life of people who go on giving themselves to me in a special way. Dear children, God blesses you day after day and desires a change of your life. Therefore, pray that you may have the strength to change your life. Thank you for having responded to my call.

June 25, 1990 Dear children! Today I desire to thank you for all your sacrifices and for all your prayers. I am blessing you with my special motherly blessing. I invite you all to decide for God, so that from day to day you will discover His will in prayer. I desire, dear children, to call all of you to a full conversion so that joy will be in your hearts. I am happy that you are here today in such great numbers. Thank you for having responded to my call.

July 25, 1990 Dear children! Today I invite you to peace. I have come here as the Queen of Peace and I desire to enrich you with my motherly peace. Dear children, I love you and I desire to bring all of you to the peace that only God gives and that enriches every heart. I invite you to become carriers and witnesses of my peace to this unpeaceful world. Let peace rule in the whole world, which is without peace and longs for peace. I bless you with my motherly blessing. Thank you for having responded to my call.

August 25, 1990 Dear children! Today I desire to invite you to take with seriousness and put into practice the messages that I am giving you. You know, little children, that I am with you and that I desire to lead you along the same path to heaven, which is beautiful for those who discover it in prayer. Therefore, little children, do not forget that these messages which I am giving you have to be put into your everyday life in order that you might be able to say, "There, I have taken the messages and try to live them." Dear children, I am protecting you before the heavenly Father by my own prayers. Thank you for having responded to my call.

September 25, 1990 Dear children! I invite you to pray with the heart in order that your prayer may be a conversation with God. I desire each one of you to dedicate more time to God. Satan is strong and wants to destroy and deceive you in many ways. Therefore, dear children, pray every day that your life will be good for yourselves and for all those you meet. I am with you and I am protecting you even though Satan wishes to destroy my plans and to hinder the desires that the Heavenly Father wants to realize here. Thank you for having responded to my call.

October 25, 1990 Dear children! Today I call you to pray in a special way and to offer up sacrifices and good deeds for peace in the world. Satan is strong, and with all his strength tries to destroy the peace that comes from God. Therefore, dear children, pray in a special way with me for peace. I am with you and I desire to help you with my prayers and I desire to guide you on the path of peace. I bless you with my motherly blessing. Do not forget to live the messages of peace. Thank you for having responded to my call.

November 25, 1990 Dear children! Today I invite you to do works of mercy with love, and out of love for me and for your and my brothers and sisters. Dear children, all that you do for others, do it with great joy and humility toward God. I am with you and, day after day, I offer your sacrifices and prayers to God for the salvation of the world. Thank you for having responded to my call.

December 25, 1990 Dear children! Today I invite you in a special way to pray for peace. Dear children, without peace you cannot experience the birth of the little Jesus, neither today nor in your daily lives. Therefore, pray to the Lord of peace that He may protect you with His mantle, and that He may help you to comprehend the greatness and the importance of peace in your hearts. In this way you shall be able to spread peace from your hearts throughout the whole world. I am with you and I intercede for you before God. Pray, because Satan wants to destroy my plans of peace. Be reconciled with one another and by means of your lives, help peace to reign on the whole earth. Thank you for having responded to my call.

January 25, 1991 Dear children! Today like never before I invite you to prayer. Your prayer should be a prayer for peace. Satan is strong and wishes not only to destroy human life but also nature and the planet on which you live. Therefore, dear children, pray that you can protect yourselves through prayer with the blessing of God's peace. God sent me to you so that I can help you. If you wish to, grasp the rosary. The rosary alone can do miracles in the world and in your lives. I bless you and I stay among you as long as it is God's will. Thank you that you will not betray my presence here and I thank you because your response is serving God and peace. Thank you for having responded to my call.

February 25, 1991 Dear children! Today I invite you to decide for God, because distance from God is the fruit of the lack of peace in your heart. God is only peace; therefore, approach Him through your personal prayer and then live peace in your hearts, and in this way peace will flow from your heart like a river into the whole world. Do not speak about peace, but make peace. I am blessing each of you and each good decision of yours. Thank you for having responded to my call.

March 25, 1991 Dear children! Again today I invite you to live the passion of Jesus in prayer, and in union with Him. Decide to give more time to God who gave you these days of grace! Therefore, dear children, pray and renew in a special way the love for Jesus in your hearts. I am with you, and I accompany you with my blessing and my prayers. Thank you for having responded to my call.

April 25, 1991 Dear children! Today I invite you all so that your prayer be prayer with the heart. Let each of you find time for prayer so that in your prayer you discover God. I do not desire you to talk about prayer, but to pray. Let your every day be filled with prayer of gratitude to God for life and for all that you have. I do not desire your life to pass by in words, but that you glorify God with deeds. I am with you, and I am grateful to God for every moment spent with you. Thank you for responding to my call.

May 25, 1991 Dear children! Today I invite all of you who have heard my message of peace to realize it with seriousness and with love in your life. There are many who think that they are doing a lot by talking about the messages but do not live them. Dear children, I invite you to life and to change all the negative in you, so that it all turns into positive and life. Dear children, I am with you and I desire to help each of you to live and, by living, to witness the good news. I am here, dear children, to help you and to lead you to heaven, and in heaven is the joy through which you can already live heaven now. Thank you for having responded to my call.

June 25, 1991 Dear children! Today, on this great day that you have given to me, I desire to bless all of you and to say: These days while I am with you are days of grace. I desire to teach you and to help you walk on the path to holiness. There are many people who do not desire to understand my messages and to accept with seriousness what I am saying. But you, I therefore call and ask that by your life and your daily living you witness my presence. If you pray, God will help you discover the true reason for my coming. Therefore, little children, pray and read the sacred Scriptures so that through my coming you discover the message in sacred Scripture for you. Thank you for having responded to my call.

July 25, 1991 Dear children! Today I invite you to pray for peace. At this time, peace is threatened in a special way, and I am seeking from you to renew fasting and prayer in your families. Dear children, I desire for you to grasp the seriousness of the situation, and that much of what will happen depends on your prayers, and you are praying [only] a little bit. Dear children, I am with you and I am inviting you to begin to pray and fast seriously, as in the first days of my coming. Thank you for having responded to my call.

August 25, 1991 Dear children! Today also I invite you to prayer now as never before when my plan has begun to be realized. Satan is strong and wants to sweep away the plan of peace and joy, and make you think that my Son is not strong in His decisions. Therefore, I call all of you, dear children, to pray and to fast still more firmly. I invite you to renunciation for nine days, so that with your help everything I wanted to realize through the secrets I began in Fatima may be fulfilled. I call you, dear children, to grasp the importance of my coming and the seriousness of the situation. I want to save all souls and present them to God. Therefore, let us pray that everything that I have begun be fully realized. Thank you for having responded to my call.

September 25, 1991 Dear children! Today in a special way I invite you to prayer and renunciation. For now as never before Satan wants to show the world his shameful face by which he wants to seduce as many people as possible onto the way of death and sin. Therefore, dear children, help my Immaculate Heart to triumph in the sinful world. I beseech all of you to offer prayers and sacrifices for my intentions so I can present them to God for what is most necessary. Forget your desire, dear children, and pray for what God desires and not for what you desire. Thank you for having responded to my call.

October 25, 1991 Dear children! Pray, pray, pray.

November 25, 1991 Dear children! This time also I am inviting you to prayer. Pray that you might be able to comprehend what God desires to tell you through my presence and through the messages I am giving you. I desire to draw you ever closer to Jesus and to His wounded Heart, that you might be able to comprehend the immeasurable Love that gave Itself for each one of you. Therefore, dear children, pray that from your heart would flow a fountain of love to every person born, even to the one who hates you and to the one who despises you. That way you will be able through Jesus' love to overcome all the misery in this world of sorrows, which is without hope for those who do not know Jesus. I am with you and I love you with the immeasurable love of Jesus. Thank you for all your sacrifices and prayers. Pray so I might be able to help you still more. Your prayers are necessary to me. Thank you for having responded to my call.

December 25, 1991 Dear children! Today in a special way I bring the little Jesus to you, that He may bless you with His blessing of peace and love. Dear children, do not forget that this is a grace that many people neither understand nor accept. Therefore, you who have said that you are mine, and seek my help, give all of yourselves. First of all, give your love and example in your families. You say that Christmas is a family feast; therefore, dear children, put God in the first place in your families, so that He may give you peace and protect you not only from war but also protect you from every satanic attack during peace. When God is with you, you have everything. But when you do not want Him, then you are miserable and lost, and you do not know on whose side you are. Therefore, dear children, decide for God and then you will get everything. Thank you for having responded to my call.[1]

January 25, 1992 Dear children! Today I am inviting you to a renewal of prayer in your families so that way every family becomes a joy to my son, Jesus. Therefore, dear children, pray and seek more time for Jesus and then you will be able to understand and accept everything, even the most difficult sicknesses and crosses. I am with you, and I desire to take you into my heart and protect you, but you have not yet decided. Therefore, dear children, I am seeking from you to pray, so through prayer you would allow me to help you. Pray, my dear little children, so that prayer would become your daily food. Thank you for having responded to my call.

February 25, 1992 Dear children! Today I invite you to draw still closer to God through prayer. Only that way will I be able to help you and to protect you from every attack of Satan. I am with you and

I intercede for you with God, that He protect you. But I need your prayers and your "Yes." You get lost easily in material and human things, and forget that God is your greatest friend. Therefore, my dear little children, draw close to God so He may protect you and guard you from every evil. Thank you for having responded to my call.

March 25, 1992 Dear children! Today as never before, I invite you to live my messages and to put them into practice in your life. I have come to you to help you, and therefore I invite you to change your life because you have taken a path of misery, a path of ruin. When I told you, "Convert, pray, fast, be reconciled," you took these messages superficially. You started to live them and then you stopped because it was difficult for you. Know, dear children, when something is good, you have to persevere in the good and not think, "God does not see me, He is not listening, He is not helping." And so, you have gone away from God and from me because of your miserable interests. I wanted to create of you an Oasis of Peace, Love and Goodness. God wanted you with your love and with His help to do miracles and thus give an example. Therefore, here's what I say to you: "Satan is playing with you and with your souls and I cannot help you because you are far from my heart." Therefore, pray, live my messages, and then you will see the miracles of God's Love in your everyday life. Thank you for having responded to my call.

April 25, 1992 Dear children! Today also I invite you to prayer. Only by prayer and fasting can war be stopped. Therefore, my dear little children, pray and by your life give witness that you are mine and that you belong to me, because Satan wishes in these turbulent days to seduce as many souls as possible. Therefore, I invite you to decide for God and He will protect you and show you what you should do and which path to take. I invite all those who have said yes to me to renew their consecration to my Son Jesus and to His heart and to me, so we can take you more intensely as instruments of peace in this unpeaceful world. Medjugorje is a sign to all of you and a call to pray and live the days of grace that God is giving you. Therefore, dear children, accept the call to prayer with seriousness. I am with you and your suffering is also mine. Thank you for having responded to my call.

May 25, 1992 Dear children! Today also, I invite you to prayer so that through prayer you come yet closer to God. I am with you and wish to lead you on the path of salvation which Jesus gives. From day to day, I am closer and closer to you although you are not conscious of it and do not want to admit that you are connected to me in prayer only a little bit. When temptations and problems arise, you say, "O God, O Mother, where are you?" And I only wait for you to give me your "Yes" so that I pass it on to Jesus and that He may bestow you with the graces. Therefore, once again, accept my call and begin anew to pray, until prayer becomes joy for you, and then you will discover that God is almighty in your everyday life. I am with you and I wait for you. Thank you for having responded to my call.

June 25, 1992 Dear children! Today I am happy although in my heart there is still some sadness for all of those who began to take this path and then abandoned it. My presence here is therefore to lead you on a new path—the path of salvation. Thus I call you day after day to conversion, because if you do not pray, you cannot say you are converting. I pray for you and intercede before God: that God may be your peace—first in your own hearts and then for those around you. Thank you for having responded to my call.

July 25, 1992 Dear children! Today again I invite all of you to prayer, a joyful prayer, so that in these sad days, none of you feels sadness in prayer, but a joyful meeting with God his Creator. Pray, little children, so that you can be closer to me, and feel through prayer what I desire from you. I am with you, and everyday I bless you with my motherly blessing, so that the Lord may bestow you with the abundance of His grace for your daily life. Thank God for the gift of my being with you, because I am telling you: This is a great Grace. Thank you for having responded to my call.

August 25, 1992 Dear children! Today, I wish to tell you that I love you. I love you with my motherly love, and I call upon you to open yourselves completely to me so that through each of you I may be enabled to convert and save the world, where there is much sin and many things that are evil. Therefore, my dear children, open yourselves completely to me so that I may be able to lead you more and more to the marvelous love of God the Creator who reveals Himself to you day by day. I am at your side and I wish to reveal to you and show you the God who loves you. Thank you for having responded to my call.

September 25, 1992 Dear children! Today also I wish to tell you: I am with you also in these restless days in which Satan wishes to destroy everything which I and my Son Jesus are building up. In a special way he wishes to destroy your souls. He wishes to guide you as far away as possible from Christian life as well as from the commandments, to which the Church is calling you so you may give them. Satan wishes to destroy everything which is holy in you and around you. Therefore, little children, pray, pray, pray, in order to be able to comprehend all which God is giving you through my comings. Thank you for having responded to my call.

October 25, 1992 Dear children! I invite you to prayer now when Satan is strong and wishes to make as many souls as possible his own. Pray, dear children, and have more trust in me, because I am here in order to help you, and to guide you on a new path towards a new life. Therefore, dear little children, listen and live what I tell you, because it is important for you, when I shall not be with you any longer, that you remember my words and all which I told you. I call you to begin to change your life from the beginning and that you decide for conversion not with words but with your life. Thank you for having responded to my call.

November 25, 1992 Dear children! Today like never before I invite you to pray. May your life become prayer in fullness. Without love you cannot pray. Therefore I invite you to first love God the creator of your life and then you shall also discover and love God in all as he loves you. Dear children, it is a grace that I am with you. Therefore accept and live my messages for your good. I love you and therefore I am with you to teach you and to guide you to a new life of renunciation and conversion. Only in this way you shall discover God and everything which is far from you now. Therefore, little children, pray. Thank you for having responded to my call.

December 25, 1992 Dear children! Today I wish to place you all under my mantle to protect you from every satanic attack. Today is the day of Peace, but throughout the whole world there is much lack of peace. Therefore, I call you to build up a new world of Peace together with me, by means of prayer. Without you, I cannot do that, and, therefore, I call all of you, with my motherly love, and God will do the rest. Therefore, open yourselves to God's plans and purposes for you to be able to cooperate with Him for peace and for good. And do not forget that your life does not belong to you, but is a gift with which you must bring joy to others and lead them to Eternal Life. May the tenderness of my little Jesus always accompany you. Thank you for having responded to my call.

January 25, 1993 Dear children! Today I call you to accept and live my messages with seriousness. These days are the days when you need to decide for God, for peace and for the good. May every hatred and jealousy disappear from your life and your thoughts, and may there only dwell love for God and for your neighbor. Thus, only thus, shall you be able to discern the signs of this time. I am with you, and I guide you into a new time, a time which God gives you as grace, so that you may get to know him more. Thank you for having responded to my call.

EPILOGUE

The tears were quiet and the wind was gentle.

An old man, suffering from cancer and a heart condition, came to Medjugorje, though he was a self-proclaimed atheist. A medical doctor, he relied on science for all answers. One hot afternoon he had a mysterious dream. He was young again, maybe forty. Two of his children were with him, and he was in the house of his boyhood. He was filled with delight and began to show his children things long ago forgotten that were actually quite dear to him.

Suddenly he heard his mother's voice. She was calling, "Help me, please help me." He rushed up the stairs to her bedroom. He opened the door, saying, "Mother, here are my children, I want you to meet them," when he was met by a thick, foglike curtain that blocked his entrance to the room. He smelled a putrid odor and sensed pain, great pain.

"You can't come in here," she cried. "Please son, please help me."

Frantic, the old man awakened. What did it mean? Then he realized his mother, whose name was Mary, had died forty years ago that very day. He was soaked with perspiration and chilled to the marrow. Where was his mother? Was there a purgatory after all? he wondered. If she could see him now, and if heaven were real, he knew his path would not be an easy one.

That afternoon he went to confession for the first time in seventy years. He didn't believe in confession—but he knew his mother did, so he went for her. And he was honest with the priest who told him his faith was as meager as the widow's mite. Was it enough faith? The priest said it was.

Then the old man took a cab to the foot of Apparition Hill. There stood Vicka. She stared at him for a moment, then she said, "Your mother prayed the rosary every day. The rosary is the chain that binds generations to eternal life."

A few Arabs came by and offered to help the old man climb the mountain. "I'm pretty weak," he said.

"No problem," they assured him as they lifted his frail body on their own arms, which they crossed to form a litter.

The old man insisted on walking part of the way. "Do you know Christ died of asphyxiation?" he volunteered. "I'm a doctor. My own lungs are filling up now from the physical strain of the climb. But the pain is nothing in comparison to the pain of a crucifixion."

"We're Moslems," the two strong men said, as they again formed the litter for the old man. He gratefully sank into their arms and was silent. At the top of the mountain, the place where the Blessed Virgin first appeared, they found a rock for him, which he used as a seat. And they handed him a rosary.

"I don't remember how to pray this," he earnestly told them.

"But we do," they smiled. The three men, two kneeling and facing Mecca, and one sitting on a rock, prayed the rosary together up there between the sky and the valley of blood. The tears were quiet and the wind was gentle.

HEAR
O children of the earth, I long for you.
Hear Me in the wind sighing and pining for you.
Come to Me, My beloved little ones.
My arms are outstretched.
My Heart is yours, My little ones.
Hear your mother's voice.

She is My choice for your journey to paradise.
Follow her voice.
Follow her ways.
Follow her heart to the Heart of Jesus.
In Jesus and through Jesus and with Jesus,
all of you are Mine forever.
The time is now.
Come, little ones.
Come.

NOTES

AUTHOR'S NOTE

1. Joseph Terelya, *Witness to Apparitions and Persecution in the U.S.S.R.* Milford, Ohio: Faith Publishing Company, 1991, 18.

2. Ricardo Montelban, Narrator, *Marian Apparitions of the Twentieth Century: A Message of Urgency*, Video Documentary. Lima, Penn.: Marian Communications Limited, 1991.

3. Montelban, *Marian Apparitions of the Twentieth Century.*

4. Teiji Yasuda, O.S.U., *The Meaning of Akita*, trans. J. Haffert. Asbury, N.J.: 101 Foundation, 1989, 2–6, 17–24.

5. Yasuda, *The Meaning of Akita*, trans. J. Haffert, 4–6.

PROLOGUE

1. Description by a pilgrim of the Miracle of the Sun:

"Around 6:15 P.M., we headed down to the church courtyard to pray the rosary and await the Blessed Mother's apparition. Pilgrims gathered outside the church where she appears, and pray as she gives messages to the visionaries. While we prayed the rosary, I noticed that it seemed very meaningful. I sort of thought about Jesus and the Blessed Mother as I was praying. And also the meaning of the mysteries. As the crowd neared the end of the rosary, I noticed that part of the group standing on the side of the church began to look up and others began to rush toward them, looking up also. To my amazement, we saw what is called the Miracle of the Sun. I have to admit, I was entirely skeptical of this being able to occur at all. But when I looked up, the sun seemed like a full moon. It did not hurt my eyes to look at it! The sun seemed to be wobbling. It was like Jell-O being shaken. Then it began to spin very fast. I have never, ever seen anything like it. Then, the sun had many colors shooting out from it: blue, pink, green, yellow, orange. Some around me not only saw Our Lady in the sun, but also told me that they had somehow received some grace that let them understand Our Lady. We were all in shock. I was crying, thinking, half praying, 'God, I was a doubting Thomas. I almost believed but needed to see the proverbial wounds in the hands of Christ.' I kept thinking to myself, 'Now I know why God sends signs.

To help our weak faith, to encourage us in times of doubt. Or, as for me, to forever erase the need to ask: Do I believe?' Then, I saw a rainbow in the sky though it had not, nor would it rain for weeks.

Betsy Connell
July 13, 1987, Medjugorje

CHAPTER 1: IN THE BEGINNING

1. Mary Craig, *Spark from Heaven*. Notre Dame, Ind.: Ave Maria Press, 1988, 11–12.

2. Craig, *Spark from Heaven*, 13.

3. Author's interview with Vicka, Medjugorje, January 1987.

4. Author's interview with Marinko, Medjugorje, May 1991.

5. Author's interview with Vicka, Medjugorje, March 1988.

6. Laurentin and Lejeune, *Messages and Teachings of Mary at Medjugorje*. Milford, Ohio: The Riehle Foundation, 1988, 9, 11–16.

7. Description of early days by Father Jozo at Tihiljina, 1988.

8. Author's interview with former pastor, Father Jozo Zovko, O.F.M., Tihiljina, Yugoslavia. Father Philip Pavich, O.F.M., translates, January 1988.

9. Author's interview with Father Jozo Zovko, O.F.M., Tihiljina, January 1988.

10. Author's interviews with Vicka, Mirjana, Jacov, Ivan, Marija, Ivanka, and eye-witness villager Jozo Vasily, Medjugorje, 1987–1991.

11. Author's interview with Father Jozo Zovko, O.F.M., Tihiljina, January 1988.

12. Author's interview with Father Jozo Zovko, O.F.M., Tihiljina, January 1988.

13. Craig, *Spark from Heaven*, 51.

14. Craig, *Spark from Heaven*, 94.

15. Author's interview with Father Robert Faricy, S.J., Pontifical Gregorian University, Rome, October 1989.

16. April 4, 1985.

17. Louis de Montfort, Saint, *True Devotion to Mary*. Rockford, Ill.: Tan Books and Publishers, 1941, 28–35.

18. Laurentin and Lejeune, *Messages and Teachings of Mary at Medjugorje*. Milford, Ohio: Riehle Foundation, 1988, 186.

19. Message of Blessed Virgin Mary to visionaries, Thursday, January 21, 1982.

20. Author's interview with Father Jozo Zovko, Tihiljina, March 1989.

21. Francis de Sales, Saint, *The Sermons of Saint Francis de Sales on Our Lady*, ed. Lewis S. Fiorelli, O.S.F.S. Rockford, Ill.: Tan Books and Publishers, 1985, 15.

22. Francis de Sales, Saint, *The Sermons of Saint Francis de Sales on Our Lady*, 18.

23. Francis de Sales, Saint, *The Sermons of Saint Francis de Sales on Our Lady*, 18.

CHAPTER 2: SIGNS, WONDERS, AND WARNINGS

1. Laurentin and Lejeune, *Messages and Teachings of Mary at Medjugorje*. Milford, Ohio: Riehle Foundation, 1988, 55.

2. Bishop Michael Pfiefer, O.M.I., of San Antonio, Texas, speaking at Medjugorje, March 1989.

3. Michel de la Sainte Trinité, *The Whole Truth about Fatima*, trans. Collorafi. Buffalo, N.Y.: 1989, i.

4. Laurentin and Lejeune, *Messages and Teachings of Mary at Medjugorje*. Milford, Ohio: Riehle Foundation, 1988, 171.

5. Jan Connell, *Queen of the Cosmos*. Orleans, Mass.: Paraclete Press, 1990, 70–72.

6. Connell, *Queen of the Cosmos*, 19.

7. Laurentin and Lejeune, *Messages and Teachings of Mary at Medjugorje*, 173.

CHAPTER 3: MARY, MOTHER OF ALL PEOPLE

1. Luke 1:26–36.

2. Venerable Mary of Agreda, *Mystical City of God*. Washington, N.J.: Ave Maria Institute, 1971, 85.

3. Ibid., 131.

4. Deut. 5:16: "Honor your Father and your Mother, as the Lord, your God has commanded you that you may have a long life and prosperity in the land which the Lord, your God, has given you."

5. Luke 2:51: "He went down with them [Mary and Joseph] and came to Nazareth and was obedient to them."

Those who subject themselves to her command know precisely what she expects, for Scripture records her simple request. "Do whatever He [Jesus] tells you."

6. Venerable Mary of Agreda, op. cit., 88.

7. Ibid., 89.

8. Ibid., 90.

9. Ibid., 31.

10. Ibid., 139.

11. Ibid., 110.

12. Ibid., 110–111.

13. John 14:20.

14. Message from the Blessed Mother to Jelena, as quoted to author by Jelena, at Medjugorje, August 1990.

CHAPTER 4: THE VISIONARIES TODAY

1. Connell, *Queen of the Cosmos*. Orleans, Mass.: Paraclete Press, 1990, 24.

2. Connell, *Queen of the Cosmos*, 140.

CHAPTER 5: MIRJANA

1. Dr. Slavko Barbaric, trained in psychological research, was called to Medjugorje in the early days of the apparition to debunk and unmask the visionaries. To the contrary, however, after thorough investigation, he has become one of the primary protectors of the visionaries and the locutionists. Expert in many languages, Dr. Barbaric patiently chronicles the miraculous nature of this phenomenon at Medjugorje.

His sister is the mother of Mirjana's husband.

2. Svetozar Kraljevic, *The Apparitions of Our Lady at Medjugorje*. Chicago, Ill.: Franciscan Herald Press, 1984, 125–126.

3. Jan Connell, *Queen of the Cosmos*. Orleans, Mass.: Paraclete Press, 1990, 29.

4. Gen. 3:15.

5. Gen. 3:15.

6. Vision of Pope Leo XIII, as described in Mark Miravalle, *Heart of the Message of Medjugorje*. Steubenville, Ohio: Franciscan University Press, 1988, 138.

7. Acts 2:17–21.

8. Louis de Montfort, Saint, *True Devotion to Mary*. Rockford, Ill.: Tan Books and Publishers, 1941, 31–35.

9. Connell, *Queen of the Cosmos*, 80.

10. "Jesus is the Mediator. Mary is Mediatrix but in a very different manner. The Savior is the Mediator of Justice. He intercedes for us,

exposing the right and reason of our cause. He produces our just claims, which are none other than His Redemption, His blood, His cross. He acknowledges to His Father that we are debtors, but He shows that He has paid for us. But the Virgin and the saints are mediators of grace. They pray for us that we may be pardoned—all through the mediation of the Passion of the Savior. They themselves have nothing to show by which we may be justified . . . If Jesus prays in Heaven, He prays in virtue of Himself; but the Virgin prays only as we do, in virtue of her Son, but with more credit and favor."

Francis de Sales, Saint, *The Sermons of Saint Francis de Sales on Our Lady*, ed. Lewis S. Fiorelli, O.S.F.S. Rockford, Ill.: Tan Books and Publishers, 1985, 21.

11. John 1:11–12.

12. Connell, *Queen of the Cosmos*, 32.

13. Joseph Terelya, *Witness to Apparitions and Persecution in the U.S.S.R.* Milford, Ohio: Faith Publishing Company, 1991, 321–324.

14. John 19:25–27.

15. Human free will is a great gift from the Creator, God, our Father. This side of eternity, "free will" is thought by many to be the power human beings possess to choose good or evil. However, this is not true. Human freedom essentially is the power to choose good. The power to choose evil is not a perfection. It is a distortion, and in reality a destruction of human freedom. Freedom or free will, which God Himself possesses, as do all the angels and saints, is a perfection. Neither God nor the angels and saints have the power to choose evil, yet they are free; they possess free will.

In order for a human being to choose evil, we must cover up the evil with lies and distortions and make the evil appear to be good. When evil is made to look good, then and only then can the human will choose it.

In heaven the human will is not destroyed or replaced but rather the human will reaches perfection. In heaven it is impossible for the human will to choose evil. The proper object of the human will is good, and even on this earth it is only at rest when it possesses the highest good, which is God.

In heaven, human freedom has the power to choose among many goods, and it does. However, the human will is drawn toward the highest good, God, and only in God can it find its highest fulfillment and rest. The power to love is in the will. Only those with free will can love; those who are in heaven love the highest good, God Himself.

Joseph W. Coyle, O.S.F.S. Written by Father Coyle for this text as an explanation, 1991.

16. Connell, *Queen of the Cosmos*, 120–121.

17. Laurentin and Lejeune, *Messages and Teachings of Mary at Medjugorje*, 189.

18. Connell, *Queen of the Cosmos*, 68.

CHAPTER 6: IVANKA

1. Connell, *Queen of the Cosmos*, 45.

2. Teiji Yasuda, O.S.U., *The Meaning of Akita*, trans. J. Haffert. Asbury, N.J.: 101 Foundation, 1989, 45.

3. When we say "Give us this day our daily bread," we are really asking for the bread of sorrow for sin. It is sorrow for sin that prepares our hearts to welcome Jesus, in the Eucharist. Jesus, in the Eucharist, is the bread of eternal life. He heals our hearts of all the sickness and pain of sin. When we are well we can see God. We can be with God forever, with the angels, with the saints, and the Blessed Mother.

4. Connell, *Queen of the Cosmos*, 54.

CHAPTER 7: JACOV

1. Connell, *Queen of the Cosmos*, 94.

2. Ibid., 95.

3. Ibid., 97.

4. Ibid., 97.

5. Ibid., 93.

6. Ibid., 24.

CHAPTER 8: VICKA

1. On February 25, 1988, Our Lady instructed Vicka to write three letters: to Father Janko Bubalo, her confessor; to the bishop's commission investigating the apparitions; to the priests in residence at the Rectory of Saint James, Medjugorje. These letters were sealed and delivered to the above-named persons. Several months later, on September 25, 1988, Vicka asked all the persons who held the sealed letters to open them in the presence of two witnesses. Each letter contained the following information: Vicka's illness was God's gift to her; it was not a punishment. The purpose of Vicka's illness was to help heal the illness of sinners. Her sacrifice would be completed on September 25, and on that date, Vicka would be healed of her illness. In fact, Vicka was healed on September 25, 1988, just as the sealed letters of February 25, 1988 had foretold.

2. On July 25, 1982, the Blessed Mother told the visionaries at Medju-

gorje: "Today many people go to hell. God permits His children to suffer in hell due to the fact that they have committed grave and unpardonable sins. Those who are in hell no longer have a chance to know a better lot."

3. Connell, *Queen of the Cosmos*, 62–63.

4. Ibid., 73.

5. Gen. 3:15.

6. Connell, *Queen of the Cosmos*, 69.

7. Ibid., 80.

CHAPTER 9: MARIJA

1. 10:40 A.M., Eastern Standard Time in the United States is the same time the daily apparition occurs in Medjugorje.

2. Message to President Reagan from Marija Pavlovic. The following was translated from the Croatian newspaper, *Sveta Bastina*, February 1988 issue; transcribed from *Medjugorje Herald*, vol. 2, no. 6—Mary's Room M R-18, 12/88.

> *Dear President Reagan:*
> *God's Holy Mother is appearing each day in this small village of Medjugorje, Yugoslavia. She is giving us a message of peace. We know your concern for world peace and are remembering you in our prayers each day. You are very close to our hearts and we want you to know that you can count on our prayers and sacrifices to help you in your great task.*
> *Our Holy Mother has said that with prayer and fasting wars can be avoided. May her message help you and her daily visits be a sign to you of God's loving concern for His people.*
> *United in prayer, and in the Heart of Jesus and Mary we send our love and greet you with the peace of the Queen of Peace.*
> *Marija Pavlovic*

In 1987 the American ambassador for Middle Europe, Alfred H. Kingon, stayed in Medjugorje for two weeks. The reason for his coming to Medjugorje was to pray for his sick son and give thanks for receiving God's graces. He accepted the messages of Medjugorje, so he regularly fasts and prays a lot. During his stay he had a meeting with the visionary, Marija Pavlovic. Just before he returned to America in a special spiritual atmosphere there was created an opinion that it would be very convenient to send over with him a spiritual peace message for President Reagan. Sincerely delighted, Kingon, Reagan's ambassador, said that he would deliver the message to the president as soon as he returned to the White House.

This message was written by Marija Pavlovic and translated into English by Kathleen Parisod. This message was given to President Reagan just before his meeting with the Russian leader Mikhail Gorbachev when the contract about destroying intermediate missiles had been signed.

On December 8, 1987, the White House made a phone call to Marija at 7:00 P.M. Parisod translated the conversation. Ambassador Kingon was the one who called, and in the very beginning of the conversation he said that President Reagan himself wanted to talk with Marija; but it was impossible because the meeting with Gorbachev was still going on. During the conversation Kingon confirmed that he, himself, gave Marija's message to the president and that Reagan was delighted with the message. Kingon emphasized that after the president read the message he cried out: "Now, with a new spirit I am going to the meeting with Gorbachev."

The same night the White House tried to call Marija but could not get through. On December 14, 1987, Kingon sent Marija a letter in which he encouraged her to send a peace message to Gorbachev. He assured her that the American ambassador, Jack Matlock, would give it to the secretary of the Russian leader. He also added that it would be beautiful if two great leaders and the two greatest countries would find out about her prayer and Our Lady's messages.

Finally on Christmas Day Marija received a picture of Ronald Reagan under which was written: "To Marija Pavlovic—With my heartfelt thanks and every good wish. God bless you. Sincerely, Ronald Reagan."

Note: Information supplied by priests of Saint James Parish, January 1988.

CHAPTER 10: IVAN

1. Connell, *Queen of the Cosmos*, 52.

CHAPTER 11: THE LOCUTIONISTS: JELENA AND MARIJANA

1. Information supplied by the Boston Center for Peace (slightly adapted).
2. Jelena's family consists of her parents, her paternal grandparents, and her five brothers and sisters. Jelena is the second oldest. The parents, Grgo and Stefica, and the grandparents attend daily Mass.
3. Lucy Rooney, S.N.D., and Robert Faricy, S.J., *Medjugorje Journal*. Essex, England: McCrimmon Publishing Co., 1987, 62.
4. Ibid., 62.
5. Slavko Barbaric: See note 1 to Chapter 5.
6. Author's interview with Father Barbaric, at Medjugorje, July 13, 1987.

7. Rooney and Faricy, *Medjugorje Journal*, "Message of Blessed Mother." Essex, England: McCrimmon Publishing Co., February 25, 1984, 75.

8. Father Slavko Barbaric, "Phenomenological comparative account of the Inner Locutions of Jelena Vasilj and Marijana Vasilj." (Unpublished paper, October 1985.)

9. Connell, *Queen of the Cosmos*, 55.

10. Laurentin and Lejeune, *Messages and Teachings of Mary at Medjugorje*, 306.

11. See *Queen of the Cosmos* and interview in this book.

12. Connell, *Queen of the Cosmos*, 19.

13. Laurentin and Lejeune, *Messages and Teachings of Mary at Medjugorje*, 204.

14. Ibid., 202.

15. Connell, *Queen of the Cosmos*, 68–69.

16. Message from the Blessed Mother on February 20, 1985.

17. Message from the Blessed Mother on February 25, 1985.

CHAPTER 12: AND THE PILGRIMS AFTER THEM

1. Author's interview with Melona Hapsburg, at Medjugorje, January 1988.

CHAPTER 13: CURES AND LUMINARY PHENOMENA

1. Laurentin and Lejeune, *Messages and Teachings of Mary at Medjugorje*, 189.

2. James Bubalo, O.F.M., *A Thousand Encounters with the Blessed Virgin Mary in Medjugorje*. Chicago: Friends of Medjugorje, 1987, 132.

3. *Queen of Peace Newsletter*. Pittsburgh, Penn.: Pittsburgh Center for Peace, Vol. 1, Issue 4, 1990, 4.

4. Ibid., 5.

5. Laurentin and Lejeune, *Messages and Teachings of Mary at Medjugorje*, 159.

6. Ibid., 168.

7. *Queen of Peace Newsletter*, Vol. 1, Issue 4, 1990, 10.

8. Connell, *Queen of the Cosmos*, 27.

9. Author's interview with Marija, at Birmingham, Alabama, 1988.

10. Medjugorje, March 1988.

CHAPTER 14: THE MESSAGES OF THE BLESSED MOTHER

1. "Live the Messages," The Messages of Mary, Mother of Jesus Christ Lord God, Mary, Queen of Peace, Medjugorje. D. R. Golob, with permission of The Riehle Foundation, P.O. Box 7, Milford, Ohio 45150, 1991. (Slightly adapted.)

SELECTED BIBLIOGRAPHY

Aquinas, St. Thomas. *Summa Theologica.* 5 vols. Westminster, Md.: Christian Classics, 1981.

Arendzen, J. P., D.D. *Purgatory and Heaven.* Rockford, Ill.: Tan Books and Publishers, 1951.

Ashton, Joan. *Mother of All Nations.* New York: Harper and Row, 1989.

Ball, Ann. *A Litany of Mary.* Huntington, Ind.: Our Sunday Visitor Publishing Division, 1988.

Barbaric, Slavko, O.F.M. *Fasting.* Steubenville, Ohio: Franciscan University Press, 1988.

———. *Pray with the Heart.* Steubenville, Ohio: Franciscan University Press, 1988.

———. *The Way of the Cross.* Medjugorje: Parish Office, 1989.

Bedard, Fr. Bob. *Medjugorje Reflections.* Toronto, Ontario, Canada: Koinonia Enterprises, 1989.

Bojorge, Horacio, S.J. *The Image of Mary According to the Evangelists* (Aloysius Owen, S.J., trans.). New York: Alba House, 1978.

Bubalo, Fr. Janko, O.F.M. *A Thousand Encounters with the Blessed Virgin Mary in Medjugorje.* Chicago: Friends of Medjugorje, 1987.

Catherine of Genoa. *Purgation and Purgatory: The Spiritual Dialogue.* New York: Paulist Press, 1979.

Connell, Jan. *Queen of the Cosmos.* Introduction by Robert Faricy, S.J. Orleans, Mass.: Paraclete Press, 1990.

Craig, Mary. *Spark from Heaven.* Notre Dame, Ind.: Ave Maria Press, 1988.

Danielow, Jean, L.J. *The Angels and Their Mission According to the Fathers of the Church.* Dublin: Newman Press, 1957.

Delaney, John J., ed. *A Woman Clothed with the Sun.* New York: Doubleday Image Books, 1960.

Dubay, Thomas, S.M. *Fire Within.* San Francisco: Ignatius Press, 1989.

Emanuele. *Medjugorje, A Portfolio of Images.* New York: Alba House, 1987.

Emmerich, Anne Catherine. *The Life of the Blessed Virgin Mary*. Rockford, Ill.: Tan Books, 1954.

Foley, Richard, S.J., ed. "Medjugorje Is a Giant" in *Medjugorje Messenger*. London: London Medjugorje Center, January 1988.

———. "Medjugorje's Call to Apostolate" in *Medjugorje Messenger*. London: London Medjugorje Center, July 1988.

———. "Medjugorje's Call to Holiness" in *Medjugorje Messenger*. London: London Medjugorje Center, April 1988.

———. "Pray Without Ceasing" in *Medjugorje Messenger*. London: London Medjugorje Center, January 1987.

———. "The World Village" in *Medjugorje Messenger*. London: London Medjugorje Center, July 1986.

Girard, G., S.SS.A.; Girard, A., S.SS.A.; and Bubalo, F., O.F.M. *Mary, Queen of Peace Stay With Us*. Montreal: Editions-Paulines, 1988.

Glenn, Msgr. Paul J. *A Tour of the Summa*. Rockford, Ill.: Tan Books, 1978.

Gobbe and Publishers, Don Stefano. *To the Priests, Our Lady's Beloved Sons* (11th ed.). Toronto, Ont.: Marian Movement of Priests, 1990.

Hakenewerth, Quentin, S.M. *The Mother of Jesus Was Here*. Dayton, Ohio: Marianist Press, 1984.

Ignatius of Loyola, St. *The Spiritual Exercises*. Translated by Anthony Mohola. New York: Doubleday Image Books, 1989.

Jelly, Frederick M., O.P. *Madonna, Mary in the Catholic Tradition*. New Huntington, Ind.: Our Sunday Visitor Publishing Division, 1986.

John of the Cross, St. *Selected Writings*. Translated by Kieran Kavanaugh, O.C.D. New York: Paulist Press, 1987.

John Paul II, Pope. "Mary: God's Yes to Man," Encyclical Letter *Mother of the Redeemer*. Introduction by Joseph Cardinal Ratzinger. San Francisco: Ignatius Press, 1987.

———. *Encyclical Letter: Mary: God's Yes to Man*. Intro. Joseph Cardinale Ratzinger. San Francisco: Ignatius Press, 1988.

Kaczmarek, Louis. *Hidden Treasure: The Riches of the Eucharist*. Manassas, Va.: Trinity Communications, 1990.

Kelsey, Morton. *Discernment: A Study in Ecstasy and Evil*. New York: Paulist Press, 1978.

Kosicki, Rev. George, C.S.B. *Spiritual Warfare: Attack Against the Woman*. Milford, Ohio: Faith Publishing, 1990.

Kraljevic, Svetozar, O.F.M. *In the Company of Mary*. Nashville, Tenn.: St. Francis Press, 1988.

———. *The Apparitions of Mary at Medjugorje*. Chicago: Franciscan Herald Press, 1984.

Laurentin, Fr. Rene. *A Year of Grace with Mary*. Dublin, Ireland: Veritas Publications, 1987.

———. *Eight Years: Reconciliation, Analysis, The Future*. Milford, Ohio: Riehle Foundation, 1989.

———. *Is the Virgin Mary Appearing at Medjugorje?* Washington, D.C.: The Word Among Us Press, 1984.

———. *Latest News of Medjugorje: June 1987*. Milford, Ohio: Riehle Foundation, 1987.

———. *Learning from Medjugorje*. Gaithersburg, Md.: The Word Among Us Press, 1988.

———. *Nine Years of Apparitions*. Milford, Ohio: Riehle Foundation, 1991.

———. *Report on Apparitions*. Milford, Ohio: Riehle Foundation, 1989.

———. *Seven Years of Apparitions: Time for the Harvest?* Milford, Ohio: Riehle Foundation, 1988.

———. *The Apparitions of Medjugorje Prolonged*. Milford, Ohio: Riehle Foundation, 1987.

———. *The Apparitions of the Blessed Virgin Mary Today*. Dublin: Veritas Publishers, 1990.

———. *The Church and Apparitions—Their Status and Function: Criteria and Reception*. Milford, Ohio: Riehle Foundation, 1989.

Laurentin, Fr. Rene, and Joyeux, Henri. *Scientific and Medical Studies on the Apparitions at Medjugorje*. Dublin: Veritas Publishers, 1987.

Laurentin, Fr. Rene, and Lejeune, Fr. R. *Messages and Teachings of Mary at Medjugorje*. Milford, Ohio: Riehle Foundation, 1988.

Malony, George A., S.J. *Entering into the Heart of Jesus*. New York: Alba House, 1988.

Marin, Jacov. *Queen of Peace in Medjugorje*. Milford, Ohio: Riehle Foundation, 1989.

Mary of Agreda, The Venerable. *Mystical City of God*. 4 vols. Washington, N.J.: Ave Maria Institute, 1971.

Miravalle, Mark, S.T.D. *Heart of the Message of Medjugorje*. Steubenville, Ohio: Franciscan University Press, 1988.

———. *The Message of Medjugorje*. Lanham, Md.: University Press of America, 1986.

Montfort, St. Louis de. *God Alone: The Collected Writings of St. Louis de Montfort*. Washington, N.J.: The Blue Army, 1989.

———. *The Secret of the Rosary*. Washington, N.J.: The Blue Army, 1951.

———. *True Devotion to Mary*. Rockford, Ill.: Tan Books, 1941.

Nageleisen, Fr. John A. *Charity for the Suffering Souls*. Rockford, Ill.: Tan Books and Publishers, 1982.

New American Bible, The.

Newman, John Henry. *Mary the Second Eve*. Rockford, Ill.: Tan Books and Publishers, 1982.

O'Carroll, Michael, C.S.Sp. *Is Medjugorje Approved?* Dublin: Veritas Publishers, 1991.

———. *Medjugorje: Facts, Documents, Theology*. Dublin: Veritas Publishers, 1986.

O'Connor, Edward, C.S.C. "The Lady Behind the Iron Curtain" (3-part series) in *Queen of All Hearts Journal*, 1986–1987.

Pelletier, Joseph, A.A. *The Queen of Peace Visits Medjugorje*. Worcester, Mass.: Assumption Publications, 1985.

———. *The Sun Danced at Fatima*. Garden City, N.Y.: Image Books, 1951.

Pervan, Tomislav, O.F.M. *Queen of Peace*. Steubenville, Ohio: Franciscan University Press, 1986.

Riehle Foundation, The, eds. *Medjugorje and Meditations*. Milford, Ohio: Riehle Foundation, 1988.

Roberto, D. *The Love of Mary*. Rockford, Ill.: Tan Books and Publishers, 1984.

Rooney, Lucy, S.N.D., and Faricy, Robert, S.J. *Mary, Queen of Peace*. New York: Alba House, 1984.

———. *Medjugorje Journal*. Essex, England: McCremmon Publishing Co., Ltd., 1987.

———. *Medjugorje Up Close*. Chicago: Franciscan Herald Books, 1985.

Rupcic, Ljudevit. *The Truth About Medjugorje*. Lubuski-Humac, 1990.

Sales, de, St. Francis. *The Sermons of Saint Francis de Sales on Our Lady*. Edited by Lewis S. Fiorelli, O.S.F.S. Rockford, Ill.: Tan Books and Publishers, 1985.

Sanford, John A. *The Kingdom Within*. San Francisco: Harper and Row, 1987.

Scanlan, Michael, T.O.R. *Deliverance From Evil Spirits*. Ann Arbor: Servant Books, 1980.

Schouppe, F. X., S.J. *The Dogma of Hell*. Rockford, Ill.: Tan Books and Publishers, 1989.

Scupoli, Dom Lorenzo. *The Spiritual Combat: A Treatise on Peace*. Rockford, Ill.: Tan Books and Publishers, 1945.

Sharkey, Don. *The Woman Shall Conquer*. Libertyville, Ill.: Franciscan Marytown Press, 1954.

Singleton, Fred. *A Short History of the Yugoslav Peoples*. Cambridge: Cambridge University Press, 1985.

Sipes, Bob, and Sipes, Toni. *The Land Between the Mountains*. Phoenix: City Lights, Inc., 1990.

Terelya, Joseph, with Michael Brown. *Witness to Apparitions and Persecution in the U.S.S.R.* Milford, Ohio: Faith Publishers, 1991.

Teresa of Avila, St. *The Way of Perfection*. Translated by E. Allison Peers. New York: Doubleday Image Books, 1991.

———. *Interior Castle*. Translated by E. Allison Peers, ed. New York: Doubleday Image Books, 1989.

Two Friends of Medjugorje. *Words from Heaven*. Birmingham, Ala.: St. James Publishing, 1990.

Valtorta, Maria. *Poem of the Man-God*. 5 vols. Sherbrooke, Can.: Editions-Paulines, 1989.

Van Kaam, Adrien, C.S.Sp. *The Mystery of Transforming Love*. Denville, N.J.: Dominican Books, Inc., 1981.

Vlasic, Tomislav, O.F.M., and Barbaric, Slavko, O.F.M. *Abandon Yourselves Totally to Me*. West Texas: Associated Friends of Medjugorje, 1988.

———. *Open Your Hearts to Mary*. Milan: Assocation of the Friends of Medjugorje, 1986.

———. *Pray with Your Heart*. West Texas: Association of the Friends of Medjugorje, 1989.

Weil, Simone. *Waiting for God*. New York: Harper and Row, 1951.

Werfel, Franz. *The Song of Bernadette*. Translated by Ludwig Lewisohn. New York: St. Martin's Press, 1970.

Zimdals-Swartz, Sandra L. *Encountering Mary from La Jolette to Medjugorje*. Princeton, N.J.: Princeton University Press, 1991.

Zovko, Fr. Jozo, O.F.M. *A Man Named Father Jozo*. Milford, Ohio: Riehle Foundation, 1989.